Petersburg City, Virginia

Hustings Court Deed Book Abstracts

1784–1787

Ruth and Sam Sparacio

HERITAGE BOOKS
2019

HERITAGE BOOKS
AN IMPRINT OF HERITAGE BOOKS, INC.

Books, CDs, and more—Worldwide

For our listing of thousands of titles see our website
at
www.HeritageBooks.com

Published 2019 by
HERITAGE BOOKS, INC.
Publishing Division
5810 Ruatan Street
Berwyn Heights, Md. 20740

International Standard Book Number
Paperbound: 978-1-68034-482-0

p.
1
A Court of Hustings held for the Town of PETERSBURG at the House of WILLIAM DURELL on Wednesday the 6th October 1784

Present   JOHN BANISTER Esqr., Mayor
CHRISTOPHER McCONNICO, Esqr., Recorder
JOHN SHORE,   )
ROBERT BOLLING'   )   Gentlemen Aldermen
ALEXR. McNABB

To all to whom these presents shall come. WHEREAS ROBERT BOLLING Esquire, late of BOLLING BROOK in County of DINWIDDIE deceased, did by his Last Will and Testament in writing bearing date the 30th day of January 1775, and recorded in the Court of DINWIDDIE County aforesaid, after disposing of his lands and such other parts of his Estate specifically as he chose so to dispose of, devise all the rest and residue of his Estate to his Wife, MARY, & his Friend, JOHN TABB (partys hereto), or to the survivor of them, with power (after making provision for payment of his Debts and such other purposes as were by his said Will directed) to divide the residue (in which residue his Negro slaves are included) among all his Children at such time and in such proportions as to them shou'd seem proper, and the partys aforesaid having delivered and assigned over to ROBERT BOLLING, the Eldest Son and Heir at Law of the Testator, sundry of the said Negro slaves of which his Father died possessed, NOW KNOW YE that we the said MARY BOLLING and JOHN TABB have released assigned & confirmed unto said ROBERT BOLLING in pursuance of the power aforesaid, thirty Negro slaves whose names are as follows, to wit, Tom, Simon, Breechy, Marcus, York, Charles, Jem, Rochester, Prince, Jem, Casar, Pero, Nicholas, Breechy, Tull, Pall, Aneka, Sue, Patience, Pall, Clitty, Jenny, Betty, Hannah, Phillis, Mary, Joan, Cate, Liddia, Phebe with all and every of their future increase; To Hold the said thirty Negro slaves and their increase unto said ROBERT BOLLING his heirs to the proper use of him the said ROBERT BOLLING and of his heirs; In Witness whereof the partys aforesaid have hereunto set their hands and affixed their seals the (blank) day of (blank) one thousand seven hundred and eighty four Sealed and Delivered in the presence of us

THOMAS ARMISTEAD,   MARY BOLLING
RICHARD STEWART JUNR., PETER MINOR   JOHN TABB
Town of Petersburg Sct, October H. Court 1784.
The above Deed from MARY BOLLING & JOHN TABB to ROBERT BOLLING was proved in open Court by the Oaths of THOMAS ARMISTEAD, RICHARD STEWART JR., & PETER MINOR and ordered to be recorded

Test   J. GRAMMER, Clk. C.H.

pp.
2-
4
THIS INDENTURE made the Tenth day of February in the year of our Lord one thousand seven hundred & eighty four Between ROBERT BOLLING Esquire of BOLLINGBROKE in County of DINWIDDIE of one part and ROBERT WATKINS & NICHOLAS WATKINS of the other part; Witnesseth that in consideration of the sum of Two hundred & fifty pounds current money of Virginia to him in hand paid by said ROBERT WATKINS and NICHOLSON WATKINS, and also in consideration of the covenants and agreements herein after mentioned to be performed by ROBERT WATKINS and NICHOLSON WATKINS said ROBERT BOLLING by these presents do bargain sell and

confirm unto ROBERT WATKINS and NICHOLSON WATKINS their heirs three certain lots of Land lying in County of DINWIDDIE in the vicinnage of the Town of PETERSBURG and near to the PUBLICK TOBACCO WAREHOUSE called "CEDAR POINT" WAREHOUSE are part of a tract of land formerly the property of ROBERT BOLLING deced., wch: has been lately laid out in Lots by the said ROBERT BOLLING (party hereto) and are known in the plan of said lots by numbers and figures following; that is to say, (26) Twenty six, (44) Forty four; (45) Forty five, the lott number (26) Twenty six lying on the South side, and lotts number 44 & 45 lying on North side of the Street called "BOLLINGBROKE" STREET; as will appear by the Plat aforesaid, recorded in the Court of the County of DINWIDDIE, And all houses and appurtenances to the lotts or parcells of land belonging; and also all the Estate right title and demand of said ROBERT BOLLING of in and to the said lots and all Deeds Evidences and writings touching the same; To have and to hold the said three lotts of land hereby conveyed and every of their appurtenances unto ROBERT WATKINS and NICHOLSON WATKINS their heirs (as joint tenants with benefit to the survivor) ;aying unto ROBERT BOLLING his heirs yearly on the first day of January the fee rent of Twenty three pounds current money in the several and respective proportions following, that is to say, for the Lot number (26) Twenty six eight pounds current money per annum, for the Lot number (44), seven pounds ten shillings per annum, for the lot number (45) seven pounds Ten shillings per annum to commence from the first day of January last past, the first years Rent to become due and payable the first day of January which shall be in the year of our Lord one thousand seven hundred and eighty five; (nearly all of page three is taken up by the conditions to apply if rent not paid on time); In Witness whereof the parties aforesaid have hereunto set their hands and affixed their seals the day and year first above written

Sealed and Delivered in the presence of us
          (no witnesses recorded)   ROBERT BOLLING JR.
                                                           RO: WATKINS
                                                           NICOLSON WATKINS

    Received the Tenth day of February 1784 of the within named ROBERT WATKINS and NICHOLSON WATKINS, the sum of two hundred & fifty pounds current money the consideration within mentioned for the said three lots or parcells of land aforesaid
                                                           ROBERT BOLLING

    Memorandum that at and before the sealing and delivery of this Indenture, it was covenanted and agreed by ROBERT WATKINS & NICHOLSON WATKINS to and with each other that they wou'd take and hold the said three lots of land and premises as joint tenants according to the form & effect thereof   RO: WATKINS
                                                           NICOLSON WATKINS

    Town of Petersburg Sct. October Hustings Court 1784
    The foregoing Indenture from ROBT. BOLLING to ROBT. WATKINS & NICOLSON WATKINS with the memorandum and receipt thereto were acknowledged by the said ROBERT BOLLING & ROBT. WATKINS and ordered to be recorded
                    Test J. GRAMMER, Cl Ct. H.

p.   THIS INDENTURE made the fifth day of October one thousand seven hundred &
5   Eighty four Between FREDERICK WILLIAMS & ANN his Wife of the Borough of
          Petersburg & State of Virginia of the one part & JOSEPH HARDING of said
Borough & State of other part; Witnesseth that for sum of Two hundred & sixty two pounds lawful money of Virginia to him in hand paid, by these presents doth bargain sell & confirm unto JOSEPH HARDING a certain parcell of land containing Four & a half acres be the same more or less, being one moiety of three lotts of land laid of by ROBERT

RAVENSCROFT and distinguished in the plan of RAVENSCROFT TOWN by the numbers thirty two, thirty three & thirty four and bounded on the East by a plain & visible Ditch, which is the dividing line between WILLIAM HARRISON & said land, Southerly by BOSWELL GOODWYNNE, Westerly by said HARDINGs line & Northerly by lott number thirty one, together with all woods water corses &c. thereunto belonging; To have and to hold the said Lotts with the appurtenances unto JOSEPH HARDING his heirs and FREDRICK WILLIAMS & ANN his Wife will warrant and for ever defend against all persons, In Witness whereof the said FREDK. WILLIAMS & ANN his Wife hath to these presents set their hands & affixed their seals the day and year above written Signed Sealed and Delivered in the presents of

(no witnesses recorded)   FREDERICK WILLIAMS
                                           ANN WILLIAMS

Town of Petersburg Sct. October Court 1784
The above Indenture was acknowledged by the therein named FREDRICK WILLIAMS and ordered to be recorded   Test J. GRAMMER, C. C. Hs.

pp.   THIS INDENTURE made this third day of May in the year of our Lord one thou-
6-   sand seven hundred and eighty four Between WILLIAM CALL of County of
7   PRINCE GEORGE, Merchant, & ELIZABETH his Wife of the first part, NANNY FEILD
         Widow & Relict of THEOPHILUS FEILD the Younger deceased of the second part
and FREDERICK WILLIAMS of Town of Petersburg, Merchant, of the third & last part; Whereas the said WILLIAM CALL, Surviver of THEOPHILUS FEILD SENR. and THEOPHILUS FEILD JUNIOR stood and now stands seized in fee simple of one lot and houses in Town of Petersburg in that part thereof generally called and known by the name of THE OLD TOWN, numbered in the plan of said town by the No. 3 (number three) and being so seized and possessed sold and disposed of the same the 16th day of December 1778 to a certain WILLIAM COOKE for the sum of Two thousand two hundred and fifty pounds, the then current money of Virginia, And whereas the said lot and houses have since come into the hands of said FREDERICK WILLIAMS who hath paid and satisfied the said COOK for the same, and in consequence thereof said COOK hath requested said CALL to make the said WILLIAMS a Deed for the same, his assent to which is hereby signified by his becoming a witness to this Indenture; NOW THIS INDENTURE WITNESSETH that said WILLIAM CALL in consideration of the premises and for the whole purchase money to him in hand paid by these presents doth bargain sell and confirm unto FREDERICK WILLIAMS and to his heirs the above mentioned Lot of Land No. 3 with all houses & improvements thereon and the appurtenances to the same belonging; To have and to hold the said lot and premises with the appurtenances unto the said WILLIAMS his heirs, And said WILLIAM CALL the said lot of land & premises to FREDERICK WILLIAMS his heirs agt. the title claim & demand of all persons claiming under him will always hereafter warrant and for ever by these presents defend; And said NANNY FEILD, as these presents further witnesseth, for the sum of Five shillings to her in hand paid by said FREDERICK WILLIAMS, by these presents doth surrender release and make over unto FREDERICK WILLIAMS and his heirs all her the said NANNY's Dower right and demand which she now has or may have in the said lot & premises; To have and to hold the said lot with the appurtenances to him the said FREDERICK WILLIAMS his heirs; In Witness whereof the said WILLIAM CALL and ELIZABETH his Wife and the said NANNY FEILD, have hereunto respectively set their hands and seals the day & year first above written Sealed and Delivered in presence of

W. J. COOKE, J. GRAMMER,   WM. CALL Survig. Partner of
RICHD. TAYLOR, JNO: BAIRD,   of FEILDs & CALL & also of FEILD

JNO. S. FEILD, JOSEPH FOWLER
P. GOODWYN

Town of Petersburg Sct. October Court 1784
The foregoing Indenture from WILLIAM CALL to FREDK. WILLIAMS was proved by the
Oaths of JOHN GRAMMER, JOHN BAIRD and PETERSON GOODWYN and ordered to be
recorded   Test J. GRAMMER, C.C. Hs.

pp.   THIS INDENTURE made this first day of October in the year of our Lord one
8-   thousand seven hundred and Eighty four Between THOMAS MASTERSON of
10   Petersburg in the County of DINWIDDIE of one part and JOSEPH JACKSON of
         (blank) County of other part; Witnesseth that THOMAS MASTERSON for the sum of
Two hundred pounds to him in hand paid by said JOSEPH JACKSON, and also in consideration of the rents covenants and agreements herein after mentioned to be paid kept
and performed by JOSEPH JACKSON his heirs, said THOMAS MASTERSON by these presents doth bargain sell and confirm unto JOSEPH JACKSON his heirs one lott or parcel of
land lying in County of DINWIDDIE in the Town of Petersburg and "contiguous to the
PUBLICK TOBACCO WAREHOUSE" called BOLLINGS CEDAR POINT and BOLLING BROOK
WAREHOUSES and are part of the lands lately laid of in lotts by ROBERT BOLLING Esquire
which lot of land is known in the plan by said ROBERT BOLLING by the number (12)
Twelve, and extending in Front on the Street called BACK STREET one hundred feet and
on the lines back from the said Street two hundred and seventeen feet nine inches as
by the plan duly recorded in the Court of the County of DINWIDDIE and appurtenances
to said one lott and the remainders rents issue and profits thereof; (the ground rent
hereafter mentioned to be reserved by and payable to the said THOMAS MASTERSON his
heirs excepted) To have and to hold the said lot or parcel of land hereby conveyed to
JOSEPH JACKSON his heirs; said JOSEPH JACKSON his heirs paying therefor unto THOMAS
MASTERSON his heirs on the first day of January yearly the fee rent of Fourteen pounds
current money of Virginia which sum of money shall be paid on the first day of January every year the first years rent to become due and payable on the first day of January which shall be in the year of our Lord one thousand seven hundred and eight five;
and if said money shall be in arrear and unpaid it may be lawfull for said THOMAS
MASTERSON his heirs into the said lott of land to re enter and have as if this Indenture
had never been made; In Witness whereof the parties aforesaid have hereunto set their
hands and affixed their seals interchangably the day and year above first written
Sealed and Delivered in presence of us
        ALEXR: SMYTH,   THOS: MASTERSON
        HENRY MORRISS, SAML. LENOX
Received the first day of October 1794 of JOSEPH JACKSON the sum of Two hundred
pounds current money of Virginia, the consideration money for the within mentioned
one lott of land In presence of us
        HENRY MORRISS,   THOS: MASTERSON
        SAML. LENOX, ALEXR. SMYTH
Town of Petersburg Sct. October Court 1784
The foregoing Indenture from THOMAS MASTERSON to JOSEPH JACKSON was acknowledged by the therein named THOMAS MASTERSON & ordered to be recorded
                        Test J. GRAMMER C. C. Hs.

pp.   THIS INDENTURE made the first day of October in the year of our Lord one thou-
11-   sand seven hundred and Eighty four Between THOMAS MASTERSON of Petersburg
13   in County of DINWIDDIE of one part and WILLIAMSON COLEMAN and CHARLES
         WILLIAMSON, both of them of the County afforesaid, of the other part; Witnes-

seth that THOMAS MASTERSON for the sum of Two hundred pounds to him in hand paid
by said WILLIAMSON COLEMAN and CHARLES WILLIAMSON, and also in consideration of
the rents and agreements herein after mentioned to be paid and performed by said
WILLIAMSON COLEMAN and CHARLES WILLIAMSON their heirs, by these presents doth
bargain sell and confirm unto WILLIAMSON COLEMAN and CHARLES WILLIAMSON their
heirs one lott or parcell of land lying in County of DINWIDDIE and Town of Petersburg
and contiguous to the PUBLICK TOBACCO WAREHOUSES called BOLINGS CEDAR POINT and
BOLLING BROOK WAREHOUSES and are a part of the lands lately laid of in lotts by ROBERT
BOLLING Esquire, which Lott of Land is known by the number Fifteen (15), and extending in front on the Street called BACK STREET one hundred feet and on the liens back
from the said Street two hundred and seventeen feet nine inches as by the plan duly
recorded in said County of DINWIDDIE will appear; and all ways and appurtenances and
the rents issues and profits thereof (the ground rent hereafter mentioned to be
reserved by and payable to THOMAS MASTERSON his heirs excepted); To have and to hold
the said one lott of land with appertainances to WILLIAMSON COLEMAN and CHARLES
WILLIAMSON their heirs; paying THOS: MASTERSON his heirs on the first day of January
yearly the rent of Eleven pounds four shillings every year the first rent to become due
and payable on the first day of January which shall be in the year of our Lord one
thousand seven hundred and Eighty five; And if the said rent or money shall be in
arrear and unpaid it may be lawfull for said THOMAS MASTERSON his heirs into the said
lott to re enter and have as if this Indenture had never been made; In Witness whereof
the parties aforesaid have hereunto set their hands and affixed their seals interchangably the day and year above first written
Sealed and Delivered in the presents of us
      HENRY MORRISS,   THOS: MASTERSON
      ALEXR. SMYTH,   CHARLES WILLIAMSON
      SAML. LENOX
   Received the first day of October 1784, of WILLIAMSON COLEMAN and CHARLES WIL-
LIAMSON two hundred and fifty pounds current money for the within one lott of land
In presence of us HENRY MORRISS   THOS: MASTERSON
      ALEXR. SMYTH, SAML. LENOX
   Town of Petersburg Sct. October Court 1784
The foregoing Indenture from THOMAS MASTERSON to WILLIAMSON COLEMAN and
CHARLES WILLIAMSON was acknowledged by the therein named THOMAS MASTERSON
and ordered to be recorded   Test J. GRAMMER, C. C. Hs.

p.   THIS INDENTURE made between W. F. BURTON and JOHN SUMMERSALL witnes-
14   seth that said BURTON doth Lease unto sd. SUMMERSALL half the lot that said
          BURTON hath got of ROBERT BOLLING JUNR., for the term of Fifteen years for
which Lease sd. SUMMERSALL is to put one house twelve by sixteen, to have the same
house built in a good workman like manner and compleat in every degree, to have the
same underpined with Brick or Stone soficient on account of the freshes and the sd.
SUMMERSALL for himself his heirs doth agree to return the same unto sd. BURTON his
heirs &c. at the expiration of the above fifteen years in a compleat situation, sd. SUM-
MERSALL his heir &c. paying the sum of Eight pounds anually to the sd. BURTON his
heirs &c., for the above term and on failour of sd. SUMMERSALL noncompliance he his
heirs &c. doth forfit the sum of Five thousand pounds; and if sd. BURTON doth molest the
sd. SUMMERSALL the sd. BURTON forfits the sum of Five thousand pounds, As Witness
our hands and seals this fourteenth day of Feby. one thousand seven hundred and
eighty four

Test ROBT. CHAPPELL   W. F. BURTON
    W. YOUNG   J. SOMERSARLL

    MEMORANDUM; I either party hath any notion of seling or renting or going into Trade the party who hath the inclination shall give other six weeks or two months notice for the refusal of buying renting or going into Trade with each other, As Witness our hands and seals this fourteenth day of Feby. one thousand seven hundred and Eighty four   W. F. BURTON
                                          J. SOMERSARLL

    Memorandum. That on the day & year within mentioned quiet and peaceable possession was given unto JOHN SOMERSALL by WM. FERGUSON BURTON of one half the lott agreable to the within writing containing Twenty five foot in front of WATER STREET and on the lines back from the said Street two hundred and seventeen feet as by the said Deed of the said Land duly recorded in the Court of the County of DINWIDDIE will appear; for the within term of years, these 25 feet of land which the said SOMERSALL is given possession of lyes next to Mr. JAMES BROOMLEYs Lott No. 58.
In presence of us JOHN H. HOLT,   W. F. BURTON
       WILLIAM HORTON
  Town of Petersburg Sct. October Court 1784
The foregoing Lease from W. F. BURTON to SUMERSALL was proven by the Oath of ROBT. CHAPELL and the memorandums on the back thereof was proven by the Oath of WILLIAM HORTON and ordered to be recorded

(Pages 15 and 16 are blank.)

p.   A Court of Hustings held for the Town of PETERSBURG at the House of WILLIAM
17   DURELL Wednesday the 3d. of November 1784
     Present JOHN BANISTER Esqr., Mayor
              CHRISTOPHER McCONNICO Esqr. Recorder
              ALEXR. G. STRACHAN, JOHN SHORE,)
              ROBERT BOLLING, ALEXR. McNABB) Gentlemen Aldermen

p.   THIS INDENTURE made this first day of November in the year of our Lord one
17   thousand seven hundred and Eighty four Between LEWIS LANIER of the County
       of SUSSEX of one part and JOHN WATLINGTON of the County of DINWIDDIE and Burrough of Petersburg of other part; Witnesseth that LEWIS LANIER for sum of Five hundred pounds current money of Virginia to him in hand paid by JOHN WATLINGTON by these presents doth bargain & sell unto JOHN WATLINGTON and to his heirs one lott or half acre of land being on North side of the Old Street in the Town & Burrough of Petersburg known in the plan of said Town by No. 8, say number Eight, and adjoining the land of GEORGE DUDGEON on the West, and the land of JOHN BATTE on the East, together with all houses gardens &c., belonging; To have and to hold the half acre of land and premises unto JOHN WATLINGTON his heirs, and said JOHN WATLINGTON to have quiet possession of said lott or half acre of land on or before the first day of November and LEWIS LANIER his heirs by these presents for ever warrant the said lott of land to JOHN WATLINGTON and to his heirs for ever; In Witness whereof the said LEWIS LANIER hath hereunto set his hand & affixed his seal the day and year first above written
Sealed & Delivered in the presence of
    WM. STEGER,   LEWIS LANIER
WM. DURELL, JNO. HARE
 Town of Petersburg Sct. November Court 1784
The above Indenture from LEWIS LANIER to JOHN WATLINGTON was proven by the Oaths

of WM. STEGER, WM. DURELL and JOHN HARE and ordered to be recorded
Test J. GRAMMER C. C. Hs.

p.   THIS INDENTURE made this first day of November in the year of our Lord one
18   thousand seven hundred & Eighty four Between WILLIAM DURELL of the County
          of DINWIDDIE & Burrough of Petersburg of one part & LEWIS LANIER of the
County of SUSSEX of other part; Witnesseth that WILLIAM DURELL for the sum of Five
hundred pounds current money of Virginia to him in hand paid by LEWIS LANIER by
these presents doth bargain & sell unto LEWIS LANIER & to his heirs one lott or half
acre of land lying on the North side of the Old Street in Burrough of Petersburg known
in the plan by No. 8, say number Eight, adjoining the land of GEORGE DUDGEON on the
WEst and the Land of JOHN BATTE on the East, together with all houses gardens &s. belonging; To have and to hold the lott or half acre of land with the appurtenances unto
LEWIS LANIER his heirs, said LEWIS LANIER to have full possession of said lott on the
day & year above written; And WILLIAM DURELL his heirs by these presents for ever
warrant the said lott to LEWIS LANIER & to his heirs; In Witness whereof WILLIAM
DURELL hath hereunto set his hand & affixed his seal the day & year above written
Sealed & Delivered in the presence of
          WM. STEGER   WM. DURELL
          JNO: WASHINGTON,   JNO: HARE
     Town of Petersburg Sct. November Court 1784
The above Indenture of Bargain & Sale from WM. DURRELL to LEWIS LANIER was ack-
nowledged by the therein named WILLIAM DURELL and ordered to be recorded
                         Test J. GRAMMER, C. C. Hs.

p.   THIS INDENTURE made this nineteenth dy of May in the year of our Lord one
19   thousand seven hundred and Eighty four Between CHARLES DUNCAN of County
          of CHESTERFIELD of one part and DONAT PERIER of the Town of BLANDFORD in
PRINCE GEORGE County of other part; Witnesseth that CHARLES DUNCAN for the sum of
Twenty pounds in hand paid by DONAT PERRIER, by these presents doth bargain sell &
confirm unto DONAT PERRIER one certain lott or parcel of land being in the new Town
of BLANDFORD in the County of PRINCE GEORGE distinguished in the plan of said Town
(number Forty One) together with all appurtenances thereunto belonging; To have
and to hold the lott or parcel of land to DONAT PERRIER & assigns & CHARLES DUNCAN
his heirs the lott of land unto DONAT PERRIER his heirs shall warrant and defend
against any person lawfully claiming any right to the same; In Witness whereof said
CHARLES DUNCAN hath hereunto set his hand & seal the day and year above written
Sealed and Delivered in presence of
          PETER POYTHRESS, WILLIAM GILLIAM,   CHARLES DUNCAN
          ROBERT BIRCHETT JUNR., JH: GALLIGO
     Town of Petersburg Sct. November Court 1784
The above Indenture of Bargain & Sale from CHARLES DUNCAN to DONAT PERRIER was
acknowledged by the above named CHARLES DUNCAN and ordered to be recorded
                         Test J. GRAMMER, C. C. Hs.

p.   THIS INDENTURE made the first day of May in the year of our Lord one thou-
20   sand seven hundred and Eighty one Between ROBERT BOLLING JR. of County of
          DINWIDDIE of one part and JAMES HALDANE of the same County of other part;
Witnesseth that in consideration of the Rents and Covenants herein after mentioned sd.
ROBERT BOLLING JR. by these presents doth demise and to farm let unto said HALDEN
one certain spot or half acre of ground lying in Town of Petersburg in County of DIN-

WIDDIE contiguous to and adjoining the land whereon standeth the MILLS known by the name of BOLLINGS & TABBS, on North side of the Main Street of said Town and whereon the said HALDANE now liveth; To have and to hold the said spott or half acre of ground with the houses thereon unto said HALDEN his heirs during the term of Ten years to commence at the time any of the houses or improvements are finished or may become useful, that said HALDANE for himself his heirs shall agrele to make upon the said spot or half acre of ground and the said HALDANE on his part doeth oblige himself to have erected with all possible speed the following improvements, to wit, one addition at the East end of the house the said HALDANE now occupies, twenty feet long and eighteen feet wide, also a Shop thirty feet wide and sixteen feet long, both the said houses to be underpined with Brick or Stone each with a good Chimney of the same on the above spot of ground, the whole to be done in the best workman like manner; all timbers and plank of sound heart Pine or wood of equal goodness and covered with good sound Cypress Shingles, and said JAMES HALDEN for himself his heirs doth agree that the property and improvements shall vest in ROBERT BOLLING JR. his heirs &c. at the expiration of the term of Ten years, paying to ROBERT BOLLING JUNR. his heirs yearly fifteen hundred pounds nett weight of sound merchantable inspected crop tobacco at any of the Petersg. Warehouses during the term; In Witness whereof the parties to these presents have hereunto interchangeably set their hands and affixed their seals the day and year first above written
Signed Sealed Agreed to and delivered in the presence of
JOHN INNIES,   ROBERT BOLLING JR.
GEORGE LONG   JAMES HALDANE
Town of Petersburg Sct. November Court 1784
The above Lease from ROBT. BOLLING JR. to JAMES HALDANE was acknowled. by the above named parties and ordered to be recorded
Teste J. GRAMMER, C. C. Hs.

p. 21   It is hereby agreed between ROBERT BOLLING JR. of the one part and JAMES HALDANE of the other part that ROBERT BOLLING for himself his heirs &c. doth hereby release and acquit said HALDANE his heirs &c. from the obligation of a certain addition to the House he now lives in as expressed in a Lease dated the 1st day of May 1781; also the said ROBERT BOLLING doth oblige himself to receive a Coppersmiths Shop (which is already built) in the same conditon that it may be in when the Lease shall expire, except that the said HALDANE is to keep that House in repair till delivered up. in consideration for the above conditions said JAMES HALDANE for himself his heirs doth hereby relinquish all use profit or claim in and to a certain house 26 feet long and 16 feet wide which is known by the Mill Kitchen with all appurtenances thereunto belonging, that is to say, the ground the said House and Chimney now stands upon, also the use and benefit of the ground back of the said House in a direct line from each end of the same till it strikes the Mill line lately laid off by Mr. WATKINS, the said HALDANE further obliges himself his heirs never to molest said ROBERT BOLLING in the possession of the House and pieces of ground or any other person holding the same under ROBERT BOLLING JR. In confirmation of the within articles of agreement the parties have hereunto bound themselves under the penalty of One hundred pounds specia to be paid by the party failing to the party complying or willing to comply with the just sense and meaning of this contract. Signed Sealed and agreed to by both parties this 7th day of October 1784 in presence of
EDMUND COOPER,   ROBT. BOLLING JR.
JAMES FAWCETT   JAMES HALDANE

Town of Petersburg Sct. November Court 1784   At a Hustings Court held for the said
Town the 3d. day of Novembr: (Wednesday) 1784
  The above Agreement or Release from ROBERT BOLLING JR. to JAMES HALDANE was
acknowledged by both parties thereto and ordered to be recorded
                              Test J. GRAMMER, C. C. Hs.

p.   I GRESSETT DAVIS of the Borough of Petersburg being fully perswaded that
22   Freedom is the natural right of all men, agreable to the Declaration of the Bill
          of Rights, upon which I conceived our present happy Constitution is established
and Whereas I have under my care one Negro man whom I have heretofore held as a
slave named Ishmael about Thirty five years old, which Negro man Ishmael I hereby
emancipate & set free and I do for myself my heirs relinquish all right title interest &
claim or pretension of claim whatsoever either to his person or to any Estate he may
hereafter acquire, which Negro Ishmael shall enjoy his full Freedom without any in-
terruption by me or any other person from by or udner authority received of me, In
Witness whereof I have hereunto set my hand & affixed my seal this third day of November Anno Dom: one thousand seven hundred & eighty four
Signed Sealed & Delivered in presence of
          (no witnesses recorded)   GRESSETT DAVIS
  At a Court of Hustings held for the Town of Petersburg on Wednesday the third day of
Novemr: 1784 The above Deed or Instrument of Writing from GRESSETT DAVIS setting
free his Negroe man Ishmael was presented in Court and acknowledged by the above
named GRESSETT DAVIS and ordered to be recorded
                              Test J. GRAMMER, C. C. Hs.

pp.   (The Deed on pages 23 and 24 has been crossed out with the notation, N. B. The above is
23-   recorded forward properly & shou'd be taken no notice of here. J. GRAMMER.) The Deed
24   is dated the Thiryeth day of November 1784 between JAMES FAWCETT of the Town of
          Petersburg, Taylor, and JAMES GEDDY of the same Town, Silver Smith. Most of page 24 is
blank, followed at the bottom by the following).
  At a Court of Hustings held for the Town of Petersburg at the House of WILLIAM
DURELL Wednesday the 1st of December 1784
          Present JOHN BANISTER Esquire, Mayor
                  CHRISTOPHER McCONNICO, Esqr., Recorder
          ALEXR. G. STRACHAN, JOHN SHORE & ALEXR. McNABB Gent. Aldermen

p.   THIS INDENTURE made this first day of December one thousand seven hundred
25   and Eighty four Between WILLIAM FERGUSON BURTON of HENRICO County of one
          part and WILLIAM COLVIN of the Borough of Petersburg of the other part; Wit-
nesseth that WILLIAM FERGUSON BURTON for the sum of One hundred Guineas current
money of Virginia to him in hand paid by WILLIAM COLVIN, by these presents doth
bargain sell and confirm unto WILLIAM COLVIN hisheirs a certain parcel of land laid off
in the Town of Petersburg and known by No. 37, lying on WATER STREET fifty foot in
front & two hundred and seventeen feet back and all things agreable to a Deed given
the said BURTON by ROBERT BOLLING Esqr. and recorded in the Court of DINWIDDIE
County, which Deed the said COLVIN is to comply with in the said manner the said BUR-
TON was; To have and to hold the said lott unto WILLIAM COLVIN his heirs and the said
BURTON his heirs against all persons shall warrant and forever by these presents defend, In Witness whereof said WILLIAM F. BURTON hath hereunto set his hand and
affixed his seal the day and year above written

Sealed and Delivered in presence of
    (no witnesses recorded)   W. F. BURTON
At a Court of Hustings held for the Town of Petersburg on Wednesday the 1st of December 1784   The above Indenture of Bargain & Sale was presented in Court and acknowledged by the above named WILLIAM FARGUSON BURTON and ordered to be recorded
               Test   J. GRAMMER C. C. Hs.

p.   THIS INDENTURE made this Thirteenth day of September in the year of our Lord
26   one thousand seven hundred and Eighty four Between ELIZABETH GILL of the
        County of CHESTERFEILD of one part and ISHAM WELLS of said County of CHES-
TERFEILD of other part; Witnesseth that ELIZABETH GILL in consideration of the sum of Fifteen pounds current money of Virginia to her in hand paid by ISHAM WELLS, doth give and confirm unto ISHAM WELLS and to his heirs one lott of land containing half an acre lying in a certain Town called WITTON TOWN, also fourty by twenty four feet by the River side as laid of by Mr. RICHARD WITTON which lotts are marked in the plan of said Town by No. Twenty Seven; To have and to hold the said Lott with all priviledges & advantages thereunto belonging to ISHAM WELLS his heirs, And ELIZABETH GILL doth for herself her heirs &c. warrant the said Lott No. 27 unto ISHAM WELLS his heirs against all persons that may claim the same; In Witness whereof the said ELIZABETH GILL hath hereunto set her hand and affixed her Seal the day & year above written
Signed Sealed and Delivered in presence of
    WM. ROWLETT JUNR.   ELIZABETH GILL
    JO: BRAWNOR, THOMAS ROWLETT
At a Court of Hustings held for the Town of Petersburg Wednesday the 1st of December 1784   The above Indenture of Bargain & Sale from ELIZABETH GILL to ISHAM WELLS was acknowledged by the above named ELIZABETH GILL and ordered to be recorded
             Test   J. GRAMMER, C. C. Hs.

p.   THIS INDENTURE made this first day of December one thousand seven hundred
27   and Eighty four Between JOSEPH HARDING and MARY his Wife of the Borough of
        Petersburg & State of Virginia of one part and GEO: BOOTH of County of SUSSEX
of other part; Witnesseth that in consideration of the sum of Eighty seven pounds Ten shillings lawful money of Virginia to him in hand paid, by these presents doth bargain sell & confirm unto GEORGE BOOTH a certain parcell of land containing one & a half acres be the same more or less being one moiety of one three acre lott of land laid off by ROBERT RAVENSCROFT and in the Plan of RAVENSCROFT TOWN by number Thirty four (34), bounded on the East by STITH PARHAMs line, Southerly by BOSWELL GOODWYNNE, Westerly by a Street & Northerly by Lott No. 33, together with all woods water courses &c. thereunto belonging; To have and to hold the said lott or parcell of land with the appurtenances unto GEO: BOOTH his heirs, And JOSEPH HARDING shall warrant and defend against the claim or claims of all persons; In Witness whereof the sd. JOS: HARDING & MARY his Wife hath hereunto set their hands and affixed their seals the day and year first above written
Signed Sealed & Delivered in the presents of
    (no witnesses recorded)   JOSEPH HARDING
                           MARY HARDING
At a Court of Hustings held for the Town of Petersburg on Wednesday the 1st of December 1784   The above Indenture of Bargain & Sale from JOSEPH HARDING and MARY his Wife to GEORGE BOOTH was acknowledged by the said JOSEPH HARDING & Wife (she being first privately examined as the Law directs) and ordered to be recorded
             Teste J. GRAMMER C. C. Hs.

pp.   THIS INDENTURE made the Thirtyeth day of November in the year of our Lord
28-   one thousand seven hundred & Eighty four Between JAMES FAWCETT of the Town
29   of Petersburg, Taylor, of one part and JAMES GEDDY of the Town aforesaid, Silver
        Smith, of other part; Witnesseth that in consideration of the sum of Six hundred
pounds current money of Virginia to him in hand paid by JAMES GEDDY by these presents do bargain sell and confirm unto JAMES GEDDY his heirs one certain lott of land
lying in Town of Petersburg being one half of a Lott or half acre of land which the said
FAWCETT purchased of JOHN PAGAN lying on the North side of the Old Street leading
through the said Town and distinguished in the plan thereof by the number (No. 2)
number Two, dividing the said lott or half acre by a line running from the centre on
the Main Street to the River, it being that part or half of the said lott lying to the East
and bounding on Lott (No. 1), number one, And all houses and appurtenances to said lott
belonging and the rents issues and profits thereof; To have and to hold the lott of land
hereby conveyed with appurtenances unto JAMES GEDDY and his heirs; the said premises now are and so for ever shall remain and be free and clear from all incumbrances whatsoever suffered or committed by said JAMES FAWCETT or any other person
claiming in the premises; In Witness whereof JAMES FAWCETT hath hereunto set his
hand and seal the day and year first above written
Sealed and Delivered in the presence of us
        (no witnesses recorded)   JAMES FAWCETT
Received the Thirtyeth day of November 1784 of the within named JAMES GEDDY the
sum of Six hundred pounds current money, the consideration within mentioned for the
said lott or parcell of land aforesaid   JAMES FAWCETT
At a Court of Hustings held for the Town of Petersburg Wednesday the first of December 1784 The foregoing Indenture of Bargain and Sale from JAMES FAWCETT to JAMES
GEDDY with the receipt thereunto annexed was presented in Court and acknowledged by
the above named JAMES FAWCETT and by the Court ordered to be recorded
                        Test J. GRAMMER, C. C. Hs.

pp.   THIS INDENTURE made this Thirtieth day of November in the year of our Lord
30-   one thousand seven hundred and Eighty four Between WILLIAM HARRISON and
31   (blank) his Wife of Town of Petersburg of one part and WILLIAM WRIGHT of the
        Town aforesaid of other part; Witnesseth that in consideration of the sum of Two
hundred pounds current money of Virginia to him in hand paid by WILLIAM WRIGHT,
by these presents doth bargain sell and confirm unto WILLIAM WRIGHT and to his
heirs one certain lott of land containing three acres lying in Town of Petersburg in
that part thereof known by the name of RAVENSCROFTs Town and distinguished in the
plan of said Town by (No. 16) number Sixteen, & bounded on the North by FREDRICK
WILLIAMS's land, on the East & South by said HARRISON's Land and on the West by
(blank) land, And all houses and appurtenances to said lott or parcell of land belonging;
and the rents issues and profits thereof, To have and to hold the lott of land hereby conveyed unto WILLIAM WRIGHT his heirs free and clear of and from all incumbrances; In
Witness whereof the said WILLIAM HARRISON and (blank) his Wife have hereunto set
their hands and affixed their seals the day and year first above written
Sealed and Delivered in the presence of us
        (no witnesses recorded)   WM. HARRISON
                                                        LUCY HARRISON
Received the thirtieth of November 1784 of WILLIAM WRIGHT the sum of Two hundred
pounds current money, the consideration within mentioned for the said lott or parcell
of land   W. HARRISON

At a Court of Hustings held for the Town of Petersburg Wednesday first of December 1784   The foregoing Indenture of Bargain & Sale from WILLIAM HARRISON and LUCY his Wife to WILLIAM WRIGHT with the memorandum of livery & seizen and receipt thereunto annexed were acknowledged by the said WM. HARRISON and Wife (she being first privately examined as the Law directs) and ordered to be recorded
                              Test. J. GRAMMER, C. C. Hs.

p.   At a Court of Hustings held for the Town of Petersburg the 1st day of December
32   1784   LUCY MASTERSON personally appeared in open Court and after being
            privily & apart from her Husband, THOMAS MASTERSON, examined did freely and voluntarily relinquish her right of Dower of in & to the lott of land & premises conveyed by said THOMAS MASTERSON, her Husband, to JOSEPH JACKSON, as by his Deed bearing date the first of October one thousand seven hundred & Eighty four indented & duly acknowledged and recorded in this Court at a Court held in October last
                              Test J. GRAMMER, C. C. Hs.

            At a Court of Hustings held for the Town of Petersburg the 1st day of December
1784   LUCY MASTERSON personally appeared in open Court and after being privily & apart from her Husband, THOMAS MASTERSON, examined, did freely and voluntarily relinquish her Right of Dower of in & to the lott of land & premises conveyed by the said THOMAS MASTERSON, her Husband, to WILLIAMSON COLEMAN & CHARLES WILLIAMSON as by his Deed bearing date the first of October one thousand seven hundred & Eighty four indented & duly acknowledged & recorded in this Court in October last
                              Test J. GRAMMER, C. C. Hs.

pp.   THIS INDENTURE made this thirtieth day of October in the year of our Lord one
33-   thousand seven hundred & Eighty four Between LEWIS LANIER of the County of
34   SUSSEX of one part and WILLIAM DURELL of the Borough of Petersburg of other
            part; Witnesseth that LEWIS LANIER in consideration of the sum of Five pounds current money of Virginia to him in hand paid by WILLIAM DURELL, by these presents doth bargain & sell unto WILLIAM DURELL & to his heirs one lott or half acre of land lying on the South side of the Old Street in the Town of Petersburg known in the plan of said Town by number Forty Five, Together with all houses yards gardens &c. belonging the the said half acre of land above mentioned except the New House lately built there-on by JOHN CRUMPLER, which said House if retain'd by said DURELL is to be paid for by said DURELL agreable to the lawfull valuation thereof as specified by Contract between said LEWIS LANIER & WILLIAM DURELL (which contract is now in the possession of said WILLIAM DURELL), belonging or any wise appurtaining, To have and to hold the half acre of land with the appurtenances unto WILLIAM DURELL his heirs, and to have quiet and immediate possession of the said lott or half acre of land and LEWIS LANIER his heirs by these presents forever warrant the said lott to WILLIAM DURELL and to his heirs for ever; In Witness whereof LEWIS LANIER hath hereunto set his hand & affixed his seal the day & year first above written
Signed Sealed & Delivered in the presents of
        WM. STEGER,   LEWIS LANIER
        RANDL. WARREN,   JNO: WATLINGTON
  Memorandum, Livery of Seizen of the within mentioned Lott and premises was made thereon the day & year within written in the presence of us
        PARKER HARE,   PHILIP OTT,
        HENRY VAUGHAN

Whereas LEWIS LANIER by Deed bearing date this thirtieth day of October one thousand seven hundred & Eighty four hath sold and conveyed unto WILLIAM DURELL one
lott or half acre of land situate in Town of Petersburg and abutting and bounding as in
the Deed, reference being had more fully will appear, To hold the same in fee simple &
hath covenanted with said DURELL to put him forthwith in peaceable & quiet possession
of the same; Now the said LEWIS LANIER in consideration of the premises doth hereby
further covenant and agree with WILLIAM DURELL his heirs that he said LEWIS
LANIER his heirs will make full satisfaction to said DURELL for all damages whatsoever
which said DURELL his heirs shall sustain by reason of the detention of the said Lott by
JOHN CRUMPLER or any other person whomsoever from the day of the date of these
presents untill WILLIAM DURELL shall obtain the actual possession of said lott with the
appurtenances, for the performance whereof the said LEWIS LANIER doth hereby bind
himself his heirs to WILLIAM DURELL his heirs in the penal sum of One thousand
pounds current money of Virginia in Gold or Silver; Sealed with the Seal of said LEWIS
LANIER and dated the day & year first above written
Signed Sealed & Delivered, the rasure in fourth line from the bottom of the first page
being first made in presence of
         PARKER HARE,   LEWIS LANIER
         PHILIP OTT, HENRY VAUGHAN
   At a Court of Hustings held for the Town of Petersburg Wednesday 1st of December
1784   The foregoing Indenture of Bargain and Sale from LEWIS LANIER to WILLIAM
DURELL was partly proven by the Oath of WILLIAM STEGER & JOHN WATLINGTON at
November Court last and the memorandum on the back thereof with the obligation
annexed was at the same Court proven by PARKER HARE, PHILIP OTT and HENRY
VAUAHAN, the witnesses thereto, And the said Indenture being now proven by RANDAL
WARREN, the third Witness thereto, is ordered to be recorded
               Test J. GRAMMER, C. C. Hs.

pp.   THIS INDENTURE made this nineteenth day of November in the year of our Lord
35-   one thousand seven hundred and Eighty four Between ROBERT BALLARD of the
36   Town of BALTIMORE in the State of MARYLAND, Merchant, of one part and JOHN
        & WILLIAM SHORE & COMPANY of the Town of Petersburg and Commonwealth of
Virginia of other part: Witnesseth that whereas ROBERT BOLLING, Gentleman, of the
Town of Petersburg by Indenture under his hand and seal duly executed bearing date
about the seventeenth day of June one thousand seven hundred and Eighty four did
demise lease and to farm let unto ROBERT BALLARD his heirs all that lott and parcell of
ground with the appurtenances lying in Town of Petersburg and distinguished on a
platt in addition to the said Town by the number 41 (Forty One) as by said Indenture
recorded in the County Court of DINWIDDIE may more fully appear; NOW THIS INDEN-
TURE Witnesseth tht ROBERT BALLARD in consideration of the sum of Three hundred
and Fifty pounds current money of Virginia to him in hand paid, by these presents doth
bargain sell set over and confirm unto said JOHN and WILLIAM SHORE & COMPANY their
heirs all that parcel of land lying in Town aforesaid being part of said lot number 41
(Forty One), and contained within the metes courses and distances, to wit, begining at
the intersection of BOLLING BROOK and SECOND STREETs, thence runing and binding on
BOLLING BROOK STREET West thirty four feet, thence runing North one hundred and
thirty feet to a private alley of Twenty feet given by ROBERT BALLARD aforesaid,
thence runing and binding on SECOND STREET South one hundred & thirty feet to the
place of begining, together with all improvements and appurtenances belonging, To
have and to hold the parcel of land with every right title and term of years by these
presents set over unto JOHN & WILLIAM SHORE and COMPANY, their heirs; as Tenants in

Common and not as joint tenants, paying therefor yearly the rent of One penny Sterling if the same shall be demanded unto ROBERT BALLARD his heirs which rent of One penny Sterling shall be and is hereby declared and agreed by and between the parties that the same shall always be understood to be in lieu of and in full discharge from any demand for any ground rent which hath been or may hereafter be claimed by ROBERT BALLARD his heirs, And ROBERT BALLARD doth further agree with JOHN & WILLIAM SHORE and COMPANY their heirs to indemnify and secure them against all legal demands or claims of the aforementioned ROBERT BOLLING his heirs for any ground rent due or pretended to be due; And it is further covenanted and agreed by the parties that JOHN & WILLIAM SHORE & COMPANY their heirs shall be chargeable with and pay all taxes and demands whatsoever for the parcel of land and further JOHN & WILLIAM SHORE & COMPANY their heirs or some or one of them shall within the space of three years from the date hereof build a good & sufficient house of Brick Stone or Wood on the parcel of land to the value of One hundred pounds under the penalties & covenants as expressed in the Original Indenture of Lease from the aforementioned ROBERT BOLLING to said ROBERT BALLARD; In Witness whereof the parties hereto have interchangeably set their hands and seals the day and year first aforementioned
Signed Sealed & Delivered in the presence of

EDMUND B. HOLLOWAY,   ROBERT BALLARD
WM. DURELL, JAMES BROMLEY,   JNO. & WM. SHORE & CO.
JNO: HARE

At a Court of Hustings held for the town of Petersburg on Wednesday the first of December 1784   The foregoing Indenture of Bargain & Sale from ROBERT BALLARD to JOHN & WILLIAM SHORE & COMPANY was proven by the witnesses thereto and by order of the said Court is truly recorded   Test J. GRAMMER, C. C. Hs.

pp.   THIS INDENTURE made this 3d. day of March in year of our Lord one thousand
37-   seven hundred & Eighty four Between ROBERT BOLLING JR. Esqr. of BOLLING
39   BROOK of one part and JNO: BAIRD JR. and JAMES TURNBULL, both of the Town of
         Petersburg of other part; Witnesseth that ROBERT BOLLING JR. in consideration
of the sum of Seventy pounds specia to him in hand well & truly paid by JNO: BAIRD JR. & JAMES TURNBULL, by these presents doth sell make over & confirm unto JOHN BAIRD JR. and JAMES TURNBULL and their heirs one certain lott or parcel of land lying in County of DINWIDDIE lying on the Main Street or Road leading therefrom towards the PUBLICK WAREHOUSEs & towards the BRIDGE of POCOHONTAS, is part of the Lands late the property of Colo. ROBERT BOLLING deced., and lately by the said ROBERT BOLLING JR. Esqr. laid off in lotts and is distinguished by the plan of said lotts by the No. 1, or One and extends (blank) feet on the Road or Street before mentioned bordering on the Street laid of called the Back Street and is in front on said Street, to wit, the Back Street, (blank) feet and the lines or boundaries of which lott is more particularly known & established by the Corner Stones or Posts affixed & planted to discribe & point out the same, with all houses profits commodities & appurtenances with the rents issues & profits thereof; To have and to hold the lott of land with appurtenances unto JOHN BAIRD JR. and JAMES TURNBULL their heirs as Tenants in Common and not as joint Tenants, that is to say, the said JOHN BAIRD JR. one moiety or half part and JAMES TURNBULL the other moiety or half part, and ROBERT BOLLING JR. doth covenant that the premises now are and so shall remain clear of and free from all former and other gifts sales & Incumbrances whatsoever (the Fee Rent of Six pounds per annum due & payable in every year only excepted and foreprized), And ROBERT BOLLING JR. and his heirs the premises hereby sold unto JNO: BAIRD JR. & JAMES TURNBULL their heirs as Tenants in Common against all persons shall warrant and forever defend by these presents; In Witness whereof

said ROBERT BOLLING JR. Esqr., hath hereunto set his hand and affixed his seal the day and year first within written
Sealed & Delivered in presence of
      PETER THWEATT,   JOSEPH THWEATT,   ROBERT BOLLING
      HUMFRIES TRAYLOR,   WM. CONWAY
  Memorandum: That at and before the sealing and delivery of this Indenture it was covenanted and agreed by the said JNO: BAIRD JR. and JAMES TURNBULL that they will hold the said lott & appurtenances as Tenants in Common and not as Joint Tenants according to the form and effect of this Indenture
In presence of us,   PETER THWEATT   J. BAIRD JR.
      WILLIAM CONWAY   JAMES TURNBULL
  Memorandum: Be it known universally by all whom it may concern, that we JNO: BAIRD JR. & JAMES TURNBULL the day & year within written in person did divide the within mentioned Lott No. 1, One, in the following manner or form, to wit. The said BAIRD's line to begin from the North West corner of sd. Lott where it adjoins the two Streets or Roads within mentioned and runing 38 feet Southwardly on the Street or Road first mentioned in this Deed, which is FIRST STREET, and from thence back in a direct line to the extreme part of the said Lott to a corner to the post planted for ye purpose of fixing the same, from the sd. Corner Northwardly to the sd. Back Street making a fourth Corner & in wch: lines lies the sd. BAIRDs seperate part; moiety or half of the sd. Lott No. One, the residue of wch: is the sd. TURNBULLs half of the sd Lott, and we seperately to pay & be answerable for our own half of the Ground Rent to become due & to be paid on the same agreable to the tenour & effect of the within Deed. Witness our hands this 3d. March 1784
Test JAMES HARRIS   JNO: BAIRD JR.
                            JAMES TURNBULL
  At a Court of Hustings held for the Town of Petersburg Wednesday the first of December 1784   The foregoing Indenture of Bargain & Sale from ROBERT BOLLING JR. to JOHN BAIRD JR. & JAMES TURNBULL was at October Court last partly proved by the Oath of PETER THWEATT & HUMFRIES TRAYLOR, two of the witnesses thereto, And the Memorandum thereon indorsed were partly proved by the Oath of PETER THWEATT a witness thereto, And the Memorandum thereon indorsed between said BAIRD & TURNBULL was at the same Court proved by the Oath of the witnesses thereto; The said Indenture being now proved by the Oath of WM. CONWAY, a third witness thereto, & the Memorandums thereon indorsed likewise proved by the Oath of the sd. CONWAY, the said Indenture and Memorandums were by the Court ordered to be recorded
                  Test J. GRAMMER, C. C. Hs.

(Page number 40 is blank.)

p.   At a Court of Hustings held for the Town of Petersburg at the House of WIL-
41   LIAM DURELL on Wednesday the fifth day of January 1785
       Present ALEXANDER G. STRACHAN,   JOHN SHORE,
          ROBERT BOLLING   ALEXANDER McNABB Gentlemen Aldermen

pp.   THIS INDENTURE made this thirtieth day of June in year of our Lord one thou-
41-   sand seven hundred & Eighty four Between PHILIP OTT of the County of DINWID-
43   DIE & Town of Petersburg of one part & JOSEPH WHITEHEAD of the same County
       of other part. Witnesseth that said PHILIP OTT for divers good causes & considerations him thereunto moving and also for the further consideration of Five shillings current money of Virginia to him in hand paid by JOSEPH WHITEHEAD, hath demised

granted & to farm letten unto JOSEPH WHITEHEAD a certain parcel of ground in the
Town of Petersburg, (situate on the Old Street adjoining the lott of ground under the
Guardianship of SARAH NEWSUM & now occupied by ABRAM EVANS), it being part of
the lott now occupied by JAMES DURELL & belonging to the said OTT; sufficient to build
one Store House thirty six feet long in front & twenty four feet wide, also one Lumber
House of thirty two feet long & eighteen feet wide, standing to the South of the said
Store House & the ends in the same direction as it does together with sufficient room for
a Waggon to pass & repass at the East end of the said Store House and also between the
Store and Lumber Houses, so that access may conveniently be had to the Doors of the
Lumber House; To have and to hold the parcell of ground unto JOSEPH WHITEHEAD &
assigns from the first day of September next ensuing the date hereof during the full
term of Fifteen years and paying therefor yearly unto PHILIP OTT & assigns the Rent of
one ear of Indian Corn on every first day of September annually, and if it shall be that
the yearly rent shall be behind for ten days at all times thereafter it shall be lawful for
PHILIP OTT or assigns into the demised parcel of ground to re enter and the same to
have again; And JOSEPH WHITEHEAD doth covenant with PHILIP OTT & assigns that he
shall at his own proper charges erect before the expiration of this present demise upon
the soil above mentioned one good Store House thirty six feet long twenty four feet
wide, two story high with three rooms below which will be either ceild or plaistered &
two in the upper story, on of which will be either caild or plaistered & the other not,
there will be four pannell & battern doors & thirteen sash window with a cellar thro:
the House, it is also to be painted; Also one Lumber House thirty two feet long & eighteen feet wide to be cield below stairs, and he shall at all times as often as it shall re-
quire at his own charges repair maintain & keep the said houses & improvements,
casualties of Tempest or Fire & the devastation of the premises which may burn or
destroy the same or any part thereof excepted; In Witness whereof the said PHILIP OTT
& JOSEPH WHITEHEAD have hereunto interchangeably set their hands & affixed their
seals the day & year first above written
Sealed & Delivered in the presence of us
          JAMES DURELL,   PHILIP OTT
          EDMUND COOPER,   JAMES BROMLEY   JOS: WHITEHEAD
     Be it known by all parties & to all persons whom it may now or hereafter concern,
That in consideration of the value received of JOHN HIX of the Town of Petersburg,
Merchant, I have and do hereby sell relinquish transfer make over & convey all my
title interest benefit & demand of in & to the above mentioned House & Houses and the
spot of ground appurtaining thereto, agreable to the tenour & letter of the within
Lease, in Testimony whereof I have voluntarily set my hand and affixed my Seal this
Tenth day of December 1784, one thousand seven hundred & Eighty four
Witness THOMAS POLLARD,   JOSEPH WHITEHEAD
          WM. DURELL
     At a Court of Hustings held for the Town of Petersburg on Wednesday the fifth day of
January 1785   The foregoing Lease from PHILIP OTT to JOSEPH WHITEHEAD was presented in Court and acknowledged by both of the parties and with the conveyance
thereunto annexed by the said WHITEHEAD to JOHN HIX (which was likewise acknowled:
by the said JOSEPH WHITEHEAD) are by the Court ordered to be recorded
                         Test J. GRAMMER, C. C. Hs.

p.   THIS INDENTURE made this Twentieth day of November in the year of Our Lord
44   one thousand seven hundred & Seventy five Between DAVID WILLIAMS & MILES
          WILLIAMS of County of DINWIDDIE of one part & WILLIAM HARRISON, Rector of
BRISTOL CHURCH & County of DINWIDDIE of other part; Witnesseth that in considera-

tion of the sum of Twenty pounds paid by WILLIAM HARRISON to said DAVID WILLIAMS & MILES WILLIAMS, by these presents do bargain sell & confirm unto said HARRISON one certain lot of land lying in County of DINWIDDIE & in the Town lay off by ROBERT RAVENSCROFT, now known by the name of RAVENSCROFT & distinguished in the plan of said Town by the number (Forty Two), And all houses gardens &c., together with all profits commodities & advantages to the same belonging; To have and to hold the said lott of land with the appurtenances unto WILLIAM HARRISON his heirs; And the said DAVID WILLIAMS & MILES WILLIAMS do for themselves their heirs warrant and for ever defend agains their heirs and all other who may claim or pretend to claim under them; In Witness whereof they the said DAVID WILLIAMS & MILES WILLIAMS have hereunto set their hands & seals the day & year above written
Sign'd Sealed & delivered in the presence of
  EDWD. PEGRAM JR. PETER JONES,   DAVID WILLIAMS
  JOHN SCOTT COLEMAN, ALEXR. GORDON
 At a Court of Hustings held for the Town of Petersburg on Wednesday the 5th of January 1785 The foregoing Indenture from DAVID WILLIAMS to WILLIAM HARRISON was partly proven at November Court last by the Oaths of JOHN SCOTT COLEMAN & ALEXANDER GORDON, two of the witnesses thereto, And being now fully proven by the Oath of EDWARD PEGRAM JR., a third witness thereto, is by the Court ordered to be recorded
       Test J. GRAMMER, C. C. Hs.

(Pages 45 and 46 are blank.)

p. At a Court of Hustings held for the Town of Petersburg at the House of WIL-
47 LIAM DURELL on Wednesday the 2d. day of February 1785
  Present   CHRISTOPHER McCONNICO, Esqr., Recorder
   ALEXANDER G. STRACHAN, JOHN SHORE)
   ROBERT BOLLING, ALEXANDER McNABB) Gentlemen Aldermen

p. THIS INDENTURE made this Second day of February in the year of our Lord one
47 thousand seven hundred and Eighty five Between ROBERT WATKINS of the County of DINWIDDIE and Town of Petersburg of one part and RICHARD GREGORY
JUNR., of the County aforesaid of other part; Witnesseth that ROBERT WATKINS in con-
sideration of the sum of Seven hundred and Fifty pounds to him in hand paid, by these presents doth bargain sell & confirm unto said RICHARD GREGORY & to his heirs one lott or half acre of ground, No. Eighteen, laying in the Town of BLANDFORD & in the County of PRINCE GEORGE which the said WATKINS purchased of a certain THOMAS GORDON (as p. Deed recorded in the County Court of PRINCE GEORGE will appear), and bounded on one side by the land of SARAH VAUGHAN & on the other by the land of JOHN McCLOUD, together with all houses gardens orchards mines minerals, profits & commodities, To have and to hold the lott or parcell of ground to RICHARD GREGORY his heirs, And ROBERT WATKINS for himself his heirs the parcell of ground with the appurtenances to RICHARD GREGORY his heirs and against all persons will warrant & for ever by these presents defend; In Witness whereof ROBERT WATKINS hath hereunto set his hand and affixed his seal the day & year first above written
Sealed & Delivered in presence of
  RD: HILL   RO: WATKINS
 At a Court of Hustings held for the Town of Petersburg on Wednesday the second day of February 1785 The above Indenture of BArgain & Sale from ROBERT WATKINS to RICHARD GREGORY was acknowledged by the above named ROBERT WATKINS & be the said Court ordered to be recorded Test J. GRAMMER, C. C. Hs.

pp.   THIS INDENTURE made this Sixth day of November Anno Domini one thousand
48-   seven hundred and Eighty four Between RICHARD HILL Esquire of the Town of
49   Petersburg of one part and Messieurs SHORE, McCONNICO & RITSON, Merchants,
          of the same of the other part; Witnesseth that for the sum of Five hundred &
Sixty two pounds, Thirteen shillings & four pence current money of Virginia to him in
hand paid by the said SHORE, McCONNICO & RITSON, and also in consideration of the
annual Ground Rent of Nine pounds Eight shillings & eight pence currency to be paid
for ever by the said SHORE, McCONNICO & RITSON their heris to ROBERT BOLLING JUNIOR
Gentleman of BOLLING BROOK and his assigns and lastly in consideration of the covenants & agrements herein after specified said HILL hath demised granted & to farm let
two thirds part of a lot of land situate on BOLLING BROOK STREET and which is known in
the plan of the Town of Petersburg by the No. Twenty Two (22), and is bounded
begining at the North West corner of the said lot & runing on BOLLING BROOK STREET
Easterly sixty six feet eight inches, then Southerly in a parrallel line with SECOND
STREET to BACK STREET, thence along the Street Westerly sixty six feet eight inches and
Northerly, thence to the begining, To have and to hold the portion of ground and its
appurtenances unto SHORE, McCONNICO & RITSON their heirs; during the term of Ninety
nine years, paying annually the sum of Nine pounds eight shillings and eight pence
current money to ROBERT BOLLING his heirs, to commence on the first day of January
Anno Domini one thousand seven hundred & Eighty five; And said SHORE, McCONNICO &
RITSON their heirs &c., will at all times pay all taxes and other duties which shall be
taxed or assessed on the above portion of land and will erect either of Brick Stone or
wood a dwelling or House of value of One hundred pounds at least & keep the same of
such value (destruction by Fire or Tempest excepted) during the term; In Witness
whereof the parties aforesaid have hereunto set their hands and affixed their seals the
day & year first above written
Sealed and Delivered in presence of us
          L. DAVIS,   RD. HILL
          RT. HEBLETHWAITE, JOHN TAYLOR   SHORE, McCONNICO & RITSON
     At a Court of Hustings held for the Town of Petersburg on Wednesday the 2d. day of
February 1785   The foregoing Indenture of Bargain & Sale from RICHARD HILL to
SHORE, McCONNICO & RITSON was acknowledged by the above named HILL and CHRISTO-
PHER McCONNICO for SHORE, McCONNICO & RITSON, and by the Court ordered to be
recorded   Test J. GRAMMER, C. C. Hs.

pp.   THIS INDENTURE made this Sixth day of November Anno Domini one thousand
50-   seven hundred and Eighty four Between RICHARD HILL Esqr., of the Town of
51   Petersburg of one part and Messrs. PAGE & LANGDON, Merchants, of the same of
          the other part; Witnesseth that in consideration of the sum of Two hundred and
Eighty three pounds six shillings & eight pence current money of Virginia to him in
hand paid by said PAGE & LANGDON, and for the consideration of the annual Ground
Rent of Four pounds Fourteen shillings and four pence currency to be paid for ever by
said PAGE & LANGDON their heirs to ROBERT BOLLING JUNIOR, Gentn., of BOLLINB BROOK
and his assigns, and lastly in consideration of the covenants and agrements herein
afterwards specified; said HILL hath demised transferred and to farm let one third part
of a lot of land situate on BOLLING BROOK STREET and is known in the Plan of the Town
by the No. Twenty Two (22) and is bounded, begining at the North East corner of the
above lot, thence running Westerly thirty three feet four inches on the Street, thence
Southerly in a parellel line with SECOND STREET to BACK STREET, thence Easterly along
the same thirty three feet four inches & thence runing Northerly to BOLLING BROOK

STREET to the begining, To have and to hold the above portion of ground and its appurtenances unto said PAGE and LANGDON their heirs paying therefor annually the sum of
four pounds fourteen shillings and four pence current money to aforesaid ROBERT
BOLLING his heirs, to commence on the first day of January Anno Domini one thousand
seven hundred and Eighty five; And it is agreed that said PAGE and LANGDON their heirs
shall at all times pay the taxes and other duties that may be levied or assessed on the
above portion of the premises; and that they will build of Brick Stone or Wood a dwelling or House of the value of One hundred pounds at the lease & keep of such value
(destruction by Fire or Tempest excepted), during the term of ninety nine years; And if
the above building shall not be finished within the term aforesaid that said PAGE &
LANGDON shall pay unto RICHARD HILL or assigns the sum of One hundred pounds current money for the above ground not so improved; In Witness whereof the parties
aforesaid have hereunto set their hands and affixed their seals the day & year first
above written
Sealed & Delivered in presence of us
        EDWD. STABLER,   RD. HILL
        CHR: McCONNICO,   HENRY MORRISS   PAGE & LANGDON
    At a Court of Hustings held for the Town of Petersburg on Wednesday the 2d. day of
February 1785   The foregoing Indenture from RICHARD HILL to PAGE & LANGDON was
acknowledged by the parties thereto & by the said Court ordered to be recorded
                        Test J. GRAMMER, C. C. Hs.

pp.   THIS INDENTURE made this fourth day of December Anno Domini one thousand
52-   seven hundred & Eighty four Between RICHARD HILL Esquire of the Town of
53   Petersburg of one part and Messieurs WILLIAM HAXALL & WILLIAM WEST, Merchants of the same Town of other part; Witnesseth that for the sum of Eight
hundred & fifty pounds current money of Virginia to him in hand paid by WILLIAM
HAXALL & WILLIAM WEST, he the said HIL has bargained transferred and to farm let
unto WILLIAM HAXALL & WILLIAM WEST a certain lot of land known in the plan of the
Town which was laid out by ROBERT BOLLING Esquire of BOLLING BROOK by the number
Twenty Three (23), situate on BOLLING BROOK STREET & is bounded, begining at the
North East corner of said lot, thence runing Westerly one hundred feet on BOLLING
BROOK STREET, thence Southerly two hundred & seventeen feet nine inches to BACK
STREET, thence along BACK STREET Easterly one hundred feet to SECOND STREET, thence
along SECOND STREET Northerly two hundred and seventeen feet nine inches to the be-
gining; And also in consideration of the rents & agrements herein afterwards
expressed RICHARD HILL hath bargained transferred and to farm let to WILLIAM
HAXALL & WILLIAM WEST To have and to hold the above lot of land with all its appertenances unto WILLIAM HAXALL & WILLIAM WEST their heirs from the first day of
January last past for the term of ninety nine years paying therefor annually the sum
of fourteen pounds three shillings current money during the term unto RICHARD HILL
his heirs to commence on the first day of January Anno Domini one thousand seven
hundred and Eighty five (1785), And it is agreed WILLIAM HAXALL & WILLIAM WEST
shall at all times pay all taxes & other dues that may be levied or assessed on the above
lot of land & premises; and within the space of two years from the date hereof build
either of Brick Stone or Wood a house or dwelling of the value of One hundred pounds
currency and keep the same of such value during the term of ninety nine years, (Destruction by Fire or Tempest excepted), In Witness whereof the aforesaid have hereunto set their hands and affixed their Seals the day & year first above written

Sealed and Delivered in presence of us
    CHR: McCONNICO,   RD. HILL
    HENRY MORRISS,   P. DAVIS   WM. HAXALL & WM. WEST
    Memorandum: That WM. HAXALL & WM. WEST are Tenants in Common
    At a Court of Hustings held for the Town of Petersburg on Wednesday the 2d. of February 1785   The foregoing Indenture from RICHARD HILL to WM. HAXALL & WM. WEST was acknowledged by the sd. HILL and WM. HAXALL & WM. WEST above written and by the said Court ordered to be recorded   Test J. GRAMMER, C. C. Hs.

p.   THIS INDENTURE made between ROBERT BOLLING JUNR. of one part and HENRY
54   LINCH of the other part on the first day of April one thousand seven hundred
            and Eighty four. Witnesseth that in consideration of the Rents and Covenants
hereinafter mentioned said ROBERT BOLLING by these presents doth demise and to farm let unto HENRY LINCH a certain spot of ground contiguous to MRS. SPENCERs to be laid off on the same side of the Road leading from PETERSBURG to POCOHONTAS BRIDGE, the above spot of ground to be fifty in front of the above mentioned Road, thence back to the Low Water mark bounded on one side by Mrs. SPENCERs line and on the other side by the lines of the Town Lots; the said LINCH on his part doth by these presents oblige himself to have erected the following buildings, to wit, one house twelve feet wide by sixteen feet long, one other house adjoining the same twenty feet long & sixteen feet wide with a Brick Chimney between the two houses with all necessary and convenient fire plces and to be well underpined with Brick and doth further agree that the houses and spot of ground shall rest in ROBERT BOLLING JUNR. his heirs at the expiration of Nine years from the date hereof and to continue in possession of said houses and spot of ground during the term provided HENRY LINCH doth apay all the taxes of every kind; To the performance of the above articles both parties do by these presents respectably bind themselves their heirs in the penal sum of One thousand pounds specia to be paid by the party failing to the party observing or willing to observe the within articles of agrement; In Testimony whereof the parties aforesaid have hereunto set their hands and affixed their seals the first day of April one thousand seven hundred and Eighty four
Test HECTOR McNEIL,   ROBT. BOLLING JR.
     LEWIS STARKE   HENRY LINCH
    Memorandum. It is hereby agreed between the within named parties that all accidents of Fire and Winds shall be excepted but HENRY LINCH doth warrant the above houses against freshes or overflowings of the River   ROBT. BOLLING
                                             HENRY LINCH
    At a Court of Hustings held for the Town of Petersburg on Wednesday the 2d. day of February 1785   The foregoing Lease from ROBERT BOLLING JR., to HENRY LINCH with the memorandum thereunto, was acknowledged by the said ROBERT BOLLING JR. & HENRY LINCH above written and by the said Court ordered to be recorded
                            Test J. GRAMMER, C. C. Hs.

pp.   THIS INDENTURE made this fifth day of January in year of our Lord one thou-
55-   sand seven hundred & Eighty four Between MARY BOLLING the Elder, ROBERT
57   BOLLING & MARY his Wife of BOLLING BROOK in Town of Petersburg of one part
            and ARDCHIBALD MIDDLEMAST of Town aforesaid of other part. Witnesseth that
MARY BOLLING, ROBERT BOLLING & MARY his Wife in consideration of the sum of seventy pounds current money of Virginia to them in hand paid by ARCHIBALD MIDDLEMAST, and also in consideration of the Rents covenants and agrements herein

after mentioned to be paid and performed by said ARCHIBALD MIDDLEMAST his heirs,
said MARY BOLLING, ROBERT BOLLING and MARY his Wife by these presents doth bargain sell and confirm unto ARCHIBALD MIDDLEMAST his heirs one certain lot or parcel
of land lying in Town of Petersburg near to and in the vicinity of the PUBLICK TOBACCO
WAREHOUSES called ROBERT BOLLINGs, is part of the land lately laid out in lots by
ROBERT BOLLING and is known in the plan of said Town by the number Fifty Six (56),
extending in front on the Street called WATER STREET one hundred and eight feet and
on the East line back from the said Street two hundred & seventeen feet nine inches
bounded on the West by a Street runing to the River and on the back sixty five feet
more or less as by the plan of said lands recorded in the Court of the County of DINWID-
DIE may appear; And all ways and appurtenances to said lot of land belonging; To have
and to hold the land hereby granted and sold unto ARCHIBALD MIDDLEMAST his heirs
paying therefor unto ROBERT BOLLING his heirs every year on the first day of January
for ever the fee rent of six pounds current money which sum shall be paid on the first
day of January in every year, the first years rent to grow due and become payable the
first day of January in the year one thousand seven hundred & eighty five; And MARY
BOLLING, ROBERT BOLLING & MARY his Wife and their heirs shall warrant and forever
defend by these presents; In Witness whereof the parties aforesaid have hereunto set
their hands and affixed their seals the day and year first above written
Sealed and Delivered in the presence of us
    WM. STEGER,   ROBERT BOLLING JR.
    JNO: HARE,   WM. DURELL   ARCHD: MIDDLEMIST
    Received the first day of January one thousand seven hundred & Eighty four of
ARCHIBALD MIDDLEMAST, the sum of Twenty pounds the consideration for the lot of
land and premises within mentioned;   ROBT. BOLLING JR.
    At a Court of Hustings held for the Town of Petersburg on Wednesday the 2d. day of
February 1785   The foregoing Indenture of Bargain & Sale from ROBERT BOLLING JR.
&c. was acknowledged by the above ROBERT BOLLING with the memorandum & receipt
thereto likewise, and the said Indenture on the part of ARCHIBALD MIDDLEMAST was
proved by the Oaths of the witnesses thereto and by the Court ordered to be recorded
                  Test J. GRAMMER, C. C. Hs.

pp.   THIS INDENTURE made this sixteenth day of August in the year of our Lord one
58-   thousand seven hundred and Eighty four Between WILLIAM BIGELOW of Town of
59   Petersburg, Merchant, of one part and JOHN BATTE of the County of PRINCE
          GEORGE, Gentleman, of other part; Whereas the said JOHN BATTE and MARY his
Wife for the sum of Twelve hundred pounds have bargained and sold unto WILLIAM
BIGELOW in fee simple a platt of ground, part of a lot of land in the afsd. Town of Petersburg No. 7 (Seven), laid off and begining at the Street that runs from the Main Street to
the River, thence up the Main Street twenty feet above the East end of the dwelling
house, which in all is seventy feet in width through the full length of the lott from the
Main Street to the River, with the dwelling house now in occupancy of said BATTE &c.,
and by their, the said JOHN and MARY's Deed of Conveyance to said BIGELOW bearing
date with these presents reference being thereunto had may more fully appear; And
whereas said BIGELOW willing and desirous to secure the said BATTE the paiment of the
said twelve hundred pounds at such times as is specified for that purpose and expressed
in eight several bonds given by him to the said BATTE for the same and all of them
bearing even date with these presents; NOW THIS INDENTURE Witnesseth that said
BIGELOW in consideration thereof as also for the further consideration of Five shillings
to him in hand paid by said BATTE, by these presents doth bargain & sell unto JOHN

BATTE and to his heirs the above mentioned platt of ground conveyed to him by said
BATTE & MARY his Wife; To have and to hold the same to JOHN BATTE his heirs, Provided
nevertheless that if WILLIAM BIGELOW his heirs do well and truly pay the sum of
Twelve hundred pounds at the times set forth in the eight Bonds for that purpose without deducting or abatement, that then these presents shall cease determine and be void;
And whereas said BIGELOW purposes to divide the aforesaid platt of ground as afsd. purchased of said BATTE into two parcells, one including the dwelling house and fifty feet
front on the Main Street, the other the remaining fifty feet front at the East end of the
house above mentioned and so to extend to the River; In Witness whereof said WILLIAM
BIGELOW & JOHN BATTE parties to these presents have interchangeably set their hands
and affixed their seals the day and year first above written
Sealed and Delivered in the presence of

JNO: BAIRD JR.,   WM. BIGELOW
WILLIAM BARKSDALE,   JOHN BATTE
LEWIS EDWARDS

At a Court of Hustings held for the Town of Petersburg on Wednesday the Second day of
February 1785   The foregoing Indenture from WILLIAM BIGELOW to JOHN BATTE was
proven by the Oaths of JNO: BAIRD JR., WM. BARKSDALE and LEWIS EDWARDS witnesses
thereto and by the said Court ordered to be recorded
                         Test J. GRAMMER, C. C. Hs.

p.   THIS INDENTURE made this the Second dy of February one thousand seven hun-
60   dred and Eighty five Between JOSEPH HARDING and MARY his Wife of the
        Borough of Petersburg and State of Virginia of one part and STITH PARHAM of
said Borough of other part; Witnesseth that for the sum of Sixty six pounds thirteen
shillings & four pence lawful money of Virginia to him in hand paid, by these presents
doth bargain sell & confirm unto STITH PARHAM a certain piece of land containing one
acre be the same more or less being two thirds of one moiety of one three acre lot of
land laid off by ROBERT RAVENSCROFT and distinguished in the plan of RAVENSCROFT
TOWN by number Thirty four (34), lying on South side of said lott adjoining BOSWELL
GOODWYN's and the East end adjoining the Revd. WILLIAM HARRISON, Together with all
woods ways water course &c. thereto belonging; To have and to hold the piece of land
with the appurtenances unto STITH PARHAM his heirs and JOSEPH HARDING shall warrant and defend against the claim of all persons; In Witness whereof said JOSEPH HAR-
DING & MARY his Wife hath hereunto set their hands and affixed their seals the day
and year first above written
Signed Sealed & Delivered in presence of
        (no witnesses recorded)   JOS: HARDING
                                                   MARY HARDING
At a Court of Hustings held for the Town of Petersburg at the House of WM. DURELL on
Wednesday the 2d. day of Feby. 1785   The foregoing Indenture of Bargain & Sale from
JOSEPH HARDING and MARY his Wife to STITH PARHAM was acknowledged by the above
subscribed JOSEPH HARDING and by the said Court ordered to be recorded
                         Test J. GRAMMER, C. C. Hs.

p.   THIS INDENTURE made this the Second day of February one thousand seven
61   hundred and Eighty five Between JOSEPH HARDING and MARY his Wife of the
        Borough of Petersburg and State of Virginia of one part and RICHARD GARRETT-
SON of said Borough of other part; Witnesseth that in consideration of the sum of Thirty
three pounds six shillings & eight pence lawful money of Virginia to him in hand paid

by these presents doth bargain sell and confirm unto RICHARD GARRETTSON a certain parcel of land containing half an acre be the same more or less being one third of one moiety of one three acre lott of land laid off by ROBERT RAVENSCROFT and distinguished in the plan of RAVENSCROFT TOWN by the number Thirty Four (34), lying on North side of the said lott adjoining lott number Thirty three and on the East end adjoining the Revd. WILLIAM HARRISON, Together with all woods ways water courses &c., thereto belonging; To have and to hold the parcel of land with the appurtenances unto RICHARD GARRETTSON his heirs and JOSEPH HARDING shall warrant and defend against the claim of any person; In Witness whereof the said JOSEPH HARDING & MARY his Wife hath hereunto set their hands and affixed their seals the day and year above written Signed sealed & delivered in presence of
        (no witnesses recorded)   JOS: HARDING
                                    MARY HARDING

At a Court of Hustings held for the town of Petersburg at the House of WM. DURELL on Wednesday the Second day of February 1785   The foregoing Indenture of Bargain & Sale from JOSEPH HARDING & MARY his Wife to RICHARD GARRETTSON was acknowledged by the above subscribed JOSEPH HARDING and by the said Court ordered to be recorded   Test J. GRAMMER, C. C. Hs.
(Most of page 62 is blank. At the bottom is the following):

p.   At a Court of Hustings held for the Town of Petersburg at the House of WILLIAM
62   DURELL on Wednesday the 2d. day of March 1785
      Present   CHRISTOPHER McCONNICO, Esqr., Recorder
               JOHN SHORE,   ROBERT BOLING   }
                   ALEXR. McNABB   } Gentlemen Aldermen

p.   THIS INDENTURE made this thirty first day of January one thousand seven hun-
63   dred and eighty five Between FREDERICK WILLIAMS of the Town of Petersburg
      of one part and ANDREW JOHNSTON of the same place of the other part; Witnesseth that in consideration of the sum of Eleven hundred & sixty five pounds to said FREDERICK in handpaid by said ANDREW, the said FREDERICK doth bargain sell & confirm unto the said ANDREW his heirs all that tract of land with appurtenances lying in that part of the Town of Petersburg called RAVENSCROFTs TOWN, being the Lots (No. 17) number Seventeen, (No. 18) number Eighteen and a divided moiety of the lots (No. 29, No. 30, No. 31) numbers twenty nine, thirty and thirty one, as they are distinguished in the plan of the Town of RAVENSCROFT, the said moiety or half part of the three last mentioned lots lying on East side of strait continued line runing thro: & equally dividing the said three lots from one and to the other the whole of the said tract of land containing all together Ten acres and a half acre, be the same more or less, together with all right title & demand of said FREDERICK in & to the premises; To have and to hold the tract of land hereby bargained & sold with every of the appurtenances unto ANDREW JOHNSTON his heirs; And the said FREDERICK & his heirs the tract of land unto ANDREW JOHNSTON his heirs against all persons shall warrant and by these presents for ever defend; In Witness whereof the said FREDERICK WILLIAMS hath hereunto set his hand & seal the day & year first above written
Signed Sealed and Delivered in presence of
     JOHN STUART,   FREDERICK WILLIAMS
     JOSH: SIMPSON,   JOHN MACKIE
At a Court of Husting held for the Town of Petersburg at the house of WM. DURELL on Wednesday the 2d. day of March 1785   The foregoing Indenture of Bargain & Sale from FREDERICK WILLIAMS & ANNE WILLIAMS his Wife personally appeared in open

Court, and after being examined privily & a part from the said FREDERICK her Husband,
did freely & voluntarily relinquish her right of Dower in the said land & premises conveyed by the said FREDERICK WILLIAMS her Husband to the said ANDREW JOHNSTON.
Whereupon the same is by the said Court ordered to be recorded
                         Test J. GRAMMER, C. C. Hs.

p.   KNOW ALL MEN by these presents that I SAMUEL DAVIES of the County of
64   PRINCE GEORGE in consideration of the sum of One hundred pounds to me paid by
        WILLIAM DAVIES of the same County, by these presents do bargain and sell unto
said WILLIAM a certain Negro lad or man slave named Peter; To have and to hold the
said Negro slave Peter unto said WILLIAM. Provided always that if said SAMUEL his
heirs shall pay or cause to be paid unto said WILLIAM or assigns the sum of One hundred pounds current money of Virginia on or before the thirty first day of December in
year of our Lord one thousand seven hundred and eighty five with lawful Interest and
without any deduction or abatement whatsoever, Then this Bill of Sale shall be void to
all intents and purposes; In Witness whereof the said SAMUEL DAVIES hath hereunto
set his hand and seal this Twenty sixth day of August in the year of our Lord one thousand seven hundred and eighty four
Sealed and delivered in the presence of
        C. A. RUSSELL,   SAM: DAVIES
        JOS: PARSONS, AUT. LAUSSAT
  At a Court of Hustings held for the Town of Petersburg at the House of WM. DURELL &
sd. Town on Wednesday the 2d. day of March 1785   The above obligation or Bill of Sale
between SAMUEL DAVIES and WILLIAM DAVIES was proved by the Oath of JOSEPH PAR-
SON a witness thereto and the same having been before proven by the Oath of LAUSSETT
another of the Witnesses thereto is by the Court ordered to be recorded
                         Test J. GRAMMER, C. C. Hs.

p.   THIS INDENTURE made this fourteenth day of January Anno Domini one thou-
65   sand seven hundred & eighty five Between ARCHIBALD MIDDLEMAST of one part
        & ROBT. LOYDD both of Town of Petersburg of the other part; Witnesseth that for
the sum of Fifty five pounds by ROBERT LOYDD to said ARCHIBALD MIDDLEMAST in hand
paid, by these presents doth bargain sell & confirm unto ROBERT LOYDD his heirs a certain parcel of land lying in Petersburg (being part of a Lot of the said MIDDLEMAST
purchased of ROBERT BOLLING Esqr., & distinguished in the plan by the number Fifty
Six (56), the said parcel of land or part of said lot containing twenty feet in front on
WATER STREET & continuing the said width of twenty feet through the length of said lot
parellel to the West side of said lot, together with all houses yards, gardens, orchards &
appurtenances to the same belonging; And ARCHIBALD MIDDLEMAST and his heirs the
premises with the appurtenances unto ROBERT LOYDD his heirs against the lawful claim
of all persons will warrant & forever defend by these presents; In Witness whereof the
said ARCHIBALD MIDDLEMAST hath hereunto set his hand & affixed his seal the day &
year above written
Sign'd Seal'd & deliver'd in presence of
        WM. DURELL,   ARCHD. MIDDLEMAST
        JNO: HARE, ABRAM: EVANS
  At a Court of Hustings held for the Town of Petersburg at the House of WM. DURELL on
Wednesday the 2d. day of March 1785   This Indenture of Bargain & Sale from ARCHI-
BALD MIDDLEMAST to ROBERT LOYDD was proved by the affirmation of WM. DURELL,
JNO: HARE & ABRAM EVANS, witnesses thereto, and by the Court is ordered to be
recorded   Test J. GRAMMER, C. C. Hs.

pp.
66-
68

THIS INDENTURE made the twenty first day of June in the year of our Lord one thousand seven hundred and Eighty four Between ROBERT BOLLING Esquire of BOLLING BROOK in County of DINWIDDIE of one part and DAVID MOORE of PRINCE GEORGE County of other part; Witnesseth that for the sum of One hundred pounds to him the said ROBERT BOLLING in hand paid by DAVID MOORE, And also in consideration of the Rents Covenants and Agreements herein after mentioned to be paid and performed by DAVID MOORE his heirs, said ROBERT BOLLING by these presents doth bargain sell and confirm unto DAVID MOORE his heirs one lott of land lying in County of DINWIDDIE below the Town of Petersburg and contiguous to the PUBLICK TOBACCO WAREHOUSES called BOLLINGS, CEDAR POINT and BOLLING BROOK, and is part of the lands lately laid off in Lots by said ROBERT BOLLING which lot aforesaid is known in the plan made by ROBERT BOLLING by the number Eight (8) extending in front on the Street called BACK STREET one hundred feet and on the lines back from the said Street two hundred seventeen feet nine inches as by the plan of said lands duly recorded in the Court of the County of DINWIDDIE will appear: And all ways and appurtenances to said lot belonging; and the rents issues and profits thereof (the Ground Rent hereafter mentioned to be reserved by and payable to ROBERT BOLLING his heirs excepted) To have and to hold the said lot or parcel of land hereby conveyed to DAVID MOORE his heirs, paying ROBERT BOLLING his heirs on the first day of January yearly the fee rent of Fourteen pounds current money, due on the first day of January one thousand seven hundred and Eighty five; and if said money shall be in arrear and unpaid it may be lawful for said ROBERT BOLLING his heirs into the said lott to re enter and have as if this Indenture had never been made; In Witness whereof the parties aforesaid have hereunto set their hands and affixed their seals the day and year first above written Sealed and Delivered in the presence of

HENRY MORRISS, THOS: MASTERSON,   ROBERT BOLLING JR.
GRESSETT DAVISS, JNO: BAIRD JR.   DAVID MOORE

Reived this twenty first day of June 1784 of DAVID MOORE the sum of One hundred pounds current money the consideration money for the within mentioned lot of land In presence of HENRY MORRISS   ROBERT BOLLING JR.

At a Court of Hustings held for the Town of Petersburg at the House of WM. DURELL on Wednesday the 2d. day of March 1785   The foregoing Indenture of Bargain & Sale from ROBERT BOLLING JR. to DAVID MOORE was proven by JOHN BAIRD JR. a witness thereto and the same having been before proven by HENRY MORRISS & GRESSETT DAVIS (& the memorandum & receipt thereto by HENRY MORRISS) witness thereto was by the said Court ordered to be recorded   Test J. GRAMMER, C. C. Hs.

pp.
69-
71

THIS INDENTURE made the twenty first day of June in the year of our Lord one thousand seven hundred and eighty four Between ROBERT BOLLING JR. Esquire of BOLLING BROOK in County of DINWIDDIE of one part and JAMES MATTHEWS, Merchant, of CECIL County, MARYLAND, of other part; Witnesseth that for sum of Two hundred pounds current money of Virginia to him in hand paid by JAMES MATTHEWS, and in consideration of the Rents Covenants & agrements herein after mentioned to be paid and performed by said MATTHEWS his heirs, said ROBERT BOLLING by these presents doth bargain sell & confirm unto JAMES MATTHEWS his heirs two parcels of land lying in County of DINWIDDIE below the Town of Petersburg and contiguous to the PUBLICK TOBACCO WAREHOUSES called BOLLINGS, CEDAR POINT and BOLLING BROOK, and are part of lands lately laid off in lots by ROBERT BOLLING which said two parcels of land are known in the plan made by ROBERT BOLLING by the number Seven (7) and Eleven (11); extending in front on the Street called BACK STREET one hundred

feet and on the lines back from said Street two hundred seventeen feet nine inches as
by the plat of said lands duly recorded in the Court of the County of DINWIDDIE will
appear; And all ways and appurtenances to said two lots belonging; and the rents issues
and profits thereof (the Ground Rent hereafter mentioned to be reserved by and payable to ROBERT BOLLING his heirs excepted), To have and to hold the two lots of land
hereby conveyed unto JAMES MATTHEWS his heirs; paying unto ROBERT BOLLING his
heirs on the first day of January yearly the fee rents on each of the two lots of land,
that is to say for lot number Seven the sum of fourteen pounds, for the lot number
Eleven the sum of Fourteen pounds current money of Virginia which sums of money
shall be paid on the first day of January every year; and if the said money shall be in
arrear and unpaid it may be lawful for ROBERT BOLLING his heirs into the said lot to re
enter and have as if this Indenture had never been made; In Witness whereof the parties aforesaid have hereunto set their hands and affixed their seals interchangeably
the day and year first above written
Sealed and Delivered in presence of us
    HENRY MORRISS,   THOS: MASTERSTON   ROBERT BOLLING JR.
    ARMSTREAT DAVES,   GRESSETT DAVIS   JAMES MATTHEWS
   Received the twenty first day of June 1784 of JAMES MATTHEWS the sum of Two hundred pounds current money of Virginia the consideration money for the within mentioned two lots of land
In presence of JNO: BAIRD JR.   ROBERT BOLLING JR.
    HENRY MORRISS,   ARMSTREAT DAVES
  At a Court of Hustings held for the Town of Petersburg at the House of WM. DURELL on
Wednesday the 2d. day of March 1785   This Indenture of Bargain and Sale from ROBERT
BOLLING Jr. to JAMES MATTHEWS was proved by the Oath of JOHN BAIRD JR. and the
same having been before proved by the Oaths of HENRY MORRISS and GRESSETT DAVIS,
two other witnesses thereto and the memorandum & receipt thereon having been
before proved by HENRY MORRISS a witness thereto are with the Indenture by the said
Court ordered to be recorded   Test J. GRAMMER C. C. Hs.

pp.   THIS INDENTURE made this first day of March Anno Domini one thousand seven
72-   hundred and Eighty five Between RICHARD HILL Esqr. of Town of Petersburg of
73   one part and NOEL WADDILL of the same Town, Jeweller, of the other part; Witnesseth that for sum of Five shillings current money of Virginia to him in hand
paid by NOEL WADDILL, and also for the annual Ground Rent of Fifteen pounds current
money to be paid for ever by said NOEL WADDILL his heirs unto RICHARD HILL his
heirs, and lastly in consideration of the covenants and agreements herein afterwards
specified, said RICHARD HILL hath demised transferred & to farm let a certain parcel of
land situate on BOLLING BROOK STREET being a portion of a lot which is known in the
Plan of the Town of Petersburg by the number Twenty Nine (29), and bounded,
Begining thirty three feet from the North West corner of the above mentioned Lot,
thence runing on BOLLING BROOK STREET twenty four feet Easterly, thence Southerly
one hundred feet (to an Alley of Seventeen feet nine inches wide), thence Westerly
along the Alley twenty four feet and then Northerly to the begining, To have and to
hold the portion of ground unto NOEL WADDILL his heirs during the term of ninety
nine years paying therefor annually the sum of Fifteen pounds current money to
RICHARD HILL his heirs to commence the first day of January last past, the first years
rent to grow due and become payable on the first day of January one thousand seven
hundred & Eighty six, And if the Ground Rent be unpaid it may be lawful for RICHARD
HILL to re-enter at any time thereafter and the same to hold untill such rent be paid;

and further NOEL WADDILL his heirs shall at all times pay the taxes and other duties which shall be taxed or assessed on the above portion of land and premises; and will erect and build either of Brick Stone or Wood a dwelling of the value of One hundred pounds at the least and keep the same of such value (destruction by fire or tempest excepted) during the whole term of ninety nine years; In Witness whereof the parties aforesaid have hereunto set their hands and affixed their seals the day and year first above written
Sealed and Delivered in presence of us
     RICHD. TAYLOR,   RD. HILL
     JOHN S. FEILD,   SOLOMON BETTON   NOELL WADDELL
   At a Court of Hustings held for the Town of Petersburg at the House of WILLIAM DURELL on Wednesday the 2d. day of March 1785   The foregoing Indenture from RICHARD HILL to NOEL WADDELL was acknowledged by each of the parties thereto as above described and by the said Court ordered to be recorded
             Test J. GRAMMER, C. C. Hs.

(Page 74 is blank.)

p.   At a Court of Hustings held for the Town of Petersburg at the House of WIL-
75   LIAM DURELL on Wednesday the 6th of April 1785
       Present   JOHN BANISTER Esqr., Mayor
            CHRISTOPHER McCONNICO Esqr., Recorder
            JOHN SHORE, ROBERT BOLLING, ALEXR.McNABB, Gentlemen Aldermen

p.   KNOW ALL MEN by these presents that I WILLIAM HILL of Petersburg in Vir-
75   ginia in consideration of the sum of One hundred and Twenty seven pounds current money of Virginia to me in hand paid by EDWARD STABLER of Petersburg by these presents do bargain sell and deliver unto EDWARD STABLER and assigns all the houshold stuff and furniture herein particularly mentioned, that is to say, three dozen of Mahogany Chairs, two arm'd chairs, 1 Desk and book case, two large tables, one writing table, one Tea table, one Chest of drawers, one dressing Table, two large looking glasses with gilt frames, two bedsteads, two feather beds with bolsters & pillows, and two setts of Curtains for ditto., all and singular which said premises are now remaining standing and being in a certain tenement situate in Petersburg which WILLIAM HILL hath rented of said STABLER; To have and to hold the houshold stuff and furniture to EDWARD STABLER and assigns; And I said RICHARD HILL for myself my heirs unto EDWARD STABLER and assigns against all persons will warrant and forever defend by these presents; In Witness whereof I have hereunto set my hand and seal the twenty fifth day of August in year of our Lord one thousand seven hundred and Eighty four
Sealed and Delivered in the presence of
     SAML. MARSAM,   WILL: HILL
     ROBT. WILLIAMS
   At a Court of Hustings held for the Town of Petersburg Wednesday the 6th of April 1785 The foregoing Bill of Sale from WILLIAM HILL to EDWARD STABLER was proved by the Oath of ROBERT WILLIAMS, a witness thereto, and the same having been before proved by the Oath of SAMUEL MARSAM, another witness thereto, is ordered to be recorded
             Test J. GRAMMER, C. C. Hs.

pp.   THIS INDENTURE made this first day of February in the year of our Lord one
76-   thousand seven hundred and Eighty five Between JAMES YOUNG and SARAH his
77   Wife of Town of PORTSMOUTH and County of NORFOLK of one part and JAMES BYRNE of Town of Petersburg in County of DINWIDDIE on the other part; Wit-

nesseth that JAMES YOUNG and SARAH his Wife for sum of Three hundred pounds current money of Virginia in hand paid by JAMES BYRNE, by these presents doth bargain and confirm unto JAMES BYRNE his heirs one lot or parcel of land in that part of the Town of Petersburg known by the name of RAVENSCROFT and distinguished by the number Twenty Four in the plan of RAVENSCROFT TOWN. To have and to hold the said lot number Twenty Four and premises with appurtenances thereto belonging to said JAMES BYRNE his heirs, And JAMES YOUNG and SARAH his Wife their heirs against all persons to JAMES BYRN his heirs shall warrant and defend by these presents; In Witness whereof the said JAMES YOUNG and SARAH his Wife hath hereunto set their hands and affixed their seals the day and year first above written
Sealed Signed & Delivered in presence of
        JAMES TAYLOR,   JAS: YOUNG
        JOHN DYSART   SARAH YOUNG
        JAMES HALLIDAY
The Commonwealth of Virginia to THOMAS VEALE & SAML. VEALE Gentlemen Greeting; Whereas (the Commission for the privy Examination of SARAH, the Wife of JAMES YOUNG), Witness JOHN GRAMMER Clerk of our said Court at his Office this third day of February 1785 in the Ninth year of the Commonwealth   J. GRAMMER, Clk. C. Hs.
By virtue of the Commission hereunto annexed this Indenture was acknowledged by the thereto subscribed SARAH YOUNG on the 25th day of Feby. 1785; she the said SARAH being first privily & apart from the sd. JAMES YOUNG, her Husband, examined (the return of the execution of the privy Examination of SARAH YOUNG); before us
            THOMAS VEALE,   SAML. VEALE
Received the day and year withinwritten the sum of Three hundred pounds being the full consideration money within mentioned
Witness THOMAS F. FENN   JAS: YOUNG
At a Court of Hustings held for the Town of Petersburg at the House of WM. DURELL on Wednesday the 6th of April 1785   An Indenture of Bargain & Sale between JAMES YOUNG & SARAH his Wife of the one part and JAMES BYRN of the other part was proved on the part of JAMES YOUNG by the Oath of JAMES TAYLOR, JOHN DYSART & JAMES HALLIDAY witnesses thereto and together with a Commission annexed and the Certificate of the execution thereof are ordered to be recorded
            Test J. GRAMMER, C. C. Hs.

p.   THIS INDENTURE made this Twenty sixth day of August one thousand seven
78   hundred & Eighty four Between SAMUEL DAVIES of County of PRINCE GEORGE
        and Commonwealth of Virginia of one part and WILLIAM DAVIES of same County and Commonwealth of other part; Witnesseth that for the sum of Seven hundred pounds current money of Virginia by said WILLIAM to said SAMUEL in hand paid, said SAMUEL by these presents doth grant and to farm let unto said WILLIAM & assigns all that lots of land whereon said SAMUEL formerly lived but now occupied by SIMON FRASER, lying in the New Town of Petersburg and County of DINWIDDIE bounded by lots of EDWARD STABLER and NEIL BUCKANAN's heiresses and the Main Street and numbered Three and Four containing in the whole by estimation Two acres more or less, together with all ways profits and appurtenances to the lots of land appurtaining, as also with all barns stables gardens and orchards; To have and to hold the lot of land hereby demised unto said WILLIAM and assigns from the day of the date hereof until the full term of one thousand years next ensuing paying yearly on the last day of December to said SAMUEL his heirs the yearly rent of one Pepper Corn if it be lawfully demaned, Provided always and upon this condition that if said SAMUEL his heirs shall pay unto said WILLIAM and assigns the sum of Seven hundred pounds current money aforesaid on or

before the Thirtieth day of December in year one thousand seven hundred and Eighty
five without any deduction or abatement for taxes or other impositions that then this
present Indenture shall be void and of no effect; In Witness whereof the parties to
these presents have hereunto set their hands and seals the day and year first above
mentioned
Sealed and Delivered in the presence of
    C. A. RUSSELL,   SAMUEL DAVIES
    JOS: PARSONS, AUT. LAUSSAT
  At a Court of Hustings held for the Town of Petersburg at the House of WILLIAM
DURELL on Wednesday the 6th day of April 1785   An Indenture of Lease from SAMUEL
DAVIES to WILLIAM DAVIES was proved by the Oath of CHARLES RUSSELL a witness
thereto and the same having been before proved by the Oaths of JOS: PARSONS and AUT.
LAUSSAT, two other witnesses thereto, is by order of the said Court truly recorded
          Test J. GRAMMER, C. C. Hs.

pp.   THIS INDENTURE made this Sixteenth day of August in the year of our Lord one
79-   thousand seven hundred and Eighty four Between JOHN BATTE and MARY his
80   Wife of PRINCE GEORGE County of one part and WILLIAM BIGELOW of the County
     of DINWIDDIE and Town of Petersburg of other part; Witnesseth that JOHN BATTE
and MARY his Wife for sum of Twelve hundred pounds current money of Virginia already in hand paid by WILLIAM BIGELOW, by these presents doth bargain sell and confirm unto WILLIAM BIGELOW his heirs part of a certain lot or half acre of land lying in
Town of Petersburg in County of DINWIDDIE which said lot or half acre of land is
known in the plan of said town by the number Seven (7); and lying on the Main Street
thereof, that is to say, begining at the Street that runs from the Main Street to the River
from thence up the Main Street twenty feet above the East end of the House which is in
all seventy feet in width through the full length of the lott from the Main Street down
to the River with the dwelling house now in Occupancy by said JOHN BATTE and all
other houses fences and other appurtenances to that part of said lot belonging and the
rents issues and profits; To have and to hold the bargained premises with the appurtenances unto WILLIAM BIGELOW his heirs, And JOHN BATTE his heirs will warrant and
forever defend by these presents against the claim of all persons; In Witness whereof
the said JOHN BATTE hath hereunto set his hand and seal the day and year above written
Sealed and Delivered in presents of
    WILLIAM BARKSDALE, JNO: BAIRD, JUNR.   JOHN BATTE
    LEWIS EDWARDS, RODK. BIGELOW
  At a Court of Hustings held for the Town of Petersburg at the House of WILLIAM
DURELL on Wednesday the 6th of April 1785   An Indenture of Bargain & Sale between
JOHN BATTE & MARY his Wife of one part & WILLIAM BIGELOW of the other part was
proved by the Oaths of WILLIAM BARKSDALE, JOHN BAIRD JR. and RODK. BIGELOW wit-
nesses thereto and by the said Court ordered to be recorded
          Test J. GRAMMER, C. C. Hs.

p.   THIS INDENTURE made this Third day of September one thousand seven hun-
81   dred and Eighty four Between WILLIAM CALL and ELIZABETH his Wife of County
     of PRINCE GEORGE of one part & RICHARD BATE & WILLIAM GRAY, Merchants,
Partners under the Firm of BATE & GRAY, of the Borough of Petersburg of the other
part; Witnesseth that WILLIAM CALL and ELIZABETH his Wife for the sum of Six hundred pounds current money of Virignia to them in hand paid by BATE & GRAY by these
presents do bargain sell and confirm unto BATE & GRAY and their assigns one certain

lott of land lying in that part of the Borough of Petersburg formerly BLANDFORD and distinguished in the plan of said town number blank begining at the River APPOMAT-TOX on the East side of the Main Street running from thence up the Main Street to the first cross street, thence down the said cross street to Lot number Fifty three, thence with the line of said lott number Fifty three to APPOMATTOX RIVER and appurtenances to said lott belonging; and the rents issues and profits thereof; To have and to hold lthe lott of land hereby conveyed unto BATE & GRAY their heirs; And WILLIAM CALL and ELIZABETH his Wife the said lott and premises unto BATE & GRAY their heirs shall warrant and forever defend by these presents against any person having or lawfully claiming any right or title to the same; In Witness whereof the said WILLIAM CALL & ELIZABETH his Wife have hereunto set their hands and affixed their seals the day & year first above written

Sealed and Delivered in presence of
    ANDREW GRAY,   WILLIAM CALL
    CHARLES JOHNSTON,   WILLIS MACLIN

Received September 3d. 1784 of BATE & GRAY Six hundred pounds being the consideration within mentioned in presence of
    ANDREW GRAY,   WM. CALL
    CHARLES JOHNSTON,   WILLIS MACLIN

At a Court of Hustings held for the Town of Petersburg at the House of WILLIAM DURELL on Wednesday the 6th day of April 1785   An Indenture of Bargain & Sale between WILLIAM CALL & ELIZABETH his Wife of the County of PRINCE GEORGE of one part and BATE & GRAY of the other part and a Receipt Indorsed were acknowledged by the above subscribed WILLIAM CALL and by the said Court ordered to be recorded

              Test J. GRAMMER, C. C. Hs.

p.   THIS INDENTURE made this Sixth day of April in the year of our Lord one thou-
82   sand seven hundred and Eighty five Between THOMAS WALKE of County of
CHESTERFEILD of one part and WILLIAM PARSONS SENR. of County of PRINCE GEORGE of other part; Witnesseth that THOMAS WALKE for the sum of one hundred pounds specia to him in hand paid by WILLIAM PARSONS, by these presents doth bargain and sell unto WILLIAM PARSONS and to his heirs one certain lot of land lying in Town of Petersburg and in the County of DINWIDDIE and distinguished in the plan of said Town by the number Fifteen, which said lot was conveyed by one WILLIAM PRIDE unto ANTHONY WALKE, Father of said THOMAS WALKE, as p Deed recorded in the County Court of PRINCE GEORGE reference thereunto will fully appear; To have and to hld the lott of land number Fifteen with the appurtenances unto WILLIAM PARSONS his heirs, And said THOMAS WALAKE for himself his heirs Executors and Administrators (but from no other persons whatsoever) doth promise WILLIAM PARSONS his heirs that he will warrant and forever defend by these presents; In Witness whereof THOMAS WALKE hath hereunto set his hand and affixed his seal the day and year above written

Sealed and Delivered in presence of
    JOHN THWEATT   THOMAS WALKE
    THOMAS FRIEND, BELFEILD STARK

At a Court of Hustings held for the Town of Petersburg at the House of WILLIAM DURELL on Wednesday the 6th of April 1785   An Indenture of Bargain and Sale between THOMAS WALKE of one part of County of CHESTERFIELD and WILLIAM PARSONS of County of PRINCE GEORGE of other part was acknowledged by the above written THOMAS WALKE and by the said Court ordered to be recorded

              Test J. GRAMMER, Clk, C. Hs.

(Pages 83 and 84 are blank.)

p.   At a Court of Hustings held for the Town of Petersburg at the House of WM.
85   DURELL on Wednesday the 4th day of May 1785
        Present   CHRISTOPHER McCONNICO, Esqr. Recorder
              JOHN SHORE, ROBERT BOLLING, ALEXANDER McNABB, Gentlemen Aldermen

pp.   THIS INDENTURE made this Twelfth day of April one thousand seven hundred
85-   and Eighty five Between FREDERICK WILLIAMS and ANNE his Wife of Town of
86   Petersburg of one part and BENJAMIN SMITH, Bricklayer, of same Town of other
        part; Witnesseth that in consideration of the sum of Five hundred pounds cur-
rent money to said FREDERICK WILLIAMS in hand paid by BENJAMIN SMITH, said
FREDERICK by these presents doth bargain sell and confirm unto BENJAMIN SMITH his
heirs one certain parcel of land with the appurtenances in Town of Petersburg being
part of a Lot of Land which said FREDERICK now dwells on & holds under a Deed from
WILLIAM CALL recorded in the Court of Hustings of the Town aforesaid distinguished in
the original plat by number Three (3) & bounded, begining at the South West corner of
the dwelling house, thence on the Main Street leading through said Town Easterly
twenty four feet to the South East corner of said Hosue, bounding on an Alley of Eight
feet six inches, thence in a direction with the end of the said House and bounded by the
said Alley Northerly to the River, thence Westerly twenty four feet, and thence
Southerly to the Street, the begining; Together with all estate right title and demand of
said FREDERICK WILLIAMS to the premises; To have and to hold the parcel of land unto
BENJAMIN SMITH his heirs, And FREDERICK WILLIAMS and his heirs the parcel of land
unto BENJAMIN SMITH his heirs against all persons will warrant and forever by these
presents defend; And lastly it is further agreed by FREDERICK WILLIAMS for himself &
his heirs with BENJAMIN SMITH hisheirs that the said Alley of Eight feet six inches on
the East side of said Lott shall for ever remain & be free and open from the Street to the
River for the use and convenience of said SMITH his heirs as well as for the use and
convenience of the holder of the remaining part of said Lot Number Three, bounding
on the East side thereof; In Witness whereof the said FREDERICK WILLIAMS and ANNE
his Wife have hereunto set their hands and affixed their seals the day and year first
above written
Sealed and Delivered in the presence of
        DAVID BUCKANAN,   FREDRICK WILLIAMS
        ROBT. BARBER, JOSEPH FAUX   ANN WILLIAMS
The Commonwealth of Virginia to CHRISTOPHER McCONNICO, ALEXANDER GLASS
STRACHAN, JOHN SHORE, ROBERT BOLLING & ALEXANDER McNABB, Gentlemen Greeting;
Whereas (the Commission for the privy Examination of ANN the Wife of FREDERICK WILLIAMS)
Witness JOHN GRAMMER, Clerk of our said Court the Thirtieth day of April in year of our
Lord one thousand seven hundred and Eighty five in the Ninth year of the Common-
wealth   J. GRAMMER Clk. C. Hs.
   By Virtue of the Commission hereunto annexed this Indenture was acknowledged by
the thereto subscribed ANN WILLIAMS on the Second day of May 1785, said ANN being
first privily and apart from the said FREDERICK, her Husband, examined (the return of the
Execution of the privy Examination of ANN WILLIAMS); before us
                            ALEXR. G. STRACHAN
                            JNO: SHORE
   At a Court of Hustings held for the Town of Petersburg on Wednesday the 4th day of
May 1785 An Indenture of Bargain and Sale between FREDERICK WILLIAMS and ANN
his Wife of one part and BENJAMIN SMITH of the other part was proved by the Oaths of
DAVID BUCKANAN, ROBERT BARBER and JOSEPH FAUX witnesses thereto, And together

with the Commission annexed and the Certificate of execution thereof are ordered to be
recorded   Test J. GRAMMER Clk. C. Hs.
(Pages 87 and 88 are blank.)

p.   At a Court of Hustings held for the Town of Petersburg at the House of WILLIAM
89   DURELL on Wednesday the 1st day of June 1785 & by Adjournment the 2d. day of
            June 1785   Present   CHRISTOPHER McCONNICO, Esqr., Recorder
            JOHN SHORE,   ROBERT BOLLING,   ALEXANDER McNABB, Gentlemen Aldermen
the first day and the same with the addition of ALEXANDER GLASS STRACHAN Gent.,
Alderman the Second day

pp.   BY THIS PUBLICK INSTRUMENT of Procuration or Letter of Attorney Be It
89-   Known that on the Fifth day of March in the year of our Lord one thousand
90   seven hundred and Eighty five before me JOSHUA OGIER, Notary Publick, dwel-
            ling in LONDON duly admitted and sworn in the presence of the Witnesses here-
after named personally appeared Sir LYONEL LYDE, Baronet, and SAMUEL LYDE Esquire,
Merchants in this City of LONDON, trading under the firm of Sir LYONEL LYDE Baronet
and Company who declared to have made and constituted MR. RICHARD HANSON of Virginia their true and lawful Attorney, giving and by these presents granting unto their
said Attorney full power and lawful authority for them the said Constituents in this
names and on their behalf to ask sue for and by all lawful ways recover and receive
from all persons whom it shall concern all sums of money goods wares merchandizes
debts and effects whatsoever; promising to ratify confirm and hold for good and valid
all their said Attorney or his substitutes shall lawfull do or cause to be done about the
premises by virtue hereof. Thus Done and passed in LONDON in the presence of
ANDREW RAMSAY, JAMES BARR, ALEXANDER MITCHELL and CHARLES SEDER, Witnesses
Sealed and Delivered (being first duly stampd) in the presence of
            ANDREW RAMSAY,   JAS. BARR,   LYONEL LYDE
            ALEXR. MITCHELL, CHARLES SEDER   SAMUEL LYDE
                        In prœmiss orum fidem JOS: OGIER Not. Pub. 1785
We the underwritten do hereby certify and attest to all whom it may concern that Mr.
JOSHUA OGIER whose firm is above is a Notary Publick practising in this City of LONDON
Witness our hands in LONDON this seventh day of March in year of our Lord one thou-
sand seven hundred and eighty four
            JNO: ATKINSON, Not: Pub: WILSON FORSTER, Not: Pub:
At a Court of Hustings held for the Town of Petersburg at the House of WILLIAM
DURELL on Wednesday the 1st day of June 1785   A Letter of Attorney from Sir LYONEL
LYDE and SAMUEL LYDE Esqr., Merchants of LONDON, under the firm of Sir. LYONEL
LYDE Baronet and Company, to RICHARD HANSON was presented in Court and proved by
the Oaths of ANDREW RAMSAY, ALEXANDER MITCHELL and CHARLES SEDER witnesses
thereto and by the said Court is ordered to be recorded
                        Test J. GRAMMER, Clk. C. Hs.

pp.   THIS INDENTURE made this Twenty fourth day of March one thousand seven
91-   hundred and Eighty five Between FREDERICK WILLIAMS of the Town of Peters-
92   burg and ANNE his Wife of one part and JAMES DURELL of the same place, Tay-
            lor, of other part; Witnesseth that for sum of One hundred and fifty pounds cur-
rent money of Virginia to said FREDERICK in hand paid by JAMES DURELL, by these
presents doth bargain sell and confirm unto JAMES DURELL hisheirs one certain parcel
of land in Town of Petersburg (being part of a Lot distinguished in the Original Plat of

said Town by Number Three (3), formerly the property of FEILD & CALL and conveyed by WILLIAM CALL, Surviving Partner to said FREDERICK WILLIAMS as by his Deed bearing date the third day of May one thousand seven hundred & eighty four recorded in the Court of Hustings of the Town of Petersburg will appear; situate and bounded, Begining at the South West corner of the said Lott number Three (3) thence runing on the Main Street that leads through the said town Easterly sixteen feet, thence Northerly to continue in a direct line parralel with the West line of the said Lot to the River, thenceup the River to the North West corner & thence Southerly on the West boundary of said lot to the begining; together with the rents issues and profits thereof, To have and to hold the spot or parcel of land unto JAMES DURELL his heirs; And FREDERICK WILLIAMS doth hereby grant for him and his heirs unto JAMES DURELL and his heirs and against all persons shall warrant and by these present forever defend; In Witness whereof said FREDERICK WILLIAMS hath hereunto set his hand and affixed his seal the day and year first above written

Sealed & Delivered in presence of

WILLIAM BARR,   FREDERICK   WILLIAMS
WILLIAM SMITH,   WILLIAM BARKSDALE

At a Court of Hustings held for the Town of Petersburg at the House of WILLIAM DURELL on Wednesday the first day of June 1785   An Indenture of Bargain & Sale between FREDERICK WILLIAMS of the one part and JAMES DURELL of the other part with a Memorandum of Livery and Seizen were proved by the Oaths of WILLIAM BARR, WILLIAM SMITH and WILLIAM BARKSDALE witnesses thereto and are ordered to be recorded   Test J. GRAMMER, Clk. C. Hs.

pp.   THIS INDENTURE made this (blank) day of (blank) in year of our Lord one thou-
93-   sand seven hundred and Eighty five Between ROBERT WATKINS and NICOLSON
95   WATKINS of one part and WILLIAM CLARKE, Merchant, of the Borough of
           Petersburg of other part; Witnesseth that for sum of Two hundred and Fifty pounds current money of Virginia to them in hand paid, and also in consideration of the Conditions Covenants and agreements herein after mentioned to be performed by WILLIAM CLARKE, said ROBERT WATKINS and NICOLSON WATKINS by these presents do bargain sell and confirm unto WILLIAM CLARKE his heirs a part or portion of a certain lot of ground known in the plans of the lots laid off by ROBERT BOLLING Esquire by the number (26), Twenty Six, lying upon BOLLING BROOK STREET near the PUBLICK TOBAC-CO WAREHOUSES called CEDAR POINT in the Borough of Petersburg which part or por-tion of ground contains forty feet upon BOLLING BROOK STREET and extends carrying the same width to the Street called BACK STREET in the said plan and is taken off and allotted from the East side of lott (26) Twenty Six, with all houses and appurtenances to said allotment belonging; and the rents issues and profits thereof; To have and to hold the allotment of No. (26) Twenty Six hereby conveyed unto WILLIAM CLARKE his heirs paying unto ROBERT BOLLING Esquire his heirs every year on the first day of January the fee rent of Three pounds four shillings current money per annum, to commence the first day of January last past, the first rent to become due and payable on the first day of January one thousand seven hundred and Eighty six; Provided Always and it is hereby covenanted and agreed between the parties herto that if said fee rent shall be unpaid and in arrear it shall be lawful for ROBERT BOLLING his heirs or Attorney to make distress untill the fee rent shall be fully paid; In Witness of all which the above mentioned premises, ROBERT WATKINS and NICOLSON WATKINS and WILLIAM CLARKE parties to these presents have hereunto respectively set their hands and affixed their seals the day and year first above written

Signed Sealed and Delivered in the presence of us
(no witnesses recorded)   ROBT. WATKINS
                                                     NICOLSON WATKINS
                                                     WM. CLARKE
At a Court of Hustings held for the Town of Petersburg at the House of WM. DURELL on
Wednesday the first day of June 1785   An Indenture of Bargain & Sale between ROBERT
WATKINS and NICOLSON WATKINS of one part and WILLIAM CLARK of the other part
was acknowledged by sd. ROBERT WATKINS, NICOLSON WATKINS and WILLIAM CLARK
and is ordered to be recorded   Test J. GRAMMER, Clk. C. Hs.

pp.   THIS INDENTURE made this Nineteenth day of February in the year of our Lord
96-   one thousand seven hundred & Eighty five Between CHAPMAN MANSON of Town
97   of SUFFOLK, Bricklayer, of one part, and WILLIAM WRIGHT of Town of Peters-
         burg of other part; Witnesseth that for the sum of Forty pounds current money
to him in hand paid by WILLIAM WRIGHT, said CHAPMAN MANSON doth by these presents bargain sell and confirm unto WILLIAM WRIGHT and to his heirs one certain spot
or half acre of ground in Town of Petersburg being in that part thereof distinguished
by the New Town of Petersburg laid of by PETER JONES deced., and is one half a lot by
the number (18) Eighteen, dividing the said lot by a line runing through the middle
from the Street to the back part thereof, it being that half of said lot situate to the West
(the other half being now in possession of ALEXANDER GORDON), and bounding on the
West side of Lot number Seventeen (17); To have and to hold the said spot or half acre of
ground with all yards gardens houses rents profits and appurtenances thereunto belonging to WILLIAM WRIGHT and his heirs; And CHAPMAN MANSON for himself & his
heirs the lot & premises will warrant and defend against all persons unto WILLIAM
WRIGHT his heirs; In Witness whereof the said CHAPMAN MANSON hath hereunto set
his hand & affixed his seal the day and year being first written
Sealed and Delivered in the presence of
        JOHN GRAMMER,   CHAPMAN MANSON
        DANIEL DODSON, ALEXR. GORDON
Received the Nineteenth day of February one thousand seven hundred & Eighty five
of WILLIAM WRIGHT the sum of Forty pounds current money the full consideration for
the within mentioned Lot of land and premises
Witness JOHN GRAMMER,   CHAPMAN MANSON
        DANIEL DODSON, ALEXR. GORDON
At a Court of Hustings held for the Town of Petersburg at the House of WILLIAM
DURELL on Wednesday the first day of June 1785   An Indenture of Bargain and Sale
between CHAPMAN MANSON of the one part and WILLIAM WRIGHT of the other part and
the memorandum of livery and seizen and the Receipt thereon endorsed were proved
by the Oath of ALEXANDER GORDON, a witness thereto, and the same having been proved
by the Oaths of JOHN GRAMMER and DANIEL DODSON,. two other witnesses thereto, are
ordered to be recorded   Test J. GRAMMER, Clk. C. Hs.

p.   THIS INDENTURE made this 26th day of May in the year of our Lord one thou-
98   sand seven hundred and Eighty five Between DANIEL MABRY of County of
         GREENSVILLE of one part and PARHAM MABRY and EDWARD MABRY of the
Borough of Petersburg of other part; Witnesseth that DANIEL MABRY for the natural
love and affection which he beareth to his Sons, PARHAM and EDWARD MABRY, by
these presents do give and confirm jointly unto my said two Sons, PARHAM and ED-
WARD MABRY their heirs one certain lot or parcel of ground containing One hundred

feet square on the Main Street of BLANDFORD in the possession of my Son, PARHAM MABRY. To have and to hold the said lot with all improvements and impertenances thereunto belonging unto said PARHAM & EDWARD MABRY their heirs; And DANIEL MABRY his heirs the said lot with appurtenances unto PARHAM and EDWARD MABRY their heirs shall warrant and forever defend against any person having or lawfully claiming any right or title to the same; In Witness whereof he (the said DANIEL MABRY) have hereunto set his hand and affixed his seal the day and year above written
Signed Sealed and Delivered in presence of
ROBT. BIRCHETT,   DANIEL MABRY
THOMAS POWELL, BEERYMAN JONES
   At a Court of Hustings held & continued for the Town of Petersburg Thursday the Second day of June 1785 An Indenture between DANIEL MABRY of the one part and PARHAM MABRY and EDWARD MABRY of the other part was proved by the Oaths of ROBERT BIRCHETT, THOMAS POWELL and BERRYMAN JONES, witnesses thereto and is ordered to be recorded   Test J. GRAMMER, Clk. C. Hs.

pp.   THIS INDENTURE made this first day of January Anno Domini one thousand
99-   seven hundred & Eighty five Between Messrs. SHORE, McCONNICO & RITSON,
100   Merchants, of Town of Petersburg of one part & Messrs. JOSHA: & NATHAN WARD
           Merchants of the same of the other part: Witnesseth that for the sume of One hundred & fifty pounds current money of Virginia to them in hand paid by said JOSHUA & NATHAN WARD, And also in consideration of the annual Ground Rent of Fifteen pounds currency to be paid for ever by JOSHUA & NATHAN WARD or assigns to said SHORE, McCONNICO & RITSON or their assigns, And lastly in consideration of the covenants and agrements herein after mentioned they the said SHORE, McCONNICO & RITSON hath demised granted and to farm let a portion of a lot of land situate on BOLLING BROOK STREET and which is distinguished in the plans of the Town of Petersburg by the No. Twenty two (22), and bounded on PAGE & LANGDONs line on BOLLING BROOK STREET, thence along said Street Westerly thirty six feet, thence Southerly in a parellel line to a Line one hundred feet, thence along said Lane to PAGE & LANGDONs line thereon, thence along said line to the begining; To have & to hold the above ground and its appurtenances unto JOSHUA & NATHAN WARD their heirs during the term of Ninety nine years paying annually the sum of Fifteen pounds current money to aforesaid SHORE, McCONNICO & RITSON, their heirs to commence the first day of January Anno Domini one thousand seven hundred & Eighty five, and if the Ground Rent be unpaid having first demanded payment of such rent in arrear to re-enter & the same to hold & receive the rents thereof until such rent in arrear be fully paid; And it is further agreed that said JOSHA: & NATHAN WARD their heirs shall pay all taxes & other dutys which shall be taxed or assessed on the above land & premises; and for the more effectual securing the above ground rent, to build either of Brick Stone or Wood within the space of two years from the date heref a dwelling house of the value of one hundred pounds at least & keep the same of such value, (destruction by fire or tempest excepted) during the whole term; In Witness whereof the parties aforesaid have hereunto set their hands & seals the day & year first above written
Sealed & deliver'd in the presence of us
   HENRY MORRISS,   SHORE, McCONNICO & RITSON
   BELFEILD STARK, WILLIAM ELLIOTT   JOSH: & N. WARD
   At a Court of Hustings held & continued for the Town of Petersburg at the House of WILLIAM DURELL Thursday the 2d. day of June 1785 An Indenture of Lease between SHORE, McCONNICO & RITSON of the one part and JOSHUA & NATHAN WARD of the other

part was acknowledged by CHRISTOPHER McCONNICO on part of SHORE, McCONNICO &
RITSON and the same having been before acknowledged by NATHAN WARD on the part
of the said JOSHUA & NATHAN WARD, is by the said Court ordered to be recorded
Test J. GRAMMER, Clk. C. Hs.

pp.
101-
103

THIS INDENTURE made this Twenty fifth day of April one thousand seven hundred and Eighty five Between FREDERICK WILLIAMS, Merchant, of the Town of
Petersburg and ANNE his Wife of one part and ALEXANDER McNABB of the same
place of other part; Witnesseth that for the sum of Five hundred pounds current
money of Virginia to FREDERICK WILLIAMS in hand well & truly paid or secured to be
paid by ALEXANDER McNABB by these presents doth bargain & sell unto ALEXANDER
McNABB and to his heirs a certain parcel of land with the appurtenances thereunto belonging lying in the Town of Petersburg and on the North side of the Old Street, it
being part of the Lott or half acre of land which FRED: WILLIAMS purchased of Colo.
WILLIAM CALL, as will appear by Records of Court of Hustings of Town of Petersburg
and which is distinguished in the Original Plan by the number (3), three, and bounded
Begining at the South East corner of the Lott No. 3 on the Street and extending in front
on the said Street Westwardly to the South West corner of a RED STORE HOUSE standing
thereon, supposed to be twenty eight feet bounding on an Alley of Eight feet six inches
from then in a direct line with the end of the said House (and bounded by the aforesaid
Alley) Northwardly to the River, from thence Eastwardly bounded by the meanders of
the River twenty eight feet to the North East corenr of the said lott where it adjoins the
lott of Mr. JAMES FAWCETT and from thence in a direct line to the Old Street aforesd. to
the place or spot at first began at; Together with all houses profits & appurtenances to
the same belonging; and the rents issues and profits thereof; To have and to hold the
parcel of land with appurtenances unto ALEXANDER McNABB his heirs, And FREDERICK
WILLIAMS and his heirs the premises hereby sold unto ALEXANDER McNABB his heirs
against all persons will warrant and forever defend by these presents; And it is further
covenanted & agreed by FREDERICK WILLIAMS for himself his heris with ALEXANDER
McNABB his heirs the aforesaid Alley supposed to be eight feet six inches on the West
side the aforesaid spot of ground shall remain open from the Street to the River for the
mutual benefit & advantage of said ALEXANDER McNABB his heirs and the Proprietor of
the part of the Lott No. 3 lately sold to BENJAMIN SMITH, which part of said lott No. 3
sold to BENJAMIN SMITH lies bounded on the West side of the said Alley, In Witness
whereof the said FREDERICK WILLIAMS & ANNE his Wife have hereunto set their hands
& affixed their seals on the day & year at first within written
Sealed & Delivered in presence of
JNO: BAIRD JR.   FREDK. his mark X   WILLIAMS
BENJN. SMITH,   ANNE WILLIAMS
THOMAS HUMPHREYS,
JAMES DURELL
In the Name of the Commonwealth to CHRISTOPHER McCONNICO, Doctor ALEXANDER G.
STRACHAN, ROBERT BOLLING & Doctor JOHN SHORE, Gentlemen Greeting. Whereas (the
Commission for the privy Examination of ANNE, the Wife of FREDERICK WILLIAMS); Witness JOHN
GRAMMER, Clk. of our said Court at his Office 29th Apl. '85
By virtue of the Commission hereunto annexed, this Indenture was acknowledged by
the thereto subscribed ANNE WILLIAMS the 2d day of May 1785, she the said ANNE being
first privily & apart from the said FREDERICK, her Husband, examined (the return of the
execution of the privy Examination of ANNE WILLIAMS) before us
ALEXR: G. STRACHAN
JNO: SHORE

At a Court of Hustings held & continued for the Town of Petersburg at the House of
WILLIAM DURELL on Wednesday the 2d. day of June 1785   An Indenture of bargain &
sale between FREDERICK WILLIAMS and ANNE his Wife of one part and ALEXANDER
McNABB of the other part was proved by the Oaths of JOHN BAIRD JUNR., BENJAMIN
SMITH and THOMAS HUMPHRIES witnesses thereto and the memorandum of Livery &
Seizen thereon indorsed was proved by the Oath of JOHN BAIRD JUNR. a witness thereto
which with the said Indenture and together with the Commission thereto annexed and
the Certificate of execution thereof, are ordered to be recorded
                              Test J. GRAMMER, Clk. C. Hs.

(Page 104 is blank).

p.   At a Court of Hustings held for the Town of Petersburg at the House of WILLIAM
105   DURELL on Wednesday the 6th July 1785
          Present CHRISTOPHER McCONNICO Esqr., Recorder
          JOHN SHORE, ROBERT BOLLING, ALEXANDER McNABB, Gentlemen Alderman

pp.   TO ALL TO WHOM THESE PRESENTS SHALL COME, We WILLIAM CALL and JAMES
105-   FEILD of PRINCE GEORGE County send Greeting; Whereas CHARLES DUNCAN of
106   CHESTERFEILD County being seized and possessed in the fee simple Estate of
          Eighty acres of land or there abouts lying in County of PRINCE GEORGE between
the upper end of the Town of BLANDFORD and the CHURCH near the said Town, common-
ly called THE BRICK CHURCH, did cause the said parcel of land to be surveyed and laid off
into one hundred lotts, vizt., twenty seven irregular lotts and seventy three regular
lotts, the latter being seventy seven yards in length and thirty three and one third in
breadth and into seven principal Streets vizt. a Main Street ninety feet wide extending
from the upper end of the Town of BLANDFORD to the CHURCH, a Street runing parallel
therewith thirty three feet wide extending from the upper end of the Lotts No. 7 & 8
near the CHURCH to the Lott No. 99, and five other Streets intersecting or crossing the
said first two mentioned Streets, being each forty two feet wide and extending from the
OLD CHURCH ROAD quite across the said piece of land, also three lanes, vizt., one of them
runing between the Town of BLANDFORD and the land aforesaid being thirty three feet
wide and extending from the lower Corner of ALEXANDER TAYLORs Lott to the CRUCK,
one other lying betweenthe Lotts No. 8, 9 & 10 and the Lotts No. 13, 14, & 15; and one
other lying between the Lotss No. 93, 94, 95 & 96 and the Lott No. 100; in the plott of the
said land, And also into one Publick Square extending across the Main Street from the
Lott No. 46 to the Lott No. 47 as by the Survey of the parcel of land hereunto annexed
will more at large appear; And CHARLES DUNCAN having regularly numbered the Lotts
and publickly advertised them for Sale by way of a Lottery, sundry persons did sub-
scribe to become Adventurers for the same agreable to the terms propsed by the said
CHARLES; as by a list of names of said Subscribers to us delivered and which is hereunto annexed will also more fully appear; NOW KNOW YE that we said WILLIAM CALL and
JAMES FEILD having been chosen and appointed Trustees to direct and superintend the
drawing of the Lottery aforesaid to see equal right & justice done to the several Adventurers therein did on the (blank) 1782 at the House of JAMES TURNBULL deced., in the
Town of Petersburg, a majority of the Adventurers or their agents being there present
and no objection being made thereto publickly proceed to the drawing of the said
Lottery and did execute the Trust reposed in us carefully and impartially when the
several lotts numbered in plott before mentoned were fairly drawn for the several
persons whose names are respectively annexed to the numbers for each of them drawn
as follows: WILLIAM MURRAY the numbers 1, 23, 74, & 79;

THOMAS GRIFFIN PEACHY	No. 3, 6, 17, 20, 26, 27, 51, 57, 59, 63, 71, 75, 76, 81, 84 & 98.		
JAMES FRENCH	No. 4 & 66.	ROBERT ARMISTEAD No. 5.	
ALLEN LOVE	No. 7, 12, 19 & 92	ROBERT TURNBALL No. 8, 9, 13, 15, 22 & 86.	
STEPHEN COCK	No. 10	RICHARD BATE No. 11 & 47.	
SIMON FRASER	No. 14, 30, 62, & 87	MARK McPHERSON No. 16 & 24.	
ISAAC HALL	No. 18 & 80	SHORE & McCONNICO. No. 21, 39, 43, 64, & 67.	
THOMAS BOLLING	No. 25, 78, 85 & 94.	THOMAS MASTERSON No. 28 & 93.	
PHILIP WHITEHEAD JACKSON No. 29 & 48.		CHRISTOPHER MANLOVE No. 31	
NATHANIEL COCK	No. 32, 35 & 55	WILLIAM WITHERS No. 2.	
WILLIAM ROBERTSON	No. 33, 44, 46 & 90	JERMAN BAKER No. 34 & 65;	
THOMAS GORDON	No. 36, 42 & 82;	JOHN ANGUS No. 37.	
WILLIAM GILLIAM	No. 38.	CHARLES DUNCAN No. 40, 52, 56 & 60;	
HUMPHRY RICHARDS	No. 41.	JOHN LANG No. 45	
ALEXANDER TAYLOR	No. 49 & 95;	ROBERT FITZGERALD No. 50 & 79;	
PETER RANDOLPH	No. 53, 69 & 88	JOHN McLEOD No. 54	
JOHN CAMPBELL	No. 58	JOHN ROCHELLE No. 61 & 100.	
DANIEL FISHER	No. 68 & 91	MATTHEW FERNANDO No. 70	
WILLIAM COLEMAN	No. 72 & 97.	JOHN SKELTON No. 73	
ROBERT GILLIAM	No. 77 & 83	ANDREW HAMILTON No. 89	
JOHN SELDEN	No. 96		

And for the information of all persons concerned and for ascertaining the just claim of the respective Adventurers before named in and to the several lotts of ground laid out and drawn for as aforesaid, We do hereby make this manifestation of the due execution of the Trust committed to us as before mentioned. In Testimony whereof we have hereunto set our hands and affixed our seals the (blank) day of July in the year one thousand seven hundred and Eighty five
Signed Sealed & Delivd. in presence of
    CAD: JONES,   WM. CALL
    F. MUIR. RICHD. TAYLOR   JAMES FEILD
   At a Court of Hustings held for the Town of Petersburg at the House of WM. DURELL Wednesday the 6th day of July 1785   A Manifestation or Certificate under the hands & seals of WILLIAM CALL & JAMES FEILD, Trustees for the superintending and drawing the Lottery for the New Town of BLANDFORD was proved by the Oaths of CADWALLADER JONES and RICHARD TAYLOR two of the witnesses thereto and together with a plott of the said NEW BLANDFORD which was with the same presented is by the said Court ordered to be recorded   The plott as follows on the next Leaf
          Test J. GRAMMER, Clk. C. Hs.
(The platt which appears on page 107 of this Deed Book is reproduced and presented in this book on the back of the title page.)
(Page 108 is blank)

p.   THIS INDENTURE made the first day of June in the year of our Lord one thou-
109   sand seven hundred & eighty five Between ROBERT TURNBALL of County of
        PRINCE GEORGE of one part and JOHN BANISTER of County of DINWIDDIE of the other part; Witnesseth that ROBERT TURNBULL for the sum of One hundred & five pounds lawful money of Virginia to him in hand paid by JOHN BANISTER, by these presents doth bargain sell & confirm unto JOHN BANISTER his heirs a certain parcel of land formerly the Estate of JOHN BANISTER late of DINWIDDIE County, & by him sold & conveyed to FREDERICK JONES, who aliened the same to ROBERT RAVENSCROFT deced., who is his life time sold & conveyed the same to CHARLES TURNBULL late of this County

under whom the said ROBERT TURNBULL now claims & holds the absolute fee therein,
lying in said County of DINWIDDIE & now in the limits of the Corporation of Petersburg
containing Three acres and seven eighth of an acre and bounded by PRIDEs line on the
East side of the RACE GROUND; by the said BANISTERs Land on the West & North; & on
the South by the PUBLICK ROAD leading thro: the said BANISTERs land to the Town of
Petersburg; To have and to hold the said tract of land with appurtenances together
with the profits and advantages to said tract of land belonging unto JOHN BANISTER his
heirs; And the said ROBERT TURNBULL for himself his heirs against the claim of all
persons to JOHN BANISTER his heirs shall warrant and forever defend; In Witness
whereof the said ROBERT TURNBULL hath hereunto set his hand & affixed his seal the
day & year above written
Signed Sealed & delivered in presence of
    JAMES KING,   ROBERT TURNBULL
    PATK: WALKER, CHARLES DUNCAN
  At a Court of Hustings held for the Town of Petersburg Wednesday the 6th day of July
1785 This Indenture of Bargain and Sale between ROBERT TURNBULL of the one part &
JOHN BANISTER of the other part was acknowledged by the above subscribed ROBERT
TURNBULL and is ordered to be recorded
        Test J. GRAMMER, Clk. C. Hs.

p.   THIS INDENTURE made the Second day of September in the year of our Lord one
110   thousand seven hundred and Eighty four Between JOHN TABB Esqr., of County of
      AMELIA of one part and KILLEN & JEFFERS of Town of Petersburg and County of
DINWIDDIE of other part; Witnesseth that for the just sum of Five shillings current
money of Virginia in hand paid to JOHN TABB Esqr. by the said KILLEN & JEFFERS and
for the farther consideration of the said KILLEN and JEFFERS having built at their own
expence part of a House or Shop twenty three by thirty two feet with a Dutch Roof on
the land of said JOHN TABB Esqr., in said Town of Petersburg on East side of the BRIDGE
on the Main Street, the said JOHN TABB Esqr. doth by these presents bargain Lease and
demise unto said KILLEN & JEFFERS their heirs the West end of the said Shop or House as
above mentioned and the ground it stands upon for and during the term of twelve years
to commence the day above mentioned; To have and to hold the said House and premises
unto KILLEN & JEFFERS their heirs paying annually if demanded one Pepper Corn, also
all Taxes during the term and at the expiration of the Lease leave the said House in
tenantable repair (Fire and other accidents excepted); In Witness whereof the parties
have hereunto interchangeably sett their hands and affixed their seals the day and
year first above written
Signed Sealed & Delivered in the presence of
    SAML. DAVIES,   JOHN TABB
    BELFIELD STARK, HENRY MORRISS
  At a Court of Hustings held for the Town of Petersburg at the House of WILLIAM
DURELL on Wednesday the Sixth day of July 1785 This Lease from JOHN TABB to
KILLEN & JEFFERS was proved by the Oths of SAMUEL DAVIES,B ELFIELD STARK and
HENRY MORRISS witnesses thereto and is ordered to be recorded
        Test J. GRAMMER, Clk. C. Hs.

pp.   THIS INDENTURE made the Eighth day of December in year of our Lord one
111-   thousand seven hundred and Eighty four Between HENRY SADLER of Town of
114   Petersburg in the County of DINWIDDIE, Merchant, of one part and JAMES COR-
    RAN of the same Town & County, Merchant, of other part; Whereas HENRY SAD-

LER and JAMES CORRAN are and stand seized of a certain lott of land in the vicinity of the Town of Petersburg as Tenants in Common which said lott of land was purchased by them of a certain ROBERT BOLLING Esquire as by Indenture bearing date the 17th day of March last, recorded in the Court of the County of DINWIDDIE, will more fully appear; the said Lott being known in the plan by ROBERT BOLLING by the number Twenty, And whereas said HENRY SADLER and JAMES CORRAN by Indenture bearing date the day before the date of these presents in consideration of the sum of Thirty three pounds Six shillings and eight pence to them in hand paid and in consideration of the Covenants and agreements in the Indenture set forth have bargained and sold unto JOHN DYSART and JOHN CATHCART, Merchants and Partners, in the Town of Petersburg one third part of said Lott of Land according to the metes and bounds in said Indenture set forth, And HENRY SADLER and JAMES CORRAN have agreed to make partition between them of the remaining two thirds of the said lott of land by metes and bounds as are herein after mentioned. NOW THIS INDENTURE Witnesseth that in consideration of the premises and also of Five shillings current money to him in hand paid by said JAMES CORRAN by these presents doth bargain sell and confirm unto JAMES CORRAN his heirs one full third part of the lott of land conveyed to them by ROBERT BOLLING or one full moiety of two thirds part thereof; after deducting one third part of the lot conveyed to JOHN DY-SART and JOHN CATHCART; which two thirds of said lot of land extends in front on the Street called BOLLINGBROKE STREET forty four feet (44); and runs the whole depth of said lot from said Street to the back line, being Two hundred & seventeen feet by even parralel lines and is the lower part of said lott being on the East side towards BOLLING-BROKE WAREHOUSES by the Lot numbered Twenty (20), and on the West or upper side of said one third part of the whole lott by the sare or third part of the whole lot which is by this Indenture conveyed by JAMES CORRAN in manner herein after set forth, and which also extends on the said Street called BOLLINGBROKE STREET twenty two (22) feet and all appurtenances thereunto belonging; To have and to hold the one third part of the lot of land number Twenty unto JAMES CORRAN his heirs; AND THIS INDENTURE FURTHER Witnesseth that JAMES CORRAN in consideration of the premises and also Five shillings current money to him in hand paid by said HENRY SADLER, by these presents doth bargain sell & confirm unto HENRY SADLER his heirs one full third part of said lot of land numbered Twenty as the same was conveyed him by ROBERT BOLLING or one moiety of two thirds part of the lot of land which one third part extends in front on the Street called BOLLINGBROKE STREET Twenty two feet (22) and runs the whole depth of the lot by paralel lines to the back thereof, and is bounded on the Eastwardly side by the parcel of land herein conveyed to JAMES CORRAN and on the Western side by the parcel of land conveyed to DYSART and CATHCART, To have and to hold the one third part of said lot of land unto HENRY SADLER his heirs; In Witness whereof the said HENRY SADLER and JAMES CORRAN have hereunto set their hands and affixed their seals interchangeably the day and year first above written
Sealed and Delivered in the presence of us

WILL: GREGG,   HENRY SADLER
THOS: ARMISTEAD,   JAMES CORRAN
JOSEPH YARBROUGH,
JAMES BYRNE SENR.

At a Court of Hustings held for the Town of Petersburg at the House of WILLIAM DURELL on Wednesday the sixth day of July 1785   This Indenture of Partition between HENRY SADLER of the one part and JAMES CORRAN of the other part was proved by the Oath of WILLIAM GREGG a witness thereto and the same having been before proved by the Oaths of THOMAS ARMISTEAD and JAMES BYRNE SENR., two other witnesses thereto is ordered to be recorded   Test J. GRAMMER, Clk. C. Hs.

pp.
115-
117
THIS INDENTURE made this Sixth day of July in year of our Lord one thousand seven hundred and Eighty five Between ARCHIBALD MIDDLEMAST of Town of Petersburg of one part and MATTHEW and WILLIAM FERNANDO of PRINCE GEORGE County of other part; Witnesseth that in consideration of the sum of Thirty pounds current money to him in hand paid by said MATTHEW and WILLIAM FERNANDO, and also in consideration of the rents covenants and agreements hereafter mentioned to be kept and performed by said MATTHEW and WILLIAM FERNANDO their heirs, said ARCHIBALD MIDDLEMAST by these presents doth bargain sell & confirm unto MATTHEW & WILLIAM FERNANDO their heirs one certain spot or parcel of land in Town of Petersburg (being the Lot which said MIDDLEMAST purchased of ROBERT BOLLING Esqr. as by his Deed recorded in the Court of Hustings of said Town will appear; which lot is situate near the River and the Bridge over to POCOHANTASS being part of the land laid off by said BOLLING and distinguished in the plan by number Fifty Six (56), bounded begining in front of the said lott on WATER STREET forty six feet from the South West corner thereof, thence on said Street Easterly twenty four feet, thence back Northerly thirty feet, thence Westerly twenty feet and thence to the said Street at the begining; and all ways rents issue (other than the Fee Rent herein after reserved) and profits thereof; To have and to hold the land hereby conveyed unto MATTHEW and WILLIAM FERNANDO and their heirs paying therefor unto ARCHIBALD MIDDLEMAST his heirs every year on the first day of January the fee rent of Two pounds eight shillings current money which sum shall be paid on the first day of January in every year, the first years rent to grow due and become payable on the first day of January in year one thousand seven hundred and Eighty five; and if said money shall be in arrear and un-paid it may be lawfull for ARCHIBALD MIDDLEMAST his heirs into the said lott to re-enter and have as if this Indenture had never been made; In Witness whereof the parties aforesaid have hereunto set their hands and affixed their seals the day and year first above written

Sealed and Delivered in the presence of us

    WM. DURELL,   ARCHD: MIDLEMIST
    ABRAM. EVANS, WILLM. STEGER

At a Court of Hustings held for the Town of Petersburg at the House of WILLIAM DURELL Wednesday the Sixth day of July 1785   An Indenture of Bargain & Sale between ARCHIBALD MIDLEMIST of one part and MATTHEW and WILLIAM FERNANDO of the other part with the memorandum of Livery and seizen thereunto were proved by the Oaths of WILLIAM STEGER, WILLIAM DURELL and ABRAM: EVANS and are ordered to be recorded   Test J. GRAMMER, Clk. C. Hs.

pp.
118-
119
THIS INDENTURE made this Sixteenth day of May in the year of our Lord one thousand seven hundred and Eighty five Between ROBERT BALLARD of County of BALTIMORE in the State of MARYLAND, Gentleman, of one part and WILLIAM KNOX, THOMAS B. USSHER and JAMES McCULLOUGH of same County and State aforesaid, Merchants, of other part; Witnesseth that ROBERT BALLARD for the sum of four hundred pounds current money to him in hand paid by said WILLIAM KNOX, THOMAS B. USHER and JAMES McCULLOUGH, by these presents doth bargain sell and confirm unto said WILLIAM KNOX, THOMAS B. USHER and JAMES McCULLOUGH and assigns all those two lotts, parts of lotts and parcells of ground lying in County of DIN-WIDDIE and Town of Petersburg and known on the platt by the Number A., and B., and containing within the following metes bounds courses and distances, to wit, Begining for the same thirty four feet West from the intersection of BOLLINGBROOKE Street and SECOND STREET and runing thence West binding on BOLLINGBROOKE STREET sixty six

feet, thence runing North one hundred and thirty feet to a private Lane or Alley laid
out by said ROBERT BALLARD of the width of Twenty feet, thence runing on said private
Alley East sixty six feet to a Lott of ground sold a certain WILLIAM SHORE, thence
runing and binding on said Lott South one hundred and thirty feet to the begining;
together with all buildings improvements streets lanes alleys benefits and advantages
to said lotts of ground belonging; And all said ROBERT BALLARDs term of years yet to
come and unexpired; To have and to hold the lotts of ground unto WILLIAM KNOX, THO-
MAS B. USHER and JAMES McCULLOUGH their assigns during the residue of the term yet
to come and unexpired; paying therefor on the first day of January each year the sum
of One penny Sterling for Lott No. A., and also the sum of Fourteen pounds three shillings Virginia current money for Lott number B., annually and in case of non payment
said ROBERT BALLARD shall have remedy for recovery thereof by distress or action of
Debt at his or their Election; In Witness whereof the said parties have hereunto set
their hands and seals the day and year above written
Signed Sealed & Delivered in presence of

WM. HAXALL,	ROBERT BALLARD
EDMUND HOLLOWAY, JAS: CUMING	WM. KNOX
J. GIBBON	

Received the day and year within mentioned of and from WILLIAM KNOX, THOMAS B.
USHER and JAMES McCULLOUGH the parties herein named the sum of Four hundred
pounds current money of Virginia, the consideration within specified
Witness J. GIBBON   ROBERT BALLARD

At a Court of Hustings held for the Town of Petersburg at the House of WILLIAM
DURELL Wednesday the Sixth day of July 1785   An Indenture of Lease between ROBERT
BALLARD of the one part and WILLIAM KNOX, THOMAS B. USHER and JAMES McCUL-
LOUGH of the other part was proved by the Oaths of WILLIAM HAXALL, JAMES GIBBON
and JAMES CUMING, three of the witnesses thereto and together with the Receipt there-
unto annexed which was proved by the Oath of JAMES GIBBON, are ordered to be
recorded   Test J. GRAMMER Clk. C. Hs.
(Page 120 is blank.)

p.   At a Court of Hustings held for the Town of Petersburg at the House of WILLIAM
121   DURELL on Wednesday the Seventh day of September 1785
          Present   JOHN BANISTER Esqr., Mayor
                    CHRISTOPHER McCONNICO Esqr., Recorder
                    ALEXR. G. STRACHAN, JOHN SHORE, Gent., Aldermen

pp.   THIS INDENTURE made this twentififth day of April in year of our Lord one
121-   thousand seven hundred and Eighty five Between FREDERICK WILLIAMS and
122   ANNE his Wife of Town of Petersburg of one part and JOHN MacRAE and JOSEPH
          HARDING, Merchants and Partners under the Firm of MacRAE & HARDING of the
same Town of other part; Witnesseth that FREDERICK WILLIAMS and ANNE his wife in
consideration of the sum of (blank) current money to them in hand paid by MacRAE &
HARDING, by these presents do bargain sell and confirm unto MacRAE & HARDING their
heirs one certain spot or parcel of land being part of lot or half acre of land (which the
said WILLIAMS held under a Deed from WILLIAM CALL, recorded in the Court of Hustings of the Town of Petersburg & distinguished by the number Three (3), in the plan
of the said Town), bounding, begining on the Main Stree that leads through the said
Town at the South West corner of the Dwelling House on the said lott number Three,
which the said WILLIAMS hath conveyed to BENJAMIN SMITH, and from thence on the
said Street Westerly to the land of JAMES DURELL, part of the said lott which said WIL-

LIAMS conveyed to him thirty five feet more or less and to extend back in the same
width by two parrelel lines to APPOTMATTOX RIVER, bounding on the land of BENJA-
MIN SMITH on the East side and that of JAMES DURELL on the West side to the said River:
And all houses gardens and appurtenances to said portion of land belonging; To have
and to hold the portion of land & premises to said MacRAE & HARDING their heirs: And
FREDERICK WILLIAMS and ANNE his Wife for themselves and their heirs the parcel of
land & premises against all persons will warrant and by these presents defend; In Wit-
ness whereof they the said FREDERICK WILLIAMS and ANNE his Wife hath hereunto set
their hands and affixed their seals the day and year first above written
Sealed and Delivered in presence of
    JNO: BAIRD JR.,   FREDK. his mark X WILLIAMS
    JOHN COOK, ALEX: McNABB
  At a Court of Hustings held for the Town of Petersburg at the House of WILLIAM
DURELL Wednesday the Seventh day of September 1785
  An Indenture of Bargain and Sale between FREDERICK WILLIAMS of one part and
MacRAE & HARDING of other part was proved by the Oath of ALEXANDER McNABB a wit-
ness thereto and the same having been before proved by the Oaths of JOHN BAIRD JR.
and JOHN COOK, two other witnesses thereto is ordered to be recorded
             Test J. GRAMMER, Clk. C. Hs.

p.   At a Court of Husting held for the Town of Petersburg Wednesday the Seventh
123   day of September and by Adjournment continued Thursday 8th September 1785
      Present CHRISTOPHER McCONNICO, Esqr., Mayor
         JOHN SHORE Esqr., Recorder
    ALEXR. G. STRACHAN, ALEXR. McNABB, ISAAC HALL, Gent., Aldermen

pp.   THIS INDENTURE made on the Eighth day of April Anno Domini 1785 Between
123- SHORE & McCONNICO, Merchants in Petersburg, on the one part and ANDREW
124   JOHNSTON, Merchant in Petersburg, on the other part; Witnesseth that in con-
      sideration of the sum of Four hundred pounds current money in hand paid to
said SHORE & McCONNICO by said ANDREW JOHNSTON & for the further sum of Twenty
pounds paid them the said SHORE & McCONNICO by ALEXANDER HORSBURGH also of
Petersburg, Merchant, have granted to bargin Lease and confirm in free Tack for the
space of seven years to ANDREW JOHNSTON his heirs to be computed & reckoned from
the date of possession given to the following subject & Houses contracted for on the
ninth day of June Seventeen hundred & Eighty four in manner following, to be built
for the use of said JOHNSTON his heirs in consideration of the sums above stated, that is
to say, a STORE HOUSE to be situated in front of the Street where there present Store
stands, vizt., BOLLING BROOK STREET & to the Eastward of their lott in that Street forty
feet ling & twenty four feet wide, two story high with a Brick Cellar underneath the
size of the house, the Store House to be finished in the same manner as the Store they at
present possess with a Bed Room and Counting Room adjoining; plaistered & finished as
their own, the upper Story to be calculated for the recption of Goods with a Door in the
front for hoisting them up to be finished by the fifteenth of November seventeen hundred & Eight four or sooner if possible & possession given; A Lumber House back of and
adjoining to the said Store House of the same size height breadth & length so as in appearance to make but one house of Eighty feet long & twenty four feet wide with a
Chimney in the middle & a Door from the Counting Room in the Store House into the
Lumber House which last house to be built joined to the former & possession given by
the first day of June next ensuing the date of finishing the Store House or sooner if

possible binding themselves that if from delay of the Carpenter possession is not given
on the respective dates above mentioned for finishing both houses to the payment of
whatever rent said JOHNSTON or his assigns shall have occasion or be under the necessity of giving for a suitable Store House &c. untill the said Store House is made tenantable and no longer; which Houses agreable to the above Contract well & truly finished
to be held by ANDREW JOHNSTON his heirs in free Tack for the space of seven years
from the day possession is given clear of Rent other than the aforesaid Four hundred &
twenty pounds to them SHORE & McCONNICO already paid, subject nevertheless to such
dues as may be imposed by the Corporation or Publik; they bind themselves to warrant
and defend unto ANDREW JOHNSTON his heirs for the seven years against the claims of
all persons; In Witness whereof said SHORE & McCONNICO do hereunto set the name of
their firm & afix their seal the date above writting, having previously ascertained with
ALEXANDER HORSBURGH, assignee of ANDREW JOHNSTON, that the commencement of the
term of Seven years as above recited shall be accounted & dated from the Fifteenth day
of February last past, the Lumber House to be finished & possession given as above on
the first day of June ensuing
Witness ROBT. HEBLETHWAITE,   CHRISTOPHER McCONNICO
        BELFEILD STARK   for self & THOS: SHORE
   I do hereby bargain and sell unto ALEXANDER HORSBURGH of Petersburg, Mercht., for
sum of Three hundred pounds currt. money of Virginia to me in hand paid and for the
further sum of Three hundred pounds currt. money to be paid to me by ALEXANDER
HORSBURGH his heirs on or before the fifteenth day of February next ensuing all my
right title & property in the above free tack & Lease of the premises above bargained to
me by the above named Messrs. SHORE & McCONNICO, And I do hereby for myself my
heirs &c. warrant and defend the same unto said HORSBURGH his heirs; In Witness
whereof I have afixed my name and seal the date above written
Signed Sealed & Delivered in presence of
        WILLIAM McKINNON,   ANDW: JOHNSTON
        DUNCAN MacRAE
   At a Court of Hustings held for the Town of Petersburg on Wednesday and by adjournment continued Thursday the 8th of Sept. 1785
   An Indenture of Lease between SHORE & McCONNICO of the one part and ANDREW
JOHNSTON of the other part was acknowled: by CHRISTOPHER McCONNICO for and in behalf of the said SHORE & McCONNICO, And the conveyance & relinquishment of the same
by said ANDREW JOHNSTON to ALEXANDER HORSBURGH which is thereunto annexed was
proved by the Oaths of WILLIAM McKINNON and DUNCAN MacRAE, witnesses thereto,
and together with the said Indenture ordered to be recorded
                    Teste J. GRAMMER, Clk. C. Hs.

p.   THIS INDENTURE made this Sixth day of July one thousand seven hundred and
125   Eighty five Between CHARLES DUNCAN of CHESTERFEILD County of one part and
        JAMES CAMPBELL of BLANDFORD of other part; Witnesseth that CHARLES DUN-
CAN in consideration of the quantity of Two thousand weight of Crop Tobacco to him in
hand paid; by these presents doth bargain sell and confirm unto said CAMPBELL his
heirs a certain parcell of land in NEW BLANDFORD No. Five adjoining the Main Street on
the brow of the Hill as by a plan of said Town recorded this day in the Court of Hustings
in this Borough will appear; And also the estate right or demand of said DUNCAN to the
said land; And CHARLES DUNCAN for himself and his heirs the lott of land against every
person to JAMES CAMPBELL his heirs will warrant and forever defend by these
presents; In Witness whereof said CHARLES DUNCAN hath hereunto set his hand and

affixed his seal the day and year above written
Signed Sealed and Delivered in the presence of us
        RT. ARMISTEAD,   CHARLES DUNCAN
        J: GRAMMER,   WILLIAM DAVIES
    Whereas the Lott within mentioned is marked upon the Platt within mentioned Town
of NEW BLANDFORD as the property of ROBERT ARMISTEAD now I the said ROBERT
ARMISTEAD do hereby relinquish all right & title to the same to the within named
JAMES CAMPBELL his heirs. In Testimony whereof I the said ROBERT ARMISTEAD have
witnessed the execution of the within Deed by CHARLES DUNCAN and have hereunto set
my hand and seal the day and year within mentioned
Witness CHARLES DUNCAN   ROBERT ARMISTEAD
    At a Court of Hustings held for the Town of Petersburg Wednesday the 7th and by ad-
journment continued Thursday the Eighth day of September 1785
    An Indenture of Bargain & Sale between CHARLES DUNCAN of CHESTERFEILD County of
the one part and JAMES CAMPBELL of BLANDFORD of the other part was acknowledged
by the above subscribed CHARLES DUNCAN and the relinquishment by ROBERT ARMI-
STEAD of all his right and title to the same which is thereon indorsed was proved by the
Oath of CHARLES DUNCAN a witness thereto and together with the said Indenture are
ordered to be recorded   Teste J. GRAMMER Clk. C. Hs.

p.   THIS INDENTURE made this fifth day of September in year of our Lord one thou-
126   sand seven hundred and Eighty five Between CHARLES DUNCAN of County of
        CHESTERFEILD in Commonwealth of Virginia, Merchant, of one part and ALLEN
LOVE of County of BRUNSWICK, Merchant, of other part; Witnesseth that for the sum of
Eighty pounds by said ALLEN to said CHARLES in hand paid said CHARLES DUNCAN by
these presents doth bargain and sell unto ALLEN LOVE his heirs Four lotts of land lying
in that part of the Town of Petersburg called NEW BLANDFORD and in the plan thereof
by the numbers 7, 12, 19 & 92; seven, twelve, nineteen and ninety two, as by said plan
now on Record in Court of Hustings of Petersburg may appear; To have and to hold the
four lotts to ALLEN LOVE his heirs; In Witness whereof the said CHARLES DUNCAN hath
hereunto set his hand and affixed his seal the day and year first above written
Sealed and Delivered in the presence of us
        (no witnesses recorded)   CHARLES DUNCAN
    At a Court of Hustings held for the Town of Petersburg on Wednesday the Seventh and
by adjournment continued Thursday the Eighth day of September 1785
    An Inventure of Bargain and Sale between CHARLES DUNCAN of County of CHESTER-
FEILD of one part and ALLEN LOVE of BRUNSWICK County of other part was acknowledged by the above subscribed CHARLES DUNCAN and ordered to be recorded
                        Teste J. GRAMMER, Clk. C. Hs.

p.   THIS INDENTURE made this Seventh day of September in year of our Lord one
127   thousand seven hundred and Eighty five Between CHARLES DUNCAN of the
        County of CHESTERFEILD of one part and JOHN McCLOUD of the Borough of
Petersburg of other part; Witnesseth that CHARLES DUNCAN in consideration of the
sum of Two thousand pounds weight of Crop Tobacco paid by JOHN McCLOUD, by these
presents doth bargain sell and confirm unto JOHN McCLOUD his heirs a lott or ground
number Fifty Four lying within the Borough of Petersburg and in that part of the Town
known by the name of NEW BLANDFORD as will appear on Record in the Borough Court;
To have and to hold the said lott of ground and all advantages appertaining unto JOHN
McCLOUD his heirs and CHARLES DUNCAN for himself his heirs doth covenant that he

the said CHARLES DUNCAN will forever warrant and defend the title to said lott of ground unto JOHN McCLOUD his heirs against every person; In Witness whereof the said CHARLES DUNCAN hath hereunto set his hand and affixed his seal the day and year as above written

Sealed and Delivered in presence of
    (no witnesses recorded)   CHARLES DUNCAN
  at a Court of Hustings held for the Town of Petersburg at the House of WILLIAM DURELL on Wednesday the Seventh and by Adjournment continued Thursday the Eighth day of September 1785   An Indenture of Bargain and Sale between CHARLES DUNCAN of the County of CHESTERFEILD of one part and JOHN McCLOUD of the Town of Petersburg of the other part was acknowledged by the above subscribed CHARLES DUNCAN and ordered to be recorded
        Teste J. GRAMMER, Clk. C. Hs.

pp. 128-129 THIS INDENTURE made this Twenty ninth day of September in yar of our Lord one thousand seven hundred and Eighty four Between RICHARD HILL of the Borough of Petersburg of one part and RICHARD WILLIAMS of County of PRINCE GEORGE of other part; Witnesseth that for the sum of Two hundred and thirty three pounds, six shillings & eight pence current money to him in hand paid by RICHARD WILLIAMS, And also for the annual ground rent of Four pounds fourteen shillings & four pence currency, to be paid for ever by said WILLIAMS his heirs for ever to RICHARD HILL and his hirs and lastly for the covenants and agreements herein afterwards specified, said HILL hath demised granted transferred and to farm lett part of a lot of land situate on BOLLING BROOK STREET and in known in the plan by the No. Twenty Nine (29), and is bounded begining at North West corner of the above lot and running Easterly thirty three feet, thence running Southerly one hundred feet to an Alley of Seventeen feet nine inches (which Alley is reserved and laid of by the said HILL for the mututal benefit use & advantage of the respective Proprietors of the above lot) thence commencing in the same direction on the South side of the said Alley & running to BACK STREET, thence along the same Westerly thirty three feet to the South West corner of the lot & thence Northerly to the beginning, To have and to hold the above portion of ground and its appurtenances unto RICHARD WILLIAMS his heirs from the date aforesaid during the term of Ninety nine years & paying therefore annually the sum of Four pounds fourteen shillings & four pence untill the full end of the said term to commence on the first day of January next (1785), And it is agreed RICHARD WILLIAMS or assigns shall pay all taxes and other duties which shall be taxed or assessed on the above portion of land and for the more effectual securing the payment of the above ground rent it is hereby agreed by RICHARD WILLIAMS for himself his heirs &c. that he or they within the space of two years from the date hereof will build either of Brick Stone or Wood a dwelling or house of two stories in height of the value of One hundred pounds current money at least & keep the same of such value (destruction by fire or tempest excepted), In Witness whereof the parties have hereunto set their hands & affixed their seals the day & year first above written

Sealed and Delivered in presence of us
  JNO: CATHCART,   RD. HILL
  RO: WATKINS, JOHN GREEN   RICHD. WILLIAMS
  At a Court of Hustings held for the Town of Petersburg at the House of WILLIAM DURELL on Wednesday the Seventh and by Adjournment Thursday the Eighth day of September 1785   An Indenture of Lease between RICHARD HILL of Petersburg of one part and RICHARD WILLIAMS of the County of PRINCE GEORGE of the other part was

acknowledged by the parties above subscribed and ordered to be recorded
Teste J. GRAMMER, Clk. C. Hs.

(Pages 130-131 are blank.)

p.   At a Court of Hustings held for the Town of Petersburg at the House of WILLIAM
132   DURELL Wednesday the fifth day of October 1785
          Present CHRISTOPHER McCONNICO Esqr., Mayor
              JOHN SHORE Esqr., Recorder
              ALEXANDER McNABB, ISAAC HALL, Gentlemen, Aldermen

pp.   THIS INDENTURE made this third day of October one thousand seven hundred
132   and Eighty five Between JOSEPH HARDING and MARY his Wife of the Town of
133   Petersburg and State of Virginia of one part and DAVID BUCHANAN of the same
          Town and State of other part; Witnesseth that for sum of Nine hundred pounds
current money of Virginia to said JOSEPH by said DAVID in hand paid, by these presents
do bargain sell and confirm unto DAVID BUCHANAN his heirs all that parcel of land
with the appurtenance lying in that part of the Town of Petersburg called RAVENS-
CROFT TOWN and containing four acres and a half acre more or less, being that part of
the lott marked upon the plott of Town of RAVENSCROFT (31), number Thirty One, which
lays on the West of a Visible Ditch running through the said lott and bounded by the
Land of JOHN LOVE on the East, along the line of the said Ditch, on the North by Lott (30)
number Thirty, on the West by a Street laid off in the plan of the Town of RAVENSCROFT
and on the South by the lott (32), number Thirty two, and also that tract of land containing the whole of lott (32) number Thirty two and bounded on the North by lott (31),
number Thirty One, on the West by the above mentioned Street, on the South by ot (33)
number Thirty Three, and on the East by the land of JOHN LOVE along the line of a
visible Dith down to a cross Ditch in the said lott number Thirty Two and on the North of
said Cross Ditch by Lot (17) number seventeen along the line as laid off by the late Commissioners who resurveyed the Town of RAVENSCROFT, Together with all ways closes,
houses feedings commons profits and appurtenances to the same belonging; and the
rents issues and services of all the premises; To have and to hold the parcell of land
with appurtenances unto DAVID BUCHANAN his heirs; And JOSEPH HARDING and MARY
his Wife do for themselves severally and for their heirs covenant with DAVID
BUCHANAN that they the tract of land unto DAVID BUCHANAN and assigns against all
persons shall warrant and by these presents forever defend; In Witness whereof the
said JOSEPH HARDING and MARY his Wife have hereunto set their hands & seals the day
and year first above written
Signd. Seald. and deliverd. in the presence of
      JOHN MacRAE, GRESSETT DAVIS,   JOS: HARDING
      STITH PARHAM, JOHN DAVIS   MARY HARDING
1785. October 4th. Then received of DAVID BUCHANAN nine hundred pounds current
money Virginia in full for the within mentioned premises
Teste STITH PARHAM,   JOSEPH HARDING
      GRESSETT DAVIS, JOHN MacRAE
At a Court of Hustings held for the Town of Petersburg at the House of WILLIAM
DURELL Wednesday the fifth day of October 1785
An Indenture of Bargain and Sale between JOSEPH HARDING and MARY his Wife of the
one part and DAVID BUCHANAN of the other part, with the memorandum & receipt
thereon indorsed were acknowledged by the said JOSEPH HARDING and ordered to be
recorded; And it is ordered that a Commission be issued to take the acknowledgment of

MARY HARDING for the relinquishing of her right of Dower of in & to the land and premises mentioned in the said Indenture
Teste J. GRAMMER, Clk. C. Hs.

p.   THIS INDENTURE made this fifth day of August one thousand seven hundred
134   and Eighty five Between GRESSETT DAVIS and MARTHA his Wife of the Town of
        Petersburg and State of Virginia of one part and JOSEPH HARDING of the said
Town of the other part; Witnesseth that in consideration of the sum of Two hundred
pounds lawfull money of Virginia to him in hand paid, said GRESSETT DAVIS and
MARTHA his Wife by these presents do bargain sell and confirm unto JOSEPH HARDING
his heirs a certain parcell of land with the appurtenances lying in that part of the
Town of Petersburg called RAVENSCROFT TOWN, and containg Three acres more or less
being the lott marked upon the plott of Town of RAVENSCROFT (22) number Twenty Two,
together with all ways water courses &c., thereto belonging; To have and to hold the lott
of land with the appurtenances unto JOSEPH HARDING his heirs, And GRESSETT DAVIS
and MARTHA his Wife their heirs covenant with JOSEPH HARDING the parcel of land to
JOSEPH HARDING his heirs will warrant and ever defend against all persons, In Witness whereof the said GRESSETT DAVIS and MARTHA his Wife hath to these presents sett
their hands and affixed their seals the day and year above written
Signed Sealed and Delivered in presents of
        STITH PARHAM,   GRESSETT DAVIS
        JOHN DAVIS, JOHN MacRAE   MARTHA DAVIS
    Petersburg 7th Septr. 1785. Received of JOSEPH HARDING two hundred pounds the full
consideration money for the within mentioned lott number Twenty two & hath given
full & quiet possession of the same
In presence of JOHN DAVIS,   GRESSETT DAVIS
        JOHN MacRAE,   STITH PARHAM
    At a Court of Hustings held for the Town of Petersburg at the House of WILLIAM
DURELL Wednesday the fifth day of October 1785
    An Indenture of Bargain & Sale between GRESSETT DAVIS and MARTHA his Wife of one
part and JOSEPH HARDING of the other part with the receipt thereon indorsed were
acknowledged by the said GRESSETT DAVIS and are ordered to be recorded; And it is
ordered that a Commission be issued to take the acknowledgment of the said MARTHA
DAVIS for the relinquishing of her right of Dower to the land & premises mentioned in
this Indenture   Teste J. GRAMMER, Clk. C. Hs.

pp.   THIS INDENTURE made this twenty seventh day of September in year of our
135   Lord one thousand seven hundred and Eighty five Between DUNCAN ROSE of
        DINWIDDIE County, Agent for BUCHANAN & SIMSON, and DAVID DALYETT and
DAVID BUCHANAN of Petersburg, present agents of the said BUCHANAN and SIMSON, and
DAVID DALYETT on the one part and GRESSETT DAVIS of Petersburg on the other part;
Witnesseth that DUNCAN ROSE and DAVID BUCHANAN for the sum of Two hundred
pounds current money of Virginia to DAVID BUCHANAN in hand paid by GRESSETT
DAVIS by these presents doth bargain sell and confirm unto GRESSETT DAVIS his heirs
one lot of land containing Three acres, be the same more or less, laying in Petersburg
incorporation being part of a tract of land laid off by ROBERT RAVENSCROFT deced. into
Forty six lots termed RAVENSCROFT TOWN and distinguished by number Forty Five (45),
To have and to hold the lott of land unto GRESSETT DAVIS his heirs And DUNCAN ROSE
and DAVID BUCHANAN in behalf of said BUCHANAN & SIMSON and DAVID DALYETT warrant and will forever defend the said lott against all persons; In Witness whereof the

said DUNCAN ROSE & DAVID BUCHANAN for themselves and for the said BUCHANAN &
SIMSON and DAVID DALYETT have hereunto set their hands and affixed their seals the
day and year above written
Sign'd Seal'd and Deliver'd in presence of
JOSEPH COLEMAN JUNR.   ) as to DUNCAN   DUN: ROSE
ROBERT BARBER   ) ROSE signing &   DAVID BUCHANAN
THOMAS CHALLENNER   ) sealing &c.
WM. BROWDER   )
JOSEPH COLEMAN   )
STITH PARHAM   ) as to DD. BUCHANAN
WILLIAM VAUGHAN   ) signing & sealing
JOSHUA SMITH   ) &c.
JOS: HARDING   )
   At a Court of Hustings held for the Town of Petersburg at the House of WILLIAM
DARELL Wednesday the fifth day of October 1785
This Indenture of Bargain and Sale from DUNCAN ROSE & DAVID BUCHANAN for and in
behalf of BUCHANAN & SIMSON and DAVID DALYETT of one part and GRESSETT DAVIS of
the other part and the memorandum of Seisen thereon indorsed were proved by the
Oaths of JOSEPH COLEMAN, ROBERT BARBER, WILLIAM BROWDER, STITH PARHAM and
JOSEPH HARDING witnesses thereto and are ordered to be recorded

p.   THIS INDENTURE made this Sixth day of September Anno Dom: one thousand
136   seven hundred and Eighty five Between MILES WILLIAMS & PRECELLA his Wife
         of BRUNSWICK County & GRESSETT DAVIS of Petersburg Town, Witnesseth that
said MILES & PRECELLA WILLIAMS for sum of Twenty pounds to them in hand paid by
GRESSETT DAVIS, by these presents do bargain & sell unto GRESSETT DAVIS his heirs one
moiety of one lot of land containing Three acres more or less being part of a tract of
land in Petersburg laid off by ROBERT RAVENSCROFT deced. into Forty six lotts & known
in the plot by (No. 42) say Forty Two, To have and to hold the one moiety of the one lott
of land with every appurtenance thereunto appertaining to GRESSETT DAVIS his heirs;
And MILES WILLIAMS & PRESCILLA his Wife will warrant & forever defend the one
moiety of said lott unto GRESSETT DAVIS his heirs against the claim of every person;
In Witness whereof the said MILES WILLIAMS & PRECELLA his Wife have hereunto set
their hands & affixed their seals the day & year above written
Signed Sealed & Delivered in presents of
    JOS: HARDING, HUMFRIES TRAYLER,   MILES WILLIAMS
    JOSEPH COLEMAN JR., STITH PARHAM
   This 6th day of September 1785, I do acknowledge the receipt of Twenty pounds in full
consideration for the within mentioned one moiety of one lot of land & hath given the
said GRESSETT DAVIS full possession of the same as witness my hand
Teste JOS: HARDING,   MILES WILLIAMS
    JOSEPH COLEMAN, STITH PARHAM
   At a Court of Hustigns held for the Town of Petersburg at the House of WILLIAM
DURELL Wednesday the fifth day of October 1785
This Indenture of Bargain & Sale between MILES WILLIAMS & PRECILLA his Wife of one
part and GRESSETT DAVIS of the other part was proved by the Oaths of JOSEPH HARDING,
HUMFRIES TRAYLOR and JOSEPH COLEMAN JR., and the receipt thereon indorsed was
proved by the Oaths of JOSEPH HARDING & JOSEPH COLEMAN witnesses thereto and toge-
ther with the said Indenture ordered to be recorded
                    Teste J. GRAMMER, Clk. C. Hs.

p.
137
THIS INDENTURE made this third day of September in year of our Lord one thousand seven hundred and Eight five Between CHARLES DUNCAN of CHESTERFEILD County of one part and ROBERT FITZGERALD of Town of Petersburg of the other part; Witnesseth that in consideration of the just and full quantity of Four thousand pounds weight of Tobacco by ROBERT FITZGERALD to CHARLES DUNCAN in hand paid; by these presents doth bargain sell and confirm unto ROBERT FITZGERALD his heirs two parcells of land lying on BLANDFORD HILL known in the plan of the Town lately laid out on said Hill by the numbers (50 & 79), Fifty and Seventy Nine; and recorded in the Borough Court of Petersburg. To have and to hold the parcells of land and all the advantages appurtaining thereto to ROBERT FITZGERALD his heirs; And CHARLES DUNCAN for himself and his heirs doth covenant with ROBERT FITZGERALD his heirs that he will forever warrant and defend the title of said parcells of land to ROBERT FITZGERALD his heirs against the lawful claims of every person. In Witness whereof, the said CHARLES DUNCAN hath hereunto set his hand and seal the day and year above written

Seal'd and Deliver'd in presence of
DOND: MacKENZIE,   CHARLES DUNCAN
JAMES DOUGLASS witness

At a Court of Hustings held for the Town of Petersburg at the House of WILLIAM DURELL Wednesday the fifth day of October 1785

An Indenture of Bargain & Sale between CHARLES DUNCAN of the one part and ROBERT FITZGERALD of the other part was acknowledged by the within mentioned CHARLES DUNCAN and is ordered to be recorded   Teste J. GRAMMER, Clk. C. Hs.

p.
138
THIS INDENTURE made this Third dy of September in year of our Lord one thousand seven hundred and Eighty five Between CHARLES DUNCAN of CHESTERFEILD County of one part and PHILIP W. JACKSON of AMELIA County, Witnesseth that in consideration of the jsut and full quantity of Four thousand pounds weight of Tobacco by said PHILIP W. JACKSON to CHARLES DUNCAN in hand paid, by these presents doth bargain sell and confirm unto PHILIP W. JACKSON his heirs two parcells of land lying on BLANDFORD HILL known in the plan of a Town lately laid out on the said Hill by the numbers of (48 & 29), Forty Eight and Twenty Nine; and recorded in the Borough of Petersburg; To have and to hold the parcells of land and all the advantages appurtaining thereto unto PHILIP W. JACKSON his heirs and CHARLES DUNCAN will for ever warrant and defend the title of said parcells of land unto PHILIP W. JACKSON his heirs against the lawful claims of every person; In Witness whereof the said CHARLES DUNCAN hath hereunto set his hand and seal the day and year above written
Seal'd & Deliver'd in presence of
DOND; MacKENZIE,   CHARLES DUNCAN
JAMES DOUGLASS witness

At a Court of Hustings held for the Town of Petersburg at the House of WILLIAM DURELL Wednesday the fifth day of October 1785

An Indenture of Bargain & Sale between CHARLES DUNCAN of one part and PHILIP W. JACKSON was acknowledged by the said CHARLES DUNCAN and is ordered to be recorded
Teste J. GRAMMER, Clk. C. Hs.

pp.
139-
140
THIS INDENTURE made this fifth day of October in the year of our Lord one thousand seven hundred & Eighty five Between CHARLES DUNCAN of CHESTERFEILD County of one part and JOHN SHORE of the Town of Petersburg of other part Witnesseth that for the sum of One hundred pounds to said CHARLES in

hand paid, by these presents doth bargain & sell unto JOHN SHORE his heirs a certain
lott of land lying in that part of the Town of Petersburg called NEW BLANDFORD and
distinguished by the number (23), Twenty Three, and the rents issues and services
thereof, To have and to hold the parcell of land with the appurtenances unto JOHN
SHORE his heirs; And CHARLES DUNCAN for himself his heirs the parcel of land unto
JOHN SHORE his heirs against all persons will warrant and by these presents forever
defend; In Witness whereof the said CHARLES hath hereunto set his hand and seal the
day & year first above written
Signed Sealed & Delivered in the presence of
    WM. MURRAY,   CHARLES DUNCAN
    WILLIAM DAVIES
  Whereas the within mentioned lot of land marked upon the plan of that part of the
Town of Petersburg called NEW BLANDFORD by the distinction of number (23) Twenty
three is noted thereon as the property of WILLIAM MURRAY and is recorded as such in
the recorded Map of NEW BLANDFORD; whereas in fact the said lot was never conveyed
to me by the within granter or any other person; Now I the said WILLIAM MURRAY to
prevent all disputes respecting the same and in consideration of the sum of Five shillings to me in hand paid, do hereby for myself & my heirs relinquish release and for
ever quit claim unto the within named JOHN SHORE his heirs all my right title & demand
whatsoever of in & to the said lot and every of its appurtenances; In Witness whereof I
have hereunto set my hand & Seal this 27th day of September in the year 1785
Signed Sealed & Delivered in presence of
    WILLIAM DAVIES   WM. MURRAY
  At a Court of Hustings held for the Town of Petersburg at the House of WILLIAM
DURELL Wednesday the fifth day of October 1785
  An Indenture of Bargain and Sale between CHARLES DUNCAN of one part and JOHN
SHORE of the other part with a memorandum of possession thereon indorsed were ack-
nowledged by the thereto subscribed CHARLES DUNCAN, And a relinquishment from
WILLIAM MURRAY to the said JOHN SHORE which is thereunto annexed, was likewise
acknowledged by the thereto subscribed WILLIAM MURRAY and together with the said
Indenture & memorandum aforesaid are ordered to be recorded
                Teste J. GRAMMER, Clk. C. Hs.

(Pages 141 and 142 are blank.)

p. 143   At a Court of Hustings held for the Town of Petersburg Wednesday the Second
day of November 1785
    Present CHRISTOPHER McCONNICO Esqr., Mayor
        JOHN SHORE Esqr., Recorder
    ALEXANDER McNABB, ISAAC HALL Gentlemen Aldermen

p. 143   THIS INDENTURE made this twenty fifth day of October one thousand seven
hundred & Eighty five Between WILLIAM HARRISON & ROBERT KIRKHAM, both
of County of DINWIDDIE & Town of Petersburg, Witnesseth that for sum of Forty
three pounds, two shillings & six pence to him in hand paid by said KIRKHAM, by these
presents doth bargain sell & confirm unto ROBERT KIRKHAM one certain plott of land
lying in Town of Petersburg & in that part of the Town laid off by ROBERT RAVENS-
CROFT deceased, being part of a lott distinguished in sd. Town by number Nine, Begining at a small drain near a Pine tree on the line of JOSEPH HARDAWAY, thence One
hundred & twenty eight feet North seventy four degrees East upon said line, thence
South sixteen degrees East one hundred & twenty feet to a Cross Street, thence South

seventy four degrees West along aid Street to the Ditch near said KIRKHAMs House &
from thence to the beginning, along said Ditch or drain, Together with all woods,
waters houses, orchards belonging; To have & to hold the lot of land with the appurtenances unto ROBERT KIRKHAM, And WILLIAM HARRISON for himself & his heirs doth
agree with ROBERT KIRKHAM his heirs the plot of land against the claim & demand of
any person shall warrant & forever defend; In Witness whereof the said WILLIAM
HARRISON hath hereunto set his hand & affixed his seal the day & year above written
Signed Sealed and Delivered in the presence of
       ALEXR. TAYLOR, JOHN ATKINSON,   W. HARRISON
       GOLLOHUN WALKER, HENRY MORRISS,
       J. GRAMMER, JOSEPH FAUX
   At a Court of Hustings held for the Town of Petersburg at the House of WM. DURELL
Wednesday the 2d. day of November 1785   An Indenture of Bargain & Sale between
WILLIAM HARRISON & ROBERT KIRKHAM both of the Town aforesaid was acknowledged
by the thereto subscribed WM. HARRISON and ordered to be recorded
                       Teste J. GRAMMER, Clk. C. Hs.

p.   At a Court of Hustings held for the Town of Petersburg at the House of WM.
144   DURELL Wednesday the Second and by adjournment continued Thursday the
         third day of November 1785
         Present CHRISTOPHER McCONNICO Esqr. Mayor;
              JOHN SHORE Esqr., Recorder
         ROBERT BOLLING, ALEXR. McNABB, ISAAC HALL, Gentlemen Aldermen

p.   THIS INDENTURE made this fifth day of October in the year One thousand seven
144   hundred and Eighty five Between SIMON FRASER of County of PRINCE GEORGE
         and Corporation of Petersburg, Merchant, of one part and ROBERT TURNBULL,
Merchant, of County of PRINCE GEORGE of other part; Witnesseth that for the sum of
Twenty pounds by said ROBERT to said SIMON in hand paid, by these presents doth bargain & sell unto ROBERT TURNBULL his heirs one lot of land lying in that part of the
Town of Petersburg called NEW BLANDFORD and in the plan thereof number Fourteen
(14), as by said plan of Record of the Court of Hustings of Petersburg may appear; and
the rents issues and profits thereof; To have and to hold the lot of land unto ROBERT
TURNBULL his heirs to the only use & behoof of ROBERT TURNBULL his heirs and for no
other intent or purpose, In Witness whereof the said SIMON FRASER hath hereunto set
his hand and affixed his seal the day & year first above written
Sealed and Delivered in the presence of
       (no witnesses recorded)   SIMON FRASER
   At a Court of Hustings held for the Town of Petersburg at the House of WM. DURELL and
continued Thursday the third day of November 1785   An Indenture of Bargain &
Sale between SIMON FRASER of the Town of Petersburg of the one part and ROBERT
TURNBULL of the County of PRINCE GEORGE of the other part was acknowledged by the
thereto subscribed SIMON FRASER and is ordered to be recorded
                       Teste J. GRAMMER, Clk. C. Hs.

pp.   THIS INDENTURE made the Second day of November one thousand seven hun-
145-   dred and Eighty five Between JAMES BROMLY and MARY BROMLY both of Peters-
147   burg in the County of DINWIDDIE & State of Virginia, Innkeepers, of one part
         and SILAS SANDFORD of the Town, County and State aforesaid, Merchant, of the
other part; Witnesseth taht for the sum of Sixty five pounds current money to him in

hand paid by SILAS SANDFORD, And also in consideration of the covenants and agreements herein after mentioned on part of SILAS SANDFORD to be performed and kept,
said JAMES BROMLY and MARY BROMLY by these presents doth bargain sell and confirm unto SILAS SANDFORD his heirs one certain lott of land lying in County of DIN-
WIDDIE in the Vicinity of the PUBLICK TOBACCO WAREHOUSES, called BOLINGs and are
part of the land lately laid out in lots by ROBERT BOLLING and known by the number
(58), which plan is recorded in the Court of the County of DINWIDDIE, the lot number
(58) extending in front on WATER STREET fifty feet nine inches, as by the said plan will
more particularly appear, And all ways and appurtenances to said lot belonging; and
the Rents (other than is herein mentioned) issues and profits thereof (the Fee Rent
hereinafter mentioned payable to ROBERT BOLLING excepted) To have and to hold the
lott of land hereby conveyed with appurtenances unto SILAS SANDFORD his heirs,
paying therefor unto ROBERT BOLLING his heirs on the first day of January every yar
the fee rent of Three pounds per annum, the first years rent to grow due and payable
on the first day of January one thousand seven hundred and Eighty six; And if said
money shall be in arrear and unpaid it may be lawful for said ROBERT BOLLING his
heirs into the said lott to re-enter and have as if this Indenture had never been made;
In Witness whereof the parties aforesaid have hereunto set their hands and seals interchangeably the day and year first above written
Sealed and Delivered in the presents of us

    J. BAIRD JR.,   JAMES BROMLEY
    THOS: WILLCOX,   MARY BROMLEY
    STEPHEN PACE, THOS: WALKE

  At a Court of Hustings held for the Town of Petersburg at the House of WILLIAM
DURELL on Wednesday the Second day of November 1785 An Indenture of Bargain and
Sale between JAMES BROMLEY and MARY BROMLEY of one part and SILAS SANDFORD of
the other part was proved by the Oaths of JOHN BAIRD JR., THOAMS WILLCOX and
STEPHEN PACE and ordered to be recorded
                        Teste J. GRAMMER, Clk. C. Hs.

pp.   THIS INDENTURE made this Twenty eighth day of September in year of our
148-   Lord one thousand seven hundred and Eighty five Between WILLIAM WRIGHT of
149   Town of Petersburg of one part and ERASMUS GILL of the same Town of other
        part; Witnesseth that for the sum of Eight hundred & Ten pounds current
money of Virginia to WILLIAM WRIGHT in hand paid by ERASMUS GILL, said WILLIAM
WRIGHT hath bargained and sold unto ERASMUS GILL and to his heirs one moiety of a
certain lot or acre of land which is distinguished in the plan of the New Town of Petersburg laid out by (blank) JONES deceased by the number (18), Eighteen, which moiety or
half acre of land in bounded Begining at the middle or center from East to West of said
Lott number (18) Eighteen on the Street and from thence running Northerly parralel
with the Original Lines and equally dividing the same to the back line thereof, thence
along the back line Westerly to the corner of said lott bounding on lott number Seventeen (17), thence along on lott number Seventeen Southerly to the Street and thence
along the Street Easterly to the begining, Together with all houses gardens and appurtenances belonging; To have and to hold the said portion or half of lott number (18) as
above discribed with its appurtenances to ERASMUS GILL his heirs; And WILLIAM
WRIGHT his heirs shall warrant and defend against the right title or demand of every
person; In Witness whereof the said WILLIAM WRIGHT hath hereunto set his hand and
affixed his seal the day and year first above written

Sealed and Delivered in presence of
    JOHN DORTON,   WILLIAM WRIGHT
    J. GRAMMER, SAML. HINTON
   At a Court of Hustings held for the Town of Petersburg at the House of WILLIAM
DURELL on Wednesday the Second day of November & by Adjournment continued
Thursday the Third 1785   An Indenture of Bargain & Sale between WILLIAM
WRIGHT of one part and ERASMUS GILL of the other part with the memorandum of
Livery & Seizen thereunto annexed were acknowledged by the thereto subscribed
WILLIAM WRIGHT and are ordered to be recorded
                    Teste J. GRAMMER, Clk. C. Hs.

p.   THIS INDENTURE made this Second day of November one thousand seven hun-
150   dred and Eight five Between CHARLES DUNCAN of County of CHESTERFEILD of one
       part and Messrs. SHORE & McCONNICO, Merchts. Petersburg of the other part;
Witnesseth that CHARLES DUNCAN for the sum of One hundred pounds by said SHORE
and McCONNICO in hand paid; by these presents doth bargain and sell unto said SHORE &
McCONNICO their heirs Five lotts of land lying in that part of the Town of Petersburg
called NEW BLANDFORD and in the plan distinguished by the numbers Twenty one,
Thirty Nine, Forty Three, Sixty Four & Sixty Seven (21, 39, 43, 64 & 67) as by the plan
now of Record in the Court of Hustings of Petersburg will appear; To have and to hold
the said five lotts with all the appurtenances unto said SHORE & McCONNICO their heirs
and CHARLES DUNCAN and his heirs and against all persons will warrant and defend
forever by these presents; In Witness whereof the said CHARLES DUNCAN hath set his
hand and affixed his Seal the day and year first above written
                    CHARLES DUNCAN
  At a Court of Hustings held for the Town of Petersburg at the House of WILLIAM
DURELL the Third day of November 1785   An Indenture of Bargain and Sale between
CHARLES DUNCAN of one part and Messrs. SHORE & McCONNICO of the other part was
acknowledged by the said CHARLES DUNCAN and is ordered to be recorded
                 Teste J. GRAMMER, Clk. C. Hs.

p.   THIS INDENTURE made this Second day of November in year of our Lord one
151   thousand seven hundred and eighty five Between CHARLES DUNCAN of County of
       CHESTERFEILD of one part and SIMON FRASER of Town of Petersburg, Merchant,
of other part; Witnesseth that CHARLES DUNCAN for sum of Five shillings by said SIMON
to said CHARLES in hand paid by these presents doth bargain and sell unto SIMON
FRASER his heirs one lott of land lying in that part of the Town of Petersburg called
NEW BLANDFORD and in the plan distinguished by the number Fourteen (14), said lott
No. 14 fourteen being in front one hundred feet and two hundred and thirty one feet in
depth, and the rents issues and profits thereof; To have and to hold the lott number
Fourteen with all the appurtenances unto SIMON FRASER his heirs for no other intent
or purpose. In Witness whereof said CHARLES DUNCAN hath hereunto set his hand &
seal the day and year first above written
Sealed and Delivered in presence of us
   (no witnesses recorded)   CHARLES DUNCAN
  At a Court of Hustings held for the Town of Petersburg at the House of WILLIAM
DURELL the Third day of November 1785   An Indenture of Bargain and Sale between
CHARLES DUNCAN of County of CHESTERFEILD of one part and SIMON FRASER of the
other part was acknowledged by the above subscribed CHARLES DUNCAN and ordered to
be recorded   Teste J. GRAMMER, Clk. C. Hs.

p.   THIS INDENTURE made this Sixth day of July in the year one thousand seven
152   hundred and Eighty five Between CHARLES DUNCAN of CHESTERFEILD County of
          one part and ROBERT TURNBULL of PRINCE GEORGE County of the other part;
Witnesseth that said CHARLES in consideration of the sum of Five shillings to him in
hand paid by said ROBERT by these presents doth bargain & sell unto ROBERT TURN-
BULL his heirs the following Six lotts of land being in that part of the Town of Petersburg known by the name of NEW BLANDFORD and in the plan thereof numbers Eight,
nine, fifteen, twenty two and Eight six as by the plan now of record in the Court of
Hustings of Petersburg may appear; To have and to hold the six lotts of land and appurtenances unto ROBERT TURNBULL his heirs free and clear from every incumbrance
whatsoever; In Witness whereof the said CHARLES DUNCAN hath hereunto set his hand
and seal the day and year above written
Sealed and Delivered in presence of
    (no witnesses recorded)   CHARLES DUNCAN
  At a Court of Hustings held for the Town of Petersburg at the House of WILLIAM
DURELL the Third day of November 1785   An Indenture of Bargain & Sale between
CHARLES DUNCAN of CHESTERFEILD County of one part and ROBERT TURNBULL of
PRINCE GEORGE County of the other part was acknowledged by the said CHARLES DUN-
CAN and ordered to be recorded   Teste J. GRAMMER, Clk. C. Hs.

p.   THIS INDENTURE made this Twenty seventh dy of October one thousand seven
153   hundred & Eighty five between CHARLES DUNCAN of CHESTERFEILD County of
          one part and WILLIAM ROBERTSON of County of PRINCE GEORGE of other part;
Witnesseth that CHARLES DUNCAN for the sum of Five shillings to him in hand paid, by
these presents doth bargain & sell unto WILLIAM ROBERTSON his heirs Four lotts of
ground in NEW BLANDFORD, numbers Thirty Three, Forty Four, Forty Six & Ninety as
by a plan of said Town recorded the first day of September 1784 in the Court of Hustings
will appear; And also all rents issues and profits thereof unto WILLIAM ROBERTSON his
heirs and CHARLES DUNCAN for himself & his heirs the lotts of land to WILLIAM
ROBERTSON his heirs shall warrant and forever defend by these presents; In Witness
whereof the said CHARLES DUNCAN hath hereunto set his hand and affixed his seal the
day above written
Signed Sealed & Delivered in presence of
    ROBT. TURNBULL,   CHARLES DUNCAN
    THOS: WITHERS, PATK. WALKER
  At a Court of Hustings held for the Town of Petersburg at the House of WILLIAM
DURELL the third day of November 1785   An Indenture of Bargain and Sale from
CHARLES DUNCAN of the County of CHESTERFEILD of one part and WILLIAM ROBERTSON
of PRINCE GEORGE County of the other part was acknowledged by the said CHARLES DUN-
CAN and ordered to be recorded   Teste J. GRAMMER, Clk. C. Hs.
(Page 154 is blank).

p.   At a Court of Hustings held for the Town of Petersburg at the House of WILLIAM
155   DURELL Wednesday the Fourth day of January 1786
          Present CHRISTOPHER McCONNICO Esqr., Mayor
             JOHN SHORE Esqr. Recorder
        ROBERT BOLLING, ALEXANDER McNABB, ISAAC HALL, Gentlemen Aldermen

p.   THIS INDENTURE made this fourth day of January one thousand seven hundred
155   and Eighty six Between WILLIAM ROBERTSON of PRINCE GEORGE County of one
          part and JOHN SHORE JR. of other part; Witnesseth that WILLIAM ROBERTSON in

consideration of the sum of Five shilgs. to him in hand paid, by these presents doth
bargain sell and confirm unto said JOHN SHORE his heirs a certain lot of land in NEW
BLANDFORD No. 46 (Forty Six) as by a plan of said Town recorded the first day of September 1784 in the Court of Hustings will appear; And also all issues rents & profits thereof;
To have and to hold lunto said JNO: SHORE JR. his heirs, And WILLIAM ROBERTSON for
himself his heirs the lot of land against every person unto JOHN SHORE JR. & his heirs
shall warrant and forever defend by these presents; In Witness whereof the said WIL-
· LIAM ROBERTSON hath hereunto set his hand & affixed his seal the day above written
Signed Sealed & Delivered in presence of
            (no witnesses recorded)   WILLIAM ROBERTSON
  At a Court of Hustings held for the Town of Petersburg Wednesday the Fourth day of
January 1786   An Indenture of Bargain & Sale between WILLIAM ROBERTSON of one
part & JOHN SHORE JR. of the other part was acknowledged by the above subscribed
WILLIAM ROBERTSON & is ordered to be recorded
                            Teste J. GRAMMER, Clk. C. Hs.
(Page 156 is blank)

pp.   THIS INDENTURE made this Twenty third day of April in year of our Lord one
157-   thousand seven hundred and Eighty five Between RICHARD BATE and WILLIAM
158   GRAY of the Town of BLANDFORD and County of PRINCE GEORGE, Merchants and
           Partners under the firm of BATE & GRAY of one part and SIMON FRASER and
ROBERT DONOLD of Petersburg, DAVID PAGAN of OSBOURNEs and JOHN MURCHIE of MAN-
CHESTER, Merchants and Partners under the Stile and firm of SIMON FRASER & CO., of
the other part; Witnesseth that said BATE & GRAY for sum of Three hundred pounds to
them in hand paid by SIMON FRASER & CO., by these presents do bargain sell and con-
firm unto SIMON FRASER & CO., their heirs as Tenants in Common and not as Joint
Tenants a parcel of land lying in that part of the Town of Petersburg called BLAND-
FORD being part of the Lott the said BATE & GRAY bought of Colo. WILLIAM CALL,
begining at the West corner of ROBERT BOLLINGs Lot (formerly belonging to MATHEW
WELLS and at present occupied by GIBSON) thence running West fifty six feet along the
Cross Street, thence down to the River, the like quantity of fifty six feet, then a South
course to the place of begining; Together with all advantages priviledges and emoluments to the same belonging; To have and to hold the parcel of land with the appurtenances unto SIMON FRASER & CO., their heirs as Tenants in Common, And BATE & GRAY
their respective heirs unto SIMON FRASER & CO., their heirs the parcel of land against
all persons shall warrant and by these presents forever defend; In Witness whereof the
said BATE & GRAY have hereunto set their hands and seals the day and year first above
written
Signed Sealed and Delivered in the presence of
      JOSEPH WEISEGAR,   BATE & GRAY
      JAMES MacFARLAND, RICHARD STUARD
   The Commonwealth of Virginia to CHRISTOPHER McCONNICO, JOHN SHORE, ROBERT
BOLLING and ALEXANDER McNABB Gentlemen, Greeting: Whereas RICHARD BATE &
WILLIAM GRAY by their certain Indenture have sold unto SIMON FRASER, ROBERT
DONOLD, DAVID PAGAN and JOHN MURCHIE, Merchants and Partners under the Stile and
firm of SIMON FRASER & CO., a parcel of land in that part of the Town of Petersburg
called BLANDFORD, And Whereas SARAH BATE and MARIA GRAY, Wives of the said
RICHARD BATE and WILLIAM GRAY cannot conveniently travel to our Court of Hustings
in the Town of Petersburg to make acknowledgment of their Right of Dower in the said
land in the conveyance mentioned (the Commission for the privy Examination of SARAH, the

Wife of RICHARD BATE, and of MARIA, the Wife of WILLIAM GRAY), Witness JOHN GRAMMER Clerk of our said Court the thirteenth day of May 1785 in the ninth year of the Common-wealth   J. GRAMMER, Clk. C. Hs.

By Virtue of the Commission hereunto annxed this Indenture was acknowledged by the said SARAH BATE & MARIA GRAY on the 14th day of May, they the said SARAH & MARIA being first privily and apart from the said RICHARD BATE and WILLIAM GRAY their Husbands, examined (the return of the execution of the privy Examination of SARAH BATE and MARIA GRAY): before us   ROBERT BOLLING
                                                      ALEXR. McNABB

At a Court of Hustings held for the Town of Petersburg at the House of WM. DURELL Wednesday the 4th day of January 1786   An Indenture of Bargain & Sale between BATE & GRAY of one part and SIMON FRASER & CO., of other part was proved by the Oath of JAMES MacFARLAND a witnsse thereto and the same having been before proved by the Oaths of JOSEPH WEISIGAR & RICHD. STUARD other witnesses thereto and together with the Commission thereto annexed & the Certificate of the Execution thereof are ordered to be recorded   Teste J. GRAMMER, Clk. C. Hs.

pp.   KNOW ALL MEN by these presents that I WILLIAM JONES of the City of BRISTOL
159-   Merchant, Surviving Partner of JOSEPH FARRELL, late of the said City, Merchant
160   deceased, by these presents do nominate and appoint RICHARD HANSON now of
         Petersburg in the State of Virginia but late of the City of LONDON, Merchant, my true and lawfull Attorney for me and in my name and for my use as surviving partner as aforesaid to ask demand sue for recover and receive of and from every person whomsoever in the Province of Virginia in North America or elsewhere in the United States allsuch sum and sums of money debts goods merchandizes and effects which now is or hereafter shall be due owing payable or belonging unto me as surviving partner as aforesaid from any person in the Province of Virginia or elsewhere wherein I shall be concerned; In Witness whereof I have hereunto set my hand and seal this third day of September in the Twenty Fifth year of the Reign of our Sovereign Lord George the Third by the grace of God of Great Britain France and Ireland, King Defender of the Faith and so forth, and in the year of our Lord one thousand seven hundred and Eighty five
Sealed and Delivered in the presence of
         JOHN GROZART,   W. JONES
         D. BALMANNO
At a Court of Hustings held for the Town of Petersburg at the House of WILLIAM DURELL Wednesday the 4th day of January 1786   A Letter of Attorney from WILLIAM JONES, Mercht., of the City of BRISTOL, Surviving Partner of FARELL & JONES, late of the same City, to RICHARD HANSON was presented in Court & proved by the Oaths of JOHN GROZART and D. BALMANNO, witnesses thereto, and is ordered to be recorded
                     Teste J. GRAMMER, Clk. C. Hs.

pp.   THIS INDENTURE made this the Twenty first day of Julyh in the year of our Lord
161-   one thousand seven hundred and Eighty five Between JOHN DYSART and JOHN
164   CATHCART, Merchants of the Town of Petersburg of one part and JOHN MORRI-
         SON & COMPANY, Merchants, of the other part; Witnesseth tht for the sum of Seven hundred and Five pounds current money to them the said JOHN DYSART and JOHN CATHCART in hand paid by JOHN MORRISON & COMPANY, also in consideration of the Rents covenants and agreements herein after mentioned to be paid and performed by JOHN MORRISON & COMPANY their heirs, said JOHN DYSART and JOHN CATHCART by

these presents do bargain sell and confirm unto JOHN MORRISON & COMPANY one certain spot or parcel of land and tenement in Town of Petersburg which spot of land JOHN
DYSART and JOHN CATHCART purchased of HENRY SADLER and JAMES CORRAN as by
their Indenture bearing date the Eighth day of July 1784 recorded in Court of Hustings
of the Town of Petersburg will shew (and is one third part of a lott of land which
HENRY SADLER and JAMES CORRAN purchased of ROBERT BOLLING Esquire distinguished
in the plott of the land laid out by ROBERT BOLLING by the number Twenty (20) containing twenty two feet in front on BOLLING BROOK STREET and extending back by
parralel lines the same width, the whole depth of the lott bounded on the West side by
the lott of land belonging to the Estate of JAMES TURNBULL deceased and on the East
side by the remaining two thirds of the said lott of land number Twenty (20), and all
ways and appurtenances to the one third part of lott number Twenty (20) and tenements thereon belonging; and the rents issues and profits thereof; To have and to hold
the parcel of hand hereby conveyed with appurtenances unto JOHN MORRISON & COM-
PANY their heirs as Tenants in Common and not as Joint Tenants, paying therefore
unto JOHN DYSART and JOHN CATHCART their heirs or to ROBERT BOLLING his heirs for
the use of them and no other use on the first day of January every year the fee rent of
Seven pounds lawfull money of Great Britain, the first years Rent to grow due and become payable on the first day of January one thousand seven hundred and Eighty six;
In Witness whereof the parties have hereunto interchangeably set their hands and
affixed their seals the day and year first above written
Sealed and Delivered in the presence of
    JAMES TAYLOR,   JOHN DYSART
    JAS. FREELAND,   JOHN CATHCART
    CHS. GALBRAITH   JO: MORISON & CO.
Memorandum That on the day and year aforesaid it was covenanted and agreed by the
said JOHN MORRISON & COMPANY that they wou'd hold the land and premises aforesaid
as Tenants in Common & not as joint tenants without benefit of Survivorship
                        JO: MORISON & CO.
Sold the within mentioned Tenement at Publick Sale the 14th day of July 1785 for the
sum of Seven hundred and five pounds to Messrs. JNO: MORRISON & CO.
                        JAMES TAYLOR, A. V. M.
Memo. Received the above sum of Seven hundred & five pounds this 22d. August 1785
                        JAMES TAYLOR, A. V. M.
At a Court of Hustings held for the Town of Petersburg at the House of WILLIAM
DURELL Wednesday the fourth day of January 1786   An Indenture of Bargain and
sale between JOHN DYSART and JOHN CATHCART of the one part and JOHN MORRISON &
CO. of the other part, and the memorandum of livery and seizen thereon indorsed were
proved by the Oath of CHARLES GALBRAITH, a witness thereto, and they have been
before proved by the Oaths of JAMES TAYLOR and JAMES FREELAND, other witnesses
thereto are, together with another memorandum, a Certificate and Receipt thereon
indorsed, ordered to be recorded   Teste J. GRAMMER, Clk. C. Hs.

p.   THIS INDENTURE made this 27th day of December in the year of our Lord one
165   thousand seven hundred and Eighty five Between WILLIAM WRIGHT of the Town
       of Petersburg of one part and ROBERT KIRKHAM of the aforesaid Town of other
part; Witnesseth that for the sum of One hundred & fifty pounds current money of Virginia to him in hand paid by ROBERT KIRKHAM, by these presentsdoth bargain sell &
confirm unto ROBERT KIRKHAM his heirs one certain lott of land containing Three
acres lying & being in Town of Petersburg in that part thereof distinguished by the

name of RAVENSCROFT TOWN, and distinguished in the plan of said Town by (No. 16),
number Sixteen; And WILLIAM WRIGHT doth grant that the premises shall remain & be
free and clear from all incumbrances; In Witness whereof the said WILLIAM WRIGHT
hath hereunto set his hand and affixed his seal the day & year first above written
    ABM. EVANS,   WM. WRIGHT
    WM. BARKSDALE, P. MARSH
At a Court of Hustings held for the Town of Petersburg at the House of WM. DURELL
Wednesday the Fourth day of January 1786   An Indenture of Bargain & Sale between
WILLIAM WRIGHT of one part & ROBERT KIRKHAM of the other part was acknowledged
by the above written WILLIAM WRIGHT and is ordered to be recorded
                Teste J. GRAMMER, Clk. C. Hs.

(Page 166 is blank.)

p.   THIS INDENTURE made this fourth day of January in year of our Lord one thou-
167   sand seven hundred and Eighty six Between SIMON FRASER of County of PRINCE
      GEORGE on the one part and WILLIAM STEGAR of County of DINWIDDIE on the
other part; Witnesseth that SIMON FRASER for sum of One hundred pounds curt. money
of Virginia in hand paid by WILLIAM STEGAR, hath bargained and sold unto WILLIAM
STEGAR his heirs one lott on the Hill in the New Town of BLANDFORD known in the plan
of said Town by the number Thirty; To have and to hold lott No. 30 and premises with all
appurtenances to WILLIAM STEGAR his heirs, And SIMON FRASER for himself his heirs
the said land against every person to WILLIAM STEGAR his heirs shall warrant and for
ever defend by these present; In Witness whereof the said SIMON FRASER hath hereunto set his hand and seal the day and year first above written
Sealed Signed and Delivered in the presence of
    (no witnesses recorded)   SIMON FRASER
At a Court of Hustings held for the Town of Petersburg at the House of WILLIAM
DURELL on Wednesday the Fourth day of January 1786   An Indenture of Bargain and
Sale between SIMON FRASER of one part and WILLIAM STEGAR of the other part was
acknowledged by the above named SIMON FRASER and is ordered to be recorded
                Teste J. GRAMMER, Clk. C. Hs.

pp.   THIS INDENTURE made this Twenty ninth day of December Anno Domini one
168- thousand seven hundred and Eighty five Between ROBERT KIRKHAM of Town of
169   Petersburg of one part & WILLIAM WRIGHT of said Town of other part; Witnes-
      seth that ROBERT KIRKHAM at the time of sealing & delivering of the presents is
& stands justly indebted to WILLIAM WRIGHT in the sum of One hundred & fifty pounds
current money of Virginia as a consideration for a certain tract of land purchased by
ROBERT KIRKHAM of WILLIAM WRIGHT at the special instance and requst of said
ROBERT KIRKHAM; Now This Indenture Witnesseth that ROBERT KIRKHAM as well for
securing the said sum of One hundred & fifty pounds to WILLIAM WRIGHT as also for
the sum of Five shillings current money of Virignia to him in hand paid by WILLIAM
WRIGHT by these presents hath granted sold and confirm'd unto WILLIAM WRIGHT his
heirs one certain lot of land containing Three acres lying in Town of Petersburg in
that part thereof known by the name of RAVENSCROFT TOWN in the plot of said Town
(No. 16) number Sixteen, Together with all profits comodities and appurtenances; To
have and tohold the lot unto WILLIAM WRIGHT his heirs IN TRUST that the premises
with the appurtenances shall by WILLIAM WRIGHT or his heirs at any time after the
Seventh day of April next ensuing the date hereof be sold to the best advantage for
ready money or so much of the bargained premises at that time as shall prove suffi-

cient to pay one third of the said sum of One hundred & Fifty pounds & the money arising by such Sale to be applied toward the discharge of one third of the aforesaid sum; And if ROBERT KIRKHAM shall fail to pay one other third before the seventh day of January Anno Domini one thousand seven hundred and Eighty seven & the other remaining third before the seventh day of January one thousand seven hundred and eighty eight, the said WRIGHT shall have lawful authority to seel the whole or any part thereof to the best advantage for ready money and the surplus to be paid to said ROBERT KIRKHAM his heirs; In Witness whereof ROBERT KIRKHAM hath hereunto set his hand and seal the day & year above written

Test J. MARSH,   ROBERT KIRKHAM
       WM. BARKSDALE, ABM. EVANS

At a Court of Hustings held for the Town of Petersburg at the House of WILLIAM DURELL Wednesday the fourth day of January 1786   An Indenture of Mortgage from ROBERT KIRKHAM of the one part to WILLIAM WRIGHT of the other part ws acknowledged by the above subscribed ROBERT KIRKHAM as his act & deed and is ordered to be recorded   Teste J. GRAMMER, Clk. C. Hs.

p.   THIS INDENTURE made this Fourth day of January in year of our Lord one thou-
170   sand seven hundred & Eighty six Between WILLIAM HARRISON of Town of
        Petersburg in County of DINWIDDIE, Clerk, and LUCY his Wife of one part and
GRESSETT DAVIS of the same place, Merchant, of other part; Witnesseth that for sum of Eight pounds six shilling and eight pence by said GRESSETT DAVIS in hand paid to WILLIAM HARRISON, by these presents do bargain sell & confirm unto GRESSETT DAVIS and to his heirs all their right title & interest that they have or may possibly have in one certain lott of land lying in that part of the Corporation of Petersburg called by the name of RAVENSCROFT TOWN and distinguished by the number (42), Forty two, it being the same lott of land that was purchased by WILLIAM HARRISON of DAVID WILLIAMS as by Deed bearing date the 20 day of November in year of our Lord one thousand seven hundred & Seventy five yet remaining of Record in the Court of the aforesaid Town in said County of DINWIDDIE; To have and to hold the lott of land with the appurtenances thereunto belonging unto GRESSETT DAVIS his heirs; And WILLIAM HARRISON & his heirs the lott of land unto GRESSETT DAVIS & his heirs against all persons will warrant & forever defend by these presents; In Witness whereof said WILLIAM HARRISON & LUCY his Wife have hereunto set their hands & affixed their seals the day & year first above written

Sealed & Delivered in the presence of us
       (no witnesses recorded)
                                                            W. HARRISON
                                                            LUCY HARRISON

At a Court of Hustings continued and held for the Town of Petersburg at the House of WILLIAM DURELL Thursday the Fifth day of January 1786   An Indenture of Bargain and Sale between WILLIAM HARRISON & LUCY his Wife of the one part and GRESSETT DAVIS of the other part was acknowledged by the said WILLIAM HARRISON and is ordered to be recorded   Teste J. GRAMMER, Clk. C. Hs.

p.   THIS INDENTURE made this Fifth day of January in the year of our Lord one
171   thousand seven hundred & Eighty six between GRESSETT DAVIS & MARTHA his
        Wife of Petersburg & ROBERT TUCKER of SUSSEX County, Witnesseth that for the
sum of One hundred pounds in hand paid by said ROBERT TUCKER, GRESSETT DAVIS & MARTHA his Wife have bargained sold & confirmed unto ROBERT TUCKER his heirs one certain lot of land laying in that part of the Corporation of Petersburg called RAVENS-

CROFT TOWN being part of Lot (No. 39), Thirty Nine, & bounded Begining in the middle of the Street as laid down in the plott of said Town on North side of Lott (No. 39) thence South sixteen degrees East along the middle of the said Street ten poles & one foot from thence West sixteen degrees South sixteen poles, from thence North sixteen degrees West ten poles & one foot & from thence East sixteen degrees North sixteen poles to the beginning; excepting always reserving twenty foot on the East end of said Lott for a Publick Street; To have and to hold the lott of land unto ROBERT TUCKER his heirs; And GRESSETT DAVIS & MARTHA his Wife their heirs will warrant & for ever defend the title of said parcel of land to ROBERT TUCKER his heirs against the claim of every person; In Witness whereof the said GRESSETT DAVIS and MARTHA his Wife have hereunto set their hands and affixed their seals the day & year above written

GRESSETT DAVIS

MARTHA DAVIS

Petersburg, 5th January 1786

This day received of ROBERT TUCKER one hundred pounds the full consideration for the within mentioned lot of land & have given full & peaceible possession thereof unto him said ROBERT TUCKER   GRESSETT TUCKER

At a Court of Hustings held and continued for the Town of Petersburg at the House of WILLIAM DURELL Thursday the Fifth day of January 1786   An Indenture of Bargain and Sale between GRESSETT DAVIS & MARTHA his Wife of the Town of Petersburg of one part and ROBERT TUCKER of SUSSEX County of other part with a receipt thereon indorsed were acknowledged by the above subscribed GRESSETT DAVIS and ordered to be recorded   Teste J. GRAMMER Clk. C. Hs.

(Page 172 is blank.)

p.   At a Court of Hustings held for the Town of Petersburg Wednesday the first day
173   of February 1786
        Present CHRISTOPHER McCONNICO, Esqr., Mayor
              JOHN SHORE Esqr., Recorder
              ROBERT BOLLING, ISAAC HALL, Gentlemen Aldermen

pp.   THIS INDENTURE made this Twenty sixth day of December in the year of our
173-   Lord one thousand seven hundred and Eighty five Between CHARLES DUNCAN of
174   one part and REVD. JOHN CAMERON of PRINCE GEORGE County of other part; Wit-
        nesseth that for the sum of One hundred pounds by JOHN CAMERON unto
CHARLES DUNCAN in hand paid, by these presents doth bargain sell and confirm unto JOHN CAMERON his heirs all those two lotts or parcells of land lying on BLANDFORD HILL known in the plan of the Town lately laid out on the said Hill by the numbers Eighty One and Eighty Two (No. 81 & 82), as by a plan of said Town of record in the Court of Hustings of Petersburg will appear; To have and to hold the said lotts of land and all the advantages appertaining thereto unto JOHN CAMERON his heirs, And CHARLES DUN-CAN doth for himself and his heirs covenant with JOHN CAMERON his heirs that he will for ever warrant and defend the title of said lotts unto JOHN CAMERON his heirs against the lawful claim of all persons; In Witness whereof the said CHARLES DUNCAN hath hereunto set his hand and seal

CHARLES DUNCAN

Memorandum. That lotts of land within mentioned are mark'd in the recorded plan of that part of the Town of Petersburg call'd NEW BLANDFORD with the numbers Eighty one & Eighty two (No. 81 & 82), and noted therein as the property of THOMAS GORDON & THOS: G. PEACHY, when in fact the said lotts were never conveyed to us the said THOMAS

GORDON & THOS: G. PEACHY by the within granted or any other person; Now we the said THOMAS GORDON & THOS: G. PEACHY to prevent all disputes respecting the same and in consideration of the sum of Five shillings current money to us paid doe hereby for our-selves and our heirs release and for ever quit claim unto JOHN CAMERON his heirs for ever all our right title interest and demand whatsoever in the said lotts and all their appurtenances; In Witness whereof we have hereunto set our hands & seals this Twenty sixth day of December in the year 1785
Signed and Sealed in presence of
    JOHN FISHER, PATRICK WALKER,   T. G. PEACHY
    HENRY WINFEILD,   JOHN ANGUS,   THOMAS GORDON
    THOS: WITHERS
  At a Court of Hustings held for the Town of Petersburg at the House of WILLIAM DURELL Wednesday the first day of February 1786   An Indenture of Bargain and sale between CHARLES DUNCAN of one part and the REVD. JOHN CAMERON of the other part was acknowledged by the said CHARLES DUNCAN and the memorandum of Relinquish-ment by THOS: G. PEACHY and THOMAS GORDON thereon indorsed was proved by the Oaths of JOHN FISHER, HENRY WINFEILD and THOMAS WITHERS witnesses thereto and together with the said Indenture are ordered to be recorded
              Teste J. GRAMMER, Clk. C. Hs.

pp.   THIS INDENTURE made the Twenty fourth day of January in year of our Lord
175-   one thousand seven hundred and Eighty six Between MATTHEW & WILLIAM
178   FERNANDO of County of PRINCE GEORGE of one part and ROBERT LOYD of Peters-
        burg of other part; Witnesseth that MATTHEW and WILLIAM FERNANDO for the sum of Sixty pounds current money of Virginia to them in hand paid by ROBERT LOYD, And also in consideration of the Rents Covenants and agreements hereafter mentioned to be paid kept and performed by said ROBERT LOYD his heirs, said MATTHEW and WIL-LIAM FERNANDO by these presents doth bargain sell and confirm unto ROBERT LOYD his heirs one part of Lott No. (56) number Fifty Six begining at the Forty six feet from the So. West corner of said lott and runing twenty feet Easterly on WATER STREET, thence back thirty feet Northerly, thence Westerly twenty feet, and then to the said Street the begining, and all appurtenances to said lott of land belonging; To have and to hold the land hereby granted with the appurtenances unto ROBERT LOYD his heirs paying therefor yearly unto MATTHEW and WILLIAM FERNANDO their heirs on the first day of January the fee rent of Two pounds eight shillings current money which said sum shall be paid on the first day of January in every year, the first rent to grow due and payable on the first day of January one thousand seven hundred and Eighty seven; And ROBERT LOYD doth covenant that he will truly pay the Fee Rent according to the intent of these presents, And if the Fee Rent shall be in arrear and unpaid it may be lawfull for said MATTHEW & WILLIAM FERNANDO their heirs into the said lott to re-enter and have as if this Indenture had never been made; In Witness whereof the parties aforesaid have hereunto set their hands and affixed their seals the day & year first above written
Sealed and Delivered in the presence of
    NOEL WADDILL,   MATTHEW FERNANDO
    WM. DURELL,   GEORGE DUDGEON   WILLIAM FERNANDO
At a Court of Hustings held for the Town of Petersburg at the House of WILLIAM DURELL Wednesday the first day of February 1786   An Indenture of Bargain and Sale between MATTHEW FERNANDO and WILLIAM FERNANDO of one part and ROBERT LOYD of the other part, and the memorandum of Livery and Seizen thereunto annexed were ack-nowledged by the said MATTHEW & WILLIAM FERNANDO and are ordered to be recorded
              Teste J. GRAMMER, Clk. C. Hs.

p.   At a Court of Hustings held for the Town of Petersburg Wednesday the first day
178   of February 1786   MARTHA DAVIS personally appeared in open Court and
          after being privily and apart from her Husband, GRESSETT DAVIS, examined, did
freely and voluntarily relinquish all her right of Dower of in & to a lott of land and
premises conveyed by the said GROSSETT DAVIS & MARTHA his Wife to JOSEPH HARDING
as by their Indenture bearing date the fifth day of August one thousand seven hundred and Eighty five duly acknowledged and record in the Court in October last
                              Teste J. GRAMMER, Clk. C. Hs.

p.   At a Court of Hustings held for the Town of Petersburg at the House of WILLIAM
178   DURELL Wednesday the first day of February 1786   MARY HARDING personally
          appeared in open Court and after being privily and apart from her Husband,
JOSEPH HARDING, examined, did freely and voluntarily relinquish all her right of
Dower of in & to a parcel of land & premises containing Four and a half acres more or
less & premises conveyed by the said JOSEPH HARDING and MARY his Wife to DAVID
BUCHANAN as by their Deed bearing date the third day of October one thousand seven
hundred & Eighty five indented & duly acknowledged & recorded in this Court in
October last   Teste J. GRAMMER, Clk. C. Hs.
(Page 179 is blank. Page 180 has a platt drawn. Page 181 has an explanation of the platt.)

p.   A Plan of 149 1/2 acres of land lying in that part of the Corporation of Peters-
181   burg formerly called RAVENSCROFT TOWN surveyed for some years past for 140
          acres and laid off into 46 lotts; since which most or all of the Stones or other
marks then sat up to ascertain the said lotts were missing or not to be found and
disputes were likely to happen among the Proprietors of the said Lotts, with respect to
the bounds thereof, they the said Proprietors entered into a written agreement and
therein appointed DUNCAN ROSE and JOHN IMRAY Commissioners, together with
WILLIAM WATKINS to resurvey the same and act with them as a Commission for
deciding all or any disputes that might happen concerning the bounds of the said lotts;
In Consequence of which Agreement, we the said Commissioners and Surveyor have
resurveyed the said land and laid off the same into 46 lotts as nearly agreable to the old
plan as might be and have caused Stones to be set up at the corner of each lott of which
this is a true plan. Certified under our hands this Sixth day of September 1785
                              DUN: ROSE   )
                              WM. WATKINS) Commrs.
Note: the Streets are run parrallel to MR. BOLLINGs line and the cross lines are run at
right angles. All the Lotts except whereon the Road and on the back line are 30 poles
by 16 out of which is deducted an equal allowance of 25 feet for the width of the Streets,
the small slip of land marked G. D., in the plan is assigned to GRESSETT DAVIS to make
good his loss by his lines not measuring so long as mentioned in the old Plan
                              WM. WATKINS, Survr.
                              DUN: ROSE
At a Hustings Court held for the Town of Petersburg the Second day of May 1787
JOHN IMRAY personally appeared in open Court and subscribed his name to a plan of
Forty six lotts of land heretofore recorded in this Court in Feby. 1786. called & distin-
guished as RAVENSCROFT TOWN for that purpose and afterwards made oath thereto
which is ordered to be Certified   Attest J. GRAMMER, Clk. C. Hs.
Teste JOHN COOK, JOSEPH COLEMAN, HUMFRIES TRAYLOR
At a Hustings Court held for the Town of Petersburg Wednesday the first day of Febru-
ary 1786,   A Plan of One hundred & forty nine & half acres of land laid out into forty

six lotts and formerly called RAVENSCROFT TOWN certified under the hands of DUNCAN ROSE and WILLIAM WATKINS, two of the Commissioners chosen for the laying off & fixing the boundaries of the same, together with a Note under the hand of the said WILLIAM WATKINS as Surveyor of the same & DUNCAN ROSE aforesd., were sworn to by the said WILLIAM WATKINS and having been before proved as to the other Commissioner by the Oath of HUMFRIES TRAYLOR a witness thereto, together with the said plan are ordered to be recorded   Atteste J. GRAMMER, Clk. C. Hs.
(Page 182 is blank.)

p.   TO ALL WHOM THESE PRESENTS SHALL COME or may concern, be it known that
183   we SAMUEL HOUGH, MAHLAN HOUGH and WILLIAM STABLER having agreable
to the Last Will and Testament of EDWARD STABLER deceased, qualified and taken upon ourselves the execution thereof according to Law, by authority thereof, we the said Executors for and in behalf of the said Estate by these presents do make and appoint WILLIAM MASSENBURG of SUSSEX County our true and lawful Attorney for us and in our names and to the use of the said Estate whereof we are Executors, to ask demand and receive of all persons all sums balances and amounts of money tobacco or other commodities either in this State of Virginia or in any of the United States of America and to enable this our said Attorney to proceed on the collections of Debts due the said Estate we have put into his possession the books bonds and balances due thereto, and upon non payment the said WILLIAM MASSENBURG is hereby authorised and empowered for us and in our names to sue implead and prosecute for the same; ratifying and holding firm and good all and whatsoever our said Attorney shall lawfully do or cause to be done in or about the premises by virtue of these presents; In Witness whereof we have hereunto set our hands and seals this (blank) day of October in the year of our Lord one thousand seven hundred and Eighty five and Tenth year of the Commonwealth
          DANIEL DOBSON,   SAMUEL HOUGH
          ROBT. MASSENBURG   MAHLAN HOUGH
                                                      WM. STABLER
    At a Court of Hustings held for the Town of Petersburg at the House of WILLIAM DURELL Wednesday the first day of February 1786   A Power of Attorney from SAMUEL HOUGH, MAHLAN HOUGH & WILLIAM STABLER, Executors of the Last Will and Testament of EDWARD STABLER deced., to WILLIAM MASSENBURG was proved by the Oaths of DANIEL DODSON & ROBERT MASSENBURG witnesses thereto and ordered to be recorded   Teste J. GRAMMER, Clk. C. Hs.
(Pages 184, 185 and 186 are blank.)

p   THIS INDENTURE made this first day of June one thousand seven hundred and
187   Eighty six Between JOSEPH HARDING and MARY his Wife of Town of Petersburg
          & State of Virginia of one part and DAVID VAUGHAN of County of DINWIDDIE of other part; Witnesseth that for the sum of One hundred and Seventy five pounds lawfull money of Virginia in hand paid, said JOSEPH HARDING hath bargained sold & confirmed unto DAVID VAUGHAN a certain parcell of land containing Three acres be the same more or less being one lott laid off by ROBERT RAVENSCROFT & distinguished in the plan of RAVENSCROFT TOWN by number Thirty three (33), together with all ways &c., thereto belonging; To have and to hold the said lot or parcel of land with the appurtenances unto DAVID VAUGHAN his heirs and JOSEPH HARDING shall warrant & defend against the claim of all persons; In Witness whereof the said JOSEPH HARDING & MARY his Wife bath hereunto set their hands & affixed their seals the day & year first above written

Signed Sealed & Delivered in presents of
(no witnesses recorded)

JOS: HARDING
MARY HARDING

At a Court of Hustings held for the Town of Petersburg at the House of WILLIAM DURELL Wednesday the seventh day of June 1786   An Indenture of Bargain and Sale between JOSEPH HARDING and MARY his Wife of one part and DAVID VAUGHAN of the other part was acknowledged by the said JOSEPH HARDING and ordered to be recorded
Teste J. GRAMMER, Clk. C. Hs.

p.   The Commonwealth of Virginia to CHRISTOPHER McCONNICO & ISAAC HALL
188   Gentlemen Greeting; Whereas WILLIAM ROBERTSON of County of PRINCE GEORGE by his certain Indenture of Bargain and Sale bearing date the fourth day of January one thousand seven hundred and Eighty six have sold and conveyed to JOHN SHORE JR. one certain lot of land in Town of Petersburg in the New Town of BLANDFORD number Forty six (No. 46), And Whereas ELIZABETH ROBERTSON, Wife of the said WILLIAM ROBERTSON cannot conveniently attend our Court of Hustings (the Commission for the privy Examination of ELIZABETH, the Wife of WILLIAM ROBERTSON); Witness JOHN GRAMMER Clerk of our said Court the Tenth day of April 1786 in the Tenth year of the Commonwealth   J. GRAMMER
By Virtue of the within Commission, the Indenture hereunto annexed was acknowledged by the thereto subscribed ELIZABETH ROBERTSON on the Eleventh day of May 1786, she the said ELIZABETH being first privily and apart from the said WILLIAM her Husband, examined, (the return of the execution of the privy Examination of ELIZABETH ROBERTSON); before us   CHR: McCONNICO
                                      ISAAC HALL
At a Court of Hustings held for the Town of Petersburg at the House of WILLIAM DURELL Wednesday the Seventh day of June 1786   A Commission annexed to an Indenture of Bargain & Sale between WILLIAM ROBERTSON of one part and JOHN SHORE JR. of the other part together with the Certificate of the execution thereof was return'd and ordered to be recorded   Teste J. GRAMMER, Clk. C. Hs.

pp   THIS INDENTURE made the Sixth day of June in year of our Lord one thousand
189-   seven hundred and Eighty six Between MARY BOLLING of the Town of Peters-
191   burg and County of DINWIDDIE, and ROBERT BOLLING of the same Town & County Esquire of one part and JOHN ANDREWS LAUSSAT of the Town of Petersburg of the other part: Whereas ROBERT BOLLING Esquire, late of the said Town of Petersburg deceased, by his Last Will and Testament in writing bearing date the Thirtieth day of January in the year one thousand and seventy five and now remaining of Record in the Court of County of DINWIDDIE as by the said Will will appear, did devise unto MARY BOLLING among other things the use of certain lands in the Town of Petersburg during her natural life with remainder to said ROBERT BOLLING in Fee, and said ROBERT BOLLING with the privity and assent of said MARY BOLLING, signified by her being party to this Indenture, and sealing and delivering the same, hath agreed to Farm unto JOHN ANDREWS LAUSSAT a certain lot of land for the considerations and upon the covenants and agreements herein after mentioned. NOW THIS INDENTURE WITNESSETH that MARY BOLLING and ROBERT BOLLING for the sum of Two hundred pounds current money of Virginia to them or some one of them in hand paid by JOHN ANDREWS LAUSSAT and also in consideration of the rents covenants and agrements herein after mentioned to be paid and performed by JOHN ANDREWS LAUSSAT, said MARY BOLLING and ROBERT BOLLING by these presents do demise and to Farm Let unto JOHN ANDREWS LAUSSAT his

heirs one certain lot of land part of the lands above mentioned lying in that part of the Town of Petersburg called BLANDFORD contiguous to the TOBACCO WAREHOUSE called OLD BLANDFORD and opposite to the Tavern now occupied by THOMAS ARMISTEAD, and containing One hundred square feet, which said lot is bounded, Begining at a wooden peg on BLANDFORD STREET ninety six feet from the HIGH TOP WAREHOUSE, thence along the said Street South 58 1/2d. West one hundred feet, thence South 25 1/2d. East one hundred feet towards the Swamp, thence North 58 1/2d. East one hundred feet parralel with the Street, thence North 25 1/2d. West one hundred feet to the begining on the Street. And all appurtenances thereunto belonging; To have and to hold the said lot unto JOHN ANDREWS LAUSSAT his heirs during the term of ninety nine years paying therefor unto ROBERT BOLLING his heirs on the first day of January every year Fee or Ground Rent of twenty eight pounds current money of Virginia, the first years Rent to become due and payable on the first day of January one thousand seven hundred and Eight five, and if the said money shall be in arrear and unpaid it may be lawfull for ROBERT BOLLING his heirs into the said lott to re-enter and have as if this Indenture had never been made; In Witness whereof the parties aforesaid have hereunto set their hands and affixed their seals the day and year first above written
Sealed and Delivered in presence of

THOMAS ARMISTEAD,	MARY BOLLING
WILLIS MACLIN	ROBERT BOLLING
JOHN WEEKS	JOHN AND: LAUSSAT

At a Court of Hustings held for the Town of Petersburg at the house of WM. DURELL in the said Town Wednesday the Seventh day of June 1786   An Indenture between MARY BOLLING and ROBERT BOLLING of the one part and JOHN ANDREWS LAUSSATT of the other part was acknowled: by the said ROBERT BOLLING and being proved on the part of MARY BOLLING and JOHN ANDREWS LAUSSATT by the Oaths of THOMAS ARMISTEAD. WILLIS MACLIN and JOHN WEEKS, witnesses thereto is ordered to be recorded
Teste J. GRAMMER, Clk. C. Hs.

p.   At a Court of Hustings held for the Town of Petersburg at the house of WILLIAM
192   DURELL Wednesday the Seventh day of June 1786
    MOLLY FAWCETT personally appeared in open Court and after being privily and apart from her Husband, JAMES FAWCETT, examined, did freely and voluntarily relinquish make over and confirm all her right of Dower and Title of Dower of in & to a certin parcel or lot of land & premises conveyed by said JAMES FAWCETT her Husband to JAMES GEDDY as by Deed bearing date the Thirtieth day of November in year of our Lord one thousand seven hundred & Eighty four duly acknowledged & recorded in this Court and declared that it was with her approbation and desire the same had been so done
Teste J. GRAMMER, Clk. C. Hs.

p.   THIS INDENTURE made this twelfth day of April in year of our Lord one thou-
193   sand seven hundred and Eighty six Between PHILIP W. JACKSON of County of
    AMELIA of one part and JOHN ANGUS of DINWIDDIE County and Town of Petersburg, Merchant, of other part; Witnesseth that PHILIP W. JACKSON for the full sum of Forty pounds currt. money to him in hand paid by JOHN ANGUS, by these presents do bargain sell & confirm unto JOHN ANGUS his heirs all that lot of ground lying in the New Town of BLANDFORD being the lot numbered (48) Forty Eight; To have and to hold the said lot with all Improvements and appertenances theretunto belonging to said JOHN ANGUS his heirs; And PHILIP W. JACKSON his heirs the said lot of ground unto JOHN ANGUS his heirs shall warrant and forever defend against any person having or

lawfully claiming any right or title in or to the same; In Witness whereof the said
PHILIP W. JACKSON have hereunto set his hand and seal the day and year above written
Signed Sealed and Delivered in the presence of
      SIMON FRASER, ROBERT DONOLD,   PHILIP W. JACKSON
      WILLIAM SHARP, HENRY MORRISS
At a Court of Hustings held for the Town of Petersburg at the House of WILLIAM
DURELL Wednesday the Seventh day of June 1786   An Indenture of Bargain and Sale
between PHILIP W. JACKSON of AMELIA County of one part and JOHN ANGUS of the Town
of Petersburg of the other part was proved by the Oaths of SIMON FRASER, ROBERT
DONOLD and WILLIAM SHARP witnesses thereto and ordered to be recorded
                Teste J. GRAMMER, Clk. C. Hs.

p.   THIS INDENTURE made this Seventh day of September in year of our Lord one
194   thousand seven hundred & Eighty five Between JOHN ANGUS of DINWIDDIE
       County & Town of Petersburg, Merchant, of one part and SAMUEL DEMOVEL of
PRINCE GEORGE County of the other part; Witnesseth that JOHN ANGUS for the full sum
of Eighty pounds to him in hand paid by SAMUEL DEMOVEL by these presents do bargain sell and confirm unto SAMUEL DEMOVEL his heirs all that lot of land lying in the
New Town of BLANDFORD being the lot number Thirty Seven; To have and to hld the said
lot of ground with all Improvements & appertenances thereunto belonging unto said
SAMUEL DEMOVEL his heirs; And said JOHN ANGUS his heirs the said lot of ground unto
SAMUEL DEMOVEL his heirs shall warrant & forever defend against any person having
or lawfully claiming any right or title in or to the same; In Witness whereof he (the
said JOHN ANGUS) have hereunto set his hand and seal the day & year above written
Signed Sealed & Delivered in presence of
      MacCALL WILLSON,   JOHN ANGUS
      THO: PAGAN, H. HARALSON
At a Court of Hustings held for the Town of Petersburg at the House of WILLIAM
DURELL Wednesday the Seventh day of June 1786   An Indenture of Bargain and Sale
between JOHN ANGUS of one part and SAMUEL DEMOVEL of the other part was acknowledged by the said JOHN ANGUS and ordered to be recorded
              Teste J. GRAMMER, Clk, C. Hs.

p.   THIS INDENTURE made this Eighth day of September in year of our Lord one
195   thousand seven hundred and Eighty five Between JOHN McCLOUD of the Borough
       of Petersburg of one part and WILLIAM PARSONS JR. of the other part; Witnes-
seth that JOHN McCLOUD for sum of One hundred pounds to him in hand paid by WIL-
LIAM PARSONS by these presents doth bargain sell and confirm unto WILLIAM PAR-
SONS his heirs a lot of ground number Fifty Four lying within the Borough of Petersburg and in that part of the Town known by the name of NEW BLANDFORD; To have and
to hold the lot of ground and all the advantages appertaining thereto unto WILLIAM
PARSONS his heirs; And JOHN McCLOUD for himself and his heirs doth covenant with
WILLIAM PARSONS his heirs that he will forever warrant and defend the title to said lot
of ground unto WILLIAM PARSONS his heirs against all persons whatsoever, In Witness
whereof the said JOHN McCLOUD hath hereunto set his hand and affixed his seal the day
and year as above written
Sealed and delivered in presence of
      ROBERT FITZGERALD,   JOHN McCLOUD
      PHILIP COLEMAN, SAML. DONOLDSON

At a Court of Hustings held for the Town of Petersburg at the House of WILLIAM DURELL in the said Town Wednesday the Seventh day of June 1786
An Indenture of Bargain and Sale between JOHN McCLOUD of the one part and WILLIAM PARSONS JR. of the other part was acknowledged by the said JOHN McCLOUD and ordered to be recorded   Teste J. GRAMMER, Clk. C. Hs.

p. 196   THIS INDENTURE made this Twentieth day of January one thousand seven hundred and Eighty six Between THOMAS RICHARDS of the Borough of Petersburg and County of CHESTERFIELD of one part and SILAS SANDFORD of the Borough aforesaid and County of DINWIDDIE of other part; Witnesseth that THOMAS RICHARDS and MARTHA his Wife hath for the sum of Forty pounds to them in hand paid by these presents do bargain sell and for ever make over unto SILAS SANDFORD his heirs one lot number Eight in POCOHONTAS and another Lot on the River number Eight also, the River lot being forty by sixty together with all priviledges profits commodities and appurtenances whatsoever; To have and to hold the above granted premises and every part thereof with the appurtenances thereunto belonging to SILAS SANDFORD his heirs In Witness whereof we have hereunto set our hands and seals this Twentieth day of January one thousand seven hundred and Eighty six.
Signed Sealed and Delivered in the presence of
Test JOHN SUMERSALL,   THOS: RICHARDS
    WILLIAM COSBY   The mark /M\ of
    BRIAN TURNER   MARTHA RICHARDS
At a Court of Hustings held for the Town of Petersburg at the House of WILLIAM DURELL Wednesday the Seventh day of June 1786   An Indenture of Bargain and Sale between THOMAS RICHARDS and MARTHA his Wife of one part and SILAS SANDFORD of the other part was acknowledged by the said THOMAS RICHARDS and the same having been acknolwedged by the said MARTHA RICHARDS (she the said MARTHA being first privily and apart from the said THOMAS, her Husband, examined as the Law directs), and is ordered to be recorded   Teste J. GRAMMER, Clk. C. Hs.

p. 197   THIS INDENTURE made this Twentieth day of January one thousand seven hundred and Eighty six Between THOMAS RICHARDS and MARTHA his Wife of the Borough of Petersburg and County of CHESTERFEILD of one part and SILAS SANDFORD of the Borough aforesaid and County of DINWIDDIW of other part; Witnesseth that THOMAS RICHARDS and MARTHA his Wife by these presents do acknowledge to have bargained and sold unto SILAS SANDFORD into full and free possession of the lots as fully mentioned by a Deed bearing date the Twentieth day of January one thousand seven hundred and Eighty six and we do hereby bind ourselves our heirs to warrant support maintain and defend the said premised lotts unto SILAS SANDFORD his heirs against the claim of any person; In Witness whereof we have hereunto set our hands this Twentieth day of January one thousand seven hundred and Eighty six
Test JOHN SUMERSALL,   THOS: RICHARDS
    WILLIAM COSBY   The mark /M\ of
    BRIAN TURNER   MARTHA RICHARDS
At a Court of Hustings held for the Town of Petersburg at the House of WILLIAM DURELL Wednesday the seventh day of June 1786   An Indenture of Bargain and Sale between THOMAS RICHARDS and MARTHA his Wife of one part and SILAS SANDFORD of the other part was acknowledged by THOMAS RICHARDS and having been before acknowledged by the said MARTHA RICHARDS (she the said MARTHA being first privily and apart from the said THOMAS her Husband examined as the Law directs) is ordered to be recorded   Teste J. GRAMMER, Clk. C. Hs.

p.   THIS INDENTURE made this first day of May in year of our Lord one thousand
198   seven hundred and Eighty six Between CHARLES DUNCAN of the one part and
        the Revd. JOHN CAMERON of County of PRINCE GEORGE of other part; Witnesseth
that for the quantity of Two thousand pounds of Inspected Tobacco by JOHN CAMERON
unto CHARLES DUNCAN in hand paid, said CHARLES DUNCAN by these presents doth
bargain sell & confirm unto JOHN CAMERON his heirs all that lot of land lying on
BLANDFORD HILL known in the plan of the Town lately laid out on the said Hill by the
nubmer Eighty Three (No. 83), as by the plan of the Town on Record in the Court of
Hustings of Petersburg will appear; To have and to hold lthe lot of land and all the advantages appertaining thereto unto JOHN CAMERON his heirs; And CHARLES DUNCAN
doth for himself and his heis covenain with JOHN CAMERON his heirs that he will for
ever Warrant and defend the title of said lot of land unto JOHN CAMERON his heirs
against the lawfull claim of every person; In Witness whereof the said CHARLES DUN-
CAN hath hereunto set his hand and seal
Signed Sealed & delivd. in presence of
         WILLIAM COLE, PATRICK WALKER,   CHARLES DUNCAN
         WM. CAMERON, THOMAS WITHERS
Memorandum. The lot of Land within mentioend is marked in the recorded plan of
that part of the Town of Petersburg called NEW BLANDFORD with the number Eighty
three (83), and noted therein as the property of ROBERT GILLIAM when in fact the said
lott was never conveyed to me, the said ROBERT GILLIAM, by the within granter or any
other person. Now I the said ROBERT GILLIAM to prevent all disputes respecting the
same & in consideration of the sum of Five Shillings current money to me paid do hereby for myself and my heirs release and for ever quit claim unto the within named JOHN
CAMERON his heris all my right title Interest and demand whatsoever in the said lot and
all its appertenances; In Witness whereof I have hereunto set my hand and seal this
first day of May in the year of our Lord God one thousand seven hundred and eighty six
Signed and Sealed in the presence of
         WM. CAMERON,   ROBERT GILLIAM
         EWEN CAMERON, ROBERT YOUNG
  At a Court of Hustings held for the Town of Petersburg at the House of WM. DURELL
Wednesday the Seventh day of June 1786   An Indenture of Bargain and Sale between
CHARLES DUNCAN of one part and the Revd. JOHN CAMERON of the other part was proved
by the Oaths of PATRICK WALKER, WILLIAM CAMERON and THOMAS WITHERS, witnesses
thereto, And the memorandum of Relinquishment &c. from ROBERT GILLIAM which is
thereon indorsed was proved by the Oaths of WM. CAMERON, EWIN CAMERON and
ROBERT YOUNG, witnesses thereto, and together with the said Indenture are ordered to
be recorded   Teste J. GRAMMER, Clk. C. Hs.

p.   THIS INDENTURE made this 22d. day of March in year of our Lord one thousand
199   seven hundred and Eighty six Between CHARLES DUNCAN of County of CHESTER-
        FEILD of one part and JOSEPH SELDEN, Brother of JOHN SELDEN deced,, of other
part; Witnesseth that CHARLES DUNCAN for sum of Two thousand pounds weight of Crop
Tobacco paid by JOSEPH SELDEN by these presents doth bargain sell and confirm unto
JOSEPH SELDEN his heirs a lot of ground number (96), Ninety Six, lying within the
Borough of Petersburg in that part of the Town known by the name of NEW BLANDFORD
To have and to hold the lot of ground and all the advantages appertaining thereto unto
JOSEPH SELDEN his heirs, And CHARLES DUNCAN for himself and his heirs doth cove-
nant with JOSEPH SELDEN his heirs that he will forever warrant and defend the title to
the said lot of ground unto JOSEPH SELDEN his heirs against all persons; In Witness

whereof the said CHARLES DUNCAN hath hereunto set his hand and affixed his seal the day and year as above written
Sealed and Delivered in presence of
     PATRICK WALKER,   CHARLES DUNCAN
     THOS: WITHERS, JOHN FISHER
  At a Court of Hustings held for the Town of Petersburg at the House of WM. DURELL in the said town Wednesday the Seventh day of June 1786   An Indenture of Bargain and Sale between CHARLES DUNCAN of one part and JOSEPH SELDEN of other part was proved by the Oaths of PATRICK WALKER, THOMAS WITHERS and JOHN FISHER witnesses thereto and is ordered to be recorded   Teste J. GRAMMER, Clk. C. Hs.

p.   THIS INDENTURE made this Twenty ninth day of April one thousand seven hun-
200   dred and Eighty six Between WILLIAM HART of the Town of Petersburg of one
       part and THOMAS HOPE of the same Town of other part; Whereas said THOMAS HOPE hath become a party with the said WILLIAM HART for securing the payment of One hundred and fifty pounds curry. money to CHRISTOPHER McCONNICO, and Whereas said WILLIAM HART being willing and desirous to secure the said THOMAS HOPE against the payment of said One hundred and fifty pounds at such time as is specified for that purpose & expressed in four several Bonds given by them the said WILLIAM HART & THOMAS HOPE to CHRISTOPHER McCONNICO for them, all of them bearing date the four-teenth day of December last past; NOW THIS INDENTURE WITNESSETH that WILLIAM HART in consideration thereof as also for the furtehr consideration of Five shillings curry. money to him in hand paid by THOMAS HOPE by these presents doth bargain sell deliver & confirm unto THOMAS HOPE and to his heirs the remainder or term yet to come in a spot of land & premises which said WILLIAM holds under Lese from JEAN BRADLEY bearing even date with the Bonds & situate on the Street or Road that leads from DURELLs TAVERN to the New Town of Petersburg, as by the said Lease more fully will shew, also one Negro boy named Stephen about eleven years old and a Negro girl named Violet about nine years old and all estate right & demand of WILLIAM HART in said spot of land and the Negroes Stephen & Violet; To have and to hold lthe same to THOMAS HOPE his heirs; Provided nevertheless that if WILLIAM HART his heris shall pay unto CHRISTOPHER McCONNICO or his assigns the aforesaid sum at the times set forth & expressed in the four Bonds without abatement or deduction that then these presents shall cease determine and be void, In Witness whereof the said WILLIAM HART hath hereunto set his hand and affixed his seal the day and year above written
Signed Seald. & delivered in presenceof
     WM. STEGAR,   WILLIAM his mark X HART
     ALEXR. McCREDIE, WM. BIGELOW
  At a Court of Hustings held for the Town of Petersburg at the House of WILLIAM DURELL Wednesday the Seventh day of June 1786   An Indenture between WILLIAM HART of one part and THOMAS HOPE of the other part was acknowledged by the said WILLIAM HART and ordered to be recorded
               Teste J. GRAMMER, Clk. C. Hs.

p.   The Commonwealth of Virginia to JOHN SHORE, ALEXANDER GLASS STRACHAN &
201   ISAAC HALL Gent. Greeting; Whereas CHARLES DUNCAN and JANE his Wife by
       their Indenture of Bargain and Sale bearing date the Second day of November 1785, have sold and confirmed unto THOMAS SHORE & CHRISTOPHER McCONNICO, five lots of land in that part of Petersburg called NEW BLANDFORD distinguished by the numbers Twenty one, Thirty nine, Forty three, Sixty four & Sixty seven (No. 21, 39, 43, 64, & 67),

And whereas the said JANE cannot conveniently travel to our Court of Hustigns held for the Town of Petersburg to make acknowledgment of the said conveyance (the Commission for the privy Examination of JANE, the Wife of CHARLES DUNCAN); Witness JOHN GRAMMER Clk. of our said Court the third day of May 1786   J. GRAMMER
In Obedience to the foregoing and within Writ to us directed, we have personally applied to the said JANE DUNCAN and received her acknowledgment of the Indenture hereto annexed (the return of the execution of the privy examination of JANE DUNCAN); Certified under our hands and seals this 3d. of May 1786   JOHN SHORE
                                                                          ISAAC HALL
    At a Court of Hustings held for the Town of Petersburg at the House of WILLIAM DURELL Wednesday the Seventh day of June 1786   A Commission annexed to an Indenture of Bargain and Sale between CHARLES DUNCAN of one part and SHORE & McCONNICO of other part (bearing date the Second day of November one thousand seven hundred and Eighty five duly acknowledged and recorded at a Court held for this Town the third day of November last past) was returned & together with the Certificate of execution thereof are ordered to be recorded   Teste J. GRAMMER, Clk. C. Hs.

p.   The Commonwealth of Virginia to CHRISTOPHER, JOHN SHORE & ISAAC HALL
202   Gentn. Greeting. Whereas CHARLES DUNCAN by his certain Indenture of Bargain and Sale bearing date the Sixth of July one thousand seven hundred and Eighty five has sold and conveyed to JAMES CAMPBELL one lot in that part of the Town of Petersburg called NEW BLANDFORD, distinguished by the number Five, And whereas JANE his Wife cannot conveniently travel to our Court of Hustings held for the said Town of Petersburg to make acknowledgment of her right of dower in the same (the Commission for the privy Examination of JANE, the Wife of CHARLES DUNCAN); Witness JOHN GRAMMER Clerk of our said Court the third day of May one thousand seven hundred and Eighty six   J. GRAMMER
In Obedience to the within Writ to us directed, we have personally applied to the said JANE DUNCAN and received her acknowledgment of right of dower to the lot of land contained in the Indenture hereunto annexed; (the return of the execution of the privy examination of JANE DUNCAN); Certified under our hands & seals this third day of May 1786
                                            CHR: McCONNICO
                                            JNO: SHORE
    At a Court of Hustings held for the Town of Petersburg at the House of WILLIAM DURELL in said Town Wednesday the Seventh day of June 1786   A Commission annexed to an Indenture of Bargain and Sale between CHARLES DUNCAN of the one part and JAMES CAMPBELL of the other part bearing date the Sixth day of July 1785 duly acknowledged and recorded at a Court held for this Town the Seventh day of September last was returned and together with a Certificate of the Execution thereof are ordered to be recorded   Teste J. GRAMMER, Clk. C. Hs.

p.   This is to certify that we the Subscribers were present and desired by Mr.
203   ANDREW JOHNSTON to take notice that he had given his Servant, Becky, her perfect & entire Freedom. Petersburg 4th May 1785
                                            NEILL BUCHANAN
                                            ROBT. HASTIE
    At a Court of Hustings held for the Town of Petersburg at the House of WILLIAM DURELL Wednesday the seventh day of June 1786   A Certificate signed by NEILL BUCHANAN and ROBERT HASTIE was presented in Court and sworn to by the said NEILL BUCHANAN and ROBERT HASTIE and ordered to be recorded
                            Teste J. GRAMMER, Clk. C. Hs.

p.   THIS INDENTURE made this Eleventh day of May in year of our Lord one thou-
204   sand seven hundred & Eighty six Between RICHARD WITTON of County of
        MECKLENBURG of one part and WILLIAM ROWLETT JUNR. of CHESTERFIELD
County of other part; Witnesseth that for the sum of Fifteen pounds current money to
said RICHARD in hand paid by said WILLIAM by these presents doth bargain sell and
confirm unto WILLIAM ROWLETT JUNR., his heirs one certain lot of land containing
half an acre more or less situate in CHESTERFEILD County in that part of the Town of
Petersburg at present called POCOHONTASS and is distinguished in the plan of the lands
laid out into lotts by RICHARD WITTON and heretofore known as WITTON TOWN, by the
number Thirty One (No.31), To have and to hold the lot of land number Thirty One with
all its premises and appertenances thereunto belonging to WILLIAM ROWLETT JUNR.
his heirs; And RICHARD WITTON his heirs doth promise with WILLIAM ROWLETT JR., his
heirs by these presents that the premises are now and herafter shall remain and be
free and clear of all incumbrances; In Witness wehreof the said RICHARD WITTON hath
hereunto set his hand and affixed his seal the day and year first above written
Sealed and Delivered in presence of
            HENRY MORRISS, ROYALL BRITTON,   RICHARD WITTON
            WM. BRITTON
   Received the day and year within mentioned of WILLIAM ROWLETT JR., the sum of Fifteen pounds current money in full of the consideration within mentioned for the
within lot of land & premises
Teste HENRY MORRISS   RICHARD WITTON
   At a Court of Hustings held for the Town of Petersburg at the House of WILLIAM
DURELL Wednesday the Seventh day of June 1786   An Indenture of Bargain and Sale
between RICHARD WITTON of one part and WILLIAM ROWLETT JUNR. of other part was
proved by the Oaths of HENRY MORRISS, ROYALL BRITTON and WILLIAM BRITTON, witnesses thereto, and together with the Receipt thereunto annexed are ordered to be
recorded   Teste J. GRAMMER, Clk. C. Hs.

pp.   THIS INDENTURE made this eleventh day of May in year of our Lord one thou-
205   sand seven hundred and Eighty six Between RICHARD WITTON of County of
        MECKLENBURG of one part and ROYAL BRITTAN of other part; Witnesseth that
for sum of Fifteen pounds current money of Virginia to RICHARD WITTON in hand paid
by ROYAL BRITTAN, by these presents doth bargain sell and confirm unto ROYAL BRIT-
TAN his heirs a certain lot of land containing half an acre more or less situate in
CHESTERFEILD County in that part of Petersburg called POAKAHUNTAS and is
distinguished in a plan of said lands laid out by RICHARD WITTON and heretofore known
as WITTON TOWN by the number Fourteen (No. 14), To have and to hold the lot of land
number Fourteen with all its premises and appurtenances unto ROYAL BRITAIN his
heirs and RICHARD WITTON for himself his heirs doth covenant that the said premises
now are and so hereafter shall remain & be free from all incumbrances; and RICHARD
WITTON at all times and forever warrant and defend the said lot of land to ROYAL
BRITTAN his heirs; In Witness whereof the said RICHARD WITTON hath hereunto set his
hand and affixed his seal the day & year first above written
Sealed and Delivered in presence of us
            HENRY MORRISS,   RICHARD WITTON
            JOHN ROWLETT, WILLIAM ROWLETT
   Received of ROYAL BRITTAN Fifteen pounds current money in full of the within con-
sideration
Teste HENRY MORRISS   RICHARD WITTON

At a Court of Hustings held for the Town of Petersburg at the House of WILLIAM
DURELL Wednesday the Seventh day of June 1786   An Indenture of Bargain and Sale
between RICHARD WITTON of one part and ROYAL BRITTAN of other part was proved by
the Oaths of HENRY MORRISS, WILLIAM ROWLETT and WILLIAM BRITTON witnesses
thereto and together with the receipt thereon indorsed are ordered to be recorded
                         Teste J. GRAMMER, Clk. C. Hs.

pp.   THIS INDENTURE made the 28th day of July in year of our Lord one thousand
208-   seven hundred and Eighty five Between ANDREW HAMILTON, JAMES CAMPBELL
209   and JOHN BAIRD the Younger, Executors of the Last Will and Testament of JAMES
           TURNBULL deceased, late of the Town of Petersburg of the one part and
WILLIAM GREGG, late of the City of PHILADELPHIA but at present of the Town of Petersburg, Merchant, of the other part; Whereas JAMES TURNBULL was in his life time and
at the time of his death possessed in Fee Simple of a certain lot of land lying in the Town
of Petersburg on FIRST STREET, known by the number Nineteen (19), which said lot
number (19) was conveyed by ROBERT BOLLING to JAMES TURNBULL by Deed duly
proved and recorded in the Court of the County of DINWIDDIE, And whereas JAMES
TURNBULL in his life time had agreed with WILLIAM GREGG to bargain and sell in fee
simple unto WILLIAM GREGG part of the aforesaid Lot number (19), that is to say, so
much thereof as a certain two story house with a Shed stands upon, and the ground
back of said House as far as a Smokehouse now standing on said lot number (19) being
twenty four feet from the rear of the said two story house on FIRST STREET, to the said
Smokehouse and comprehending the whole length of the said House for the sum of
Nine hundred pounds current money and also in consideration of the Rents and Agreements herein set forth to be paid and performed by WM. GREGG, And whereas the said
JAMES TURNBULL by his Last Will and Testament bearing date the fourteenth day of
October in year of our Lord one thousand seven hundred and Eighty four duly proved
and recorded in the Court of Hustings for the Town of Petersburg did desire and direct
the said ANDREW HAMILTON, JAMES CAMPBELL and JOHN BAIRD the Younger his Executors in the said Will named to make good the Contract, said JAMES TURNBULL had with
WILLIAM GREGG, in and about the premises as by the said Will of JAMES TURNBULL will
appear; NOW THIS INDENTURE WITNESSETH that ANDREW HAMILTON, JAMES CAMPBELL
and JOHN BAIRD, Executors as aforesaid of JAMES TURNBULL deceased for the sum of
Nine hundred pounds current money to them or some of them in hand paid by WIL-
LIAM GREGG, and also in further consideration of the Rents covenants and Agrements
hereinafter mentioned to be paid and performed by WILLIAM GREGG his heirs so far as
they are authorised and to the fullest extent of the powers vested in them by the Will
aforesaid of JAMES TURNBULL deceased, by these presents do bargain sell and confirm
unto WILLIAM GREGG his heirs the parcel of land part of lots number (19) and all
houses and appertenances to said premises belonging; (the Ground Rent hereafter
mentoned always excepted), To have and to hold the lands hereby conveyed unto WIL-
LIAM GREGG his heirs paying unto ANDREW HAMILTON, JAMES CAMPBELL and JOHN
BAIRD, Executors as aforesaid, every year the ground rent of Fifty shillings current
money of Virginia the first years rent to become due and payable the sixth day of
November one thousand seven hundred and eighty five; In Witness whereof the parties
aforesaid have hereunto set their hands and affixed their seals the day and year first
written
Sealed & Delivered in the presence of
      ALEXR. McNABB,   ) for HAMILTON,   ANDW. HAMILTON
      JNO: JEFFERS   ) BAIRD &   JAMES CAMPBELL

JAS: BYRNE   ) GREGG   JNO: BAIRD JR., Exor
                                          WILL: GREGG

Received the 28th day of July 1785 the sum of Nine hundred pounds current money of
Virginia the consideration money for the within mentioned parcel of land and premises; Thirty four pounds 3/ wch: sum Mr. GREGG witholds for that sum he conceives
himself intitled for inconveniences he alledges he has sustained from the Cellar of the
within mentioned House not being in a different situation from what it was, and in
order to determine the propriety & equity of his claim a Bill is to be exhibited immedi-
ately in the Hustings Court of this place Petersburg or any other step taken that may be
more proper for the recovery or determination thereof
In presence of   JNO: BAIRD, Acting Exor.
             Note the above agreed to by me in presence of
        Witness ALEXR. McNABB   WILL: GREGG
   At a Court of Hustings held for the Town of Petersburg at the House of WILLIAM
DURELL Wednesday the Seventh day of June 1786   An Indenture of Bargain and Sale
between ANDREW HAMILTON, JAMES CAMPBELL and JOHN BAIRD JR., Executors of the
Last Will and Testament of JAMES TURNBULL deceased of one part and WILLIAM GREGG
of other part was acknowledged by ANDREW HAMILTON, JAMES CAMPBELL and
WILLIAM GREGG, three of the parties thereto, and the same having been before acknowledged by JOHN BAIRD JR. another party thereto, together with the Receipt thereon
indorsed are ordered to be recorded   Teste J. GRAMMER, Clk. C. Hs.

pp.   THIS INDENTURE made this Twenty sixth day of April in the year of our Lord
210-   one thousand seven hundred and Eighty five Between RICHARD YARBROUGH of
212   County of DINWIDDIE of one part and SAMUEL LOGAN of Town of Petersburg of
         other part; Witnesseth that for the sum of Six hundred pounds current money
of Virginia to him in hand paid by SAMUEL LOGAN said RICHARD YARBROUGH by these
presents doth bargain & sell unto SAMUEL LOGAN his heirs one certain parcell of land
lying in Town of Petersburg near the PUBLIC TOBACCO WAREHOUSES called CEDAR POINT
which said parcell of ground is part of a lott purchased of ROBERT BOLLING by said
YARBROUGH & known by the number Twenty seven (27), begining at the North West
corner of said lott & runing nearly East along the Street of BOLLING BROOK twenty five
feet, thence in a paralel with the sd. YARBROUGHs West line, thence along the said line
to the begining, And all houses and appertenances to said parcel belonging; To have
and to hold the parcel of land hereby conveyed with their appertenances unto SAMUEL
LOGAN his heirs, paying therefor unto RICHARD YARBROUGH his heirs every year on
the first day of January the Fee Rent of Two pounds current money to commence & be
computed from the first day of January last past, the first years rent to become due and
payable on the first day of January one thousand seven hundred & eighty six; In Witness whereof the parties aforesaid have hereunto set their hands and affixed their
seals the day & year first above written
Sealed and Delivered in presence of
        M. ALEXANDER,
        F. RANDOLPH, JOHN KILLEN   RICHARD YARBROUGH
        JOHN GRAMMER   SAMUEL LOGAN
   The Commonwealth of Virginia to ROBERT BOLLING and ALEXANDER McNABB Gentlemen Greeting, Whereas (the Commission for the privy Examination of SARAH, the Wife of
RICHARD YARBROUGH), Witness JOHN GRAMMER Clerk of our said Court the Eleventh day
of March in the Tenth year of the Commonwealth   J. GRAMMER
   By virtue of the Commission hereunto annexed, this Indenture was acknowledged by

SARAH YARBROUGH on the 11th day of March 1786, she the said SARAH being first privily and apart from the said RICHARD YARBROUGH her Husband, examined, (the return of the execution of the privy examination of SARAH YARBROUGH); before us

ROBERT BOLLING
ALEXR: McNABB

At a Court of Hustings held for the Town of Petersburg at the House of WILLIAM DURELL Wednesday the Seventh day of June 1786   An Indenture of Bargain and Sale between RICHARD YARBROUGH of the one part and SAMUEL LOGAN of the other part was proved by the Oath of JOHN GRAMMER a witness thereto and the same having been before partly proved by the Oaths of MARK ALEXANDER and JOHN KILLEN, two other witnesses thereto, together with the Commission thereunto annexed, and the Certificate of the Execution thereof, are ordered to be recorded

Teste J. GRAMMER, Clk. C. Hs.

pp.   THIS INDENTURE made this Twentieth day of March in year of our Lord one
213-   thousand seven hundred and Eighty six Between CHARLES DUNCAN & JANE his
214   Wife of CHESTERFEILD County of one part & DANIEL FISHER of GREENESVILLE
          County of the other part; Witnesseth that for the sum of Forty pounds by
DANIEL FISHER unto CHARLES DUNCAN in hand paid, said CHARLES DUNCAN & JANE his Wife by these presents doth bargain & sell unto DANIEL FISHER his heirs all those two lotts of land lying on BLANDFORD HILL known and lately laid out on the HILL by the numbers (68 & 91), Sixty Eight & Ninety One, To have and to hold the lotts of land and all the advantages appertaining thereto unto DANIEL FISHER his heirs; And CHARLES DUNCAN doth for himself his heirs covenant with DANIEL FISHER his heris that he will for ever warrant and defend the title of said lots of land unto DANIEL FISHER his heirs against the lawfull claim of every person; In Witness whereof the said CHARLES DUNCAN hath hereunto set his hand & seal the day and year above written
Witness WM. DAVIES,   CHARLES DUNCAN
        RICHD: GREGORY,   JANE DUNCAN
        HENRY MORRISS

The Commonwealth of Virginia to ISAAC HALL, CHRISTOPHER McCONNICO and JOHN SHORE, Gent., Greeting, Whereas (the Commission for the privy examination of JANE the Wife of CHARLES DUNCAN); Witness JNO: GRAMMER Clerk of our said Court the third day of May
1786   J. GRAMMER

In Obedience to the within Commission to us directed, we have personally applied to the said JANE DUNCAN and received her acknowledgment of the Indenture hereto annexed and have also examined her privily and apart from her Husband, (the return of the execution of the privy examination of JANE DUNCAN); Certified under our hands & seals this 3d. day of May 1786   CHR: McCONNICO
                                            ISAAC HALL

At a Court of Hustings held for the Town of Petersburg at the House of WILLIAM DURELL Wednesday the Seventh day of June 1786   An Indenture of Bargain and Sale between CHARLES DUNCAN and JANE his Wife of one part and DANIEL FISHER of other part was proved by the Oaths of WILLIAM DAVIES, RICHARD GREGORY and HENRY MORRISS witnesses thereto and together with the Commission thereto annexed and the Certificate of execution thereof are ordered to be recorded

Teste J. GRAMMER, Clk. C. Hs.

pp.   The Commonwealth of Virginia to ROBERT BOLLING & ALEXANDER McNABB
215-   Gentlemen Greeting. Whereas CHARLES DUNCAN of County of CHESTERFEILD,
216   Merchant, by certain Deeds of Bargain and Sale hath sold and conveyed unto
ROBERT FITZGERALD, PHILIP W. JACKSON, ALLEN LOVE, JOHN McCLOUD, (blank)
PERRIE, WM. STARK, JOHN ANGUS, JAMES CAMPBELL, ROBERT TURNBULL, NATHL.
COCKS, WILLM. ROBERTSON, SIMON FRASER, (blank) DOWNMAN, JOHN CAMERON,
CHARLES RUSSELL, JAMES FRENCH, THOMAS GRIFFIN PEACHY, JOHN ROCHELL, THOMAS
GORDON, ISAAC HALL, PETER RANDOLPH, DANL. FISHER, WILLIAM EDWARDS, WM.
COLEMAN, WM. GILLIAM, Dr. JOHN SHORE, ANDREW HAMILTON and ALEXANDER TAYLOR
unto each of them respectively the fee simple Estate in certain lotts of ground lying on
BLANDFORD HILL and on The CHURCH HILL, which lotts of ground are part of Eighty
acres of Land surveyed and laid out by CHARLES DUNCAN into lotts & streets for a Town
joining to the Old Town of BLANDFORD, and were disposed of by him by way of Lottery
and the several Adventurers for the same becoming intitled to a fee simple estate in the
lot or lotts drawn by each agreable to said Lotter, many of them as before named, or
their assigns, have obtained from said CHARLES DUNCAN grants for the same and he
hath also given sufficient powers to THOMAS GRIFFIN PEACHY and ROBERT TURNBULL,
his Attorneys in fct. to grant unto all other intitled thereto, Deeds of Bargain and Sale
for suchof said lotts as are not already conveyed for vesting a fee simple estate in each
of the said Adventurers his heris agreable to their several and respective rights which
Deeds of Bargain and Sale first above mentioned together with the plan of the lotts and
streets so as aforesaid laid out with the Adventurers names thereon noted are of Record
in the Court of Hustings for the Town of Petersburg; And Whereas JANE, the Wife of said
CHARLES cannot conveniently travel to the Court aforesaid to make her acknowledg-
ments of the Deeds aforesaid, or to make relinquishment of her right of dower in the
Eighty acres of land or in the lotts of ground, Therefore we give (the Commission for the
privy Examination of JANE, the Wife of CHARLES DUNCAN); Witness JOHN GRAMMER, Clerk of
our said Court the third day of May in the tenth year of our Independence
  By virtue and authority of the within Commission the said Conveyances of Bargain and
Sale together with the balance and residue of the Eighty acres of land yet to be conveyed to the several differenct persons within mentioned and their heirs were acknowledged by said JANE DUNCAN on the third day of May 1786, she the said JANE being
first privily and apart from the said CHARLES DUNCAN, examined (the return of the execution of the privy examination of JANE DUNCAN), before us   ROBERT BOLLING JR.
                                              ALEX: McNABB
  At a Court of Hustings held for the Town of Petersburg at the House of WM. DURELL
Wednesday the Seventh day of June 1786   A Commission for the privy Examination &
Relinquishmt. &c., of JANE DUNCAN of in & to Eighty acres of land laid out in Lotts &
disposed of by her Husband, CHARLES DUNCAN, was returned & together with the Cer-
tificate of execution thereof, are ordered to be recorded
                 Teste J. GRAMMER, Clk. C. Hs.
(Pages 217 and 218 are blank.)

p.   The Commonwealth of Virginia to ROBERT BOLLING and ALEXANDER McNABB
219   Gentlemen Greeting. Whereas WILLIAM HARRISON and LUCY his Wife by their
        certain Indenture of Bargain and Sale bearing date the Fourth day of January
1786, have sold and conveyed unto GRESSETT DAVIS of Town of Petersburg all their
right & title of in & to a certain lot or parcell of land in Town of Petersburg distinguished in the plan of RAVENSCROFT TOWN by the number Forty Two (42), And whereas
said LUCY HARRISON cannot conveniently travel to our Court of Hustings of the Town of

Petersburg to make acknowledgment of the said conveyance; Therefore we do give (the Commission for the privy Examination of LUCY, the Wife of WILLIAM HARRISON); Witness JOHN GRAMMER Clerk of our said Court the Twenty third day of January 1786 and in the tenth year of the Commonwealth   J. GRAMMER

By virtue of the Commission hereunto annexed, this Indenture was acknowledged by the within subscribed LUCY HARRISON on the 11th February 1786, she the said LUCY being first privily and apart from the said WILLIAM HARRISON her Husband examined; and declared that she did the same freely and voluntarily without his persuasions or threats and that she was willing and desirous that the same should be recorded in the Court of the Town of Petersburg, before us   ROBERT BOLLING
                                                                                                              ALEX: McNABB

At a Hustings Court held for the Town of Petersburg at DURRELLs in said Town Wednesday the fifth day of July 1786   A Commission annexed to an Indenture of Bargain and Sale between WILLIAM HARRISON & LUCY his Wife of one part and GRESSETT DAVIS of other part bearing date the fourth day of January 1786 and duly acknowledged and recorded in our said Court the fifth day of January last, was returned and together with the Certificate of the Execution thereof are ordered to be recorded
                                                  Teste J. GRAMMER, Clk. C. Hs.

pp.   THIS INDENTURE made this Twenty second day of April in year of our Lord one
220-   thousand seven hundred and Eighty five Between SHORE & McCONNICO, Mer-
221   chants and Partners, of the Town of Petersburg of one part and JAMES COLQU-
             HOUN & COMPANY, Merchants of NORFOLK, of other part; Witnesseth that said
SHORE & McCONNICO for sum of One hundred & fifty pounds current money of Virginia to them in hand paid by JAMES COLQUHOUN & COMPY., and also for the annual Ground Rent of Ten pounds current money to be paid forever by JAMES COLQUHOUN & COMPY. their heirs to said SHORE & McCONNICO, and in consideration of the covenants and agrements herein after mentioned, said SHORE & McCONNICO by these presents do bargain sell and confirm unto JAMES COLQUHOUN & COMPY. their heirs one moiety or part of a lot of land laid off by ROBERT BOLLING Esqr. and distinguished in the platt of the lands recorde in the Court of DINWIDDIE County by the number Thirty Eight (38), bounding, begining on BOLLING BROOK STREET thirty six feet Easterly of the Southwest Corner of said lot number Thirty Eight, thence on the said Street Easterly twenty four feet, thence Northerly eighty feet to the back line of said lot, thence along the said back line Westerly twenty four feet, thence Southerly to BOLLING BROOK STREET, the begining, (leaving Alleys of nine feet in width on each side, which said Alleys are to be for ever kept free and open for the mutual use & benefit of those bounding thereon); And all houses and appertenances to said spot of land belonging, and the rents issues and profits thereof; To have and to hold the parcel of land hereby conveyed with appertenances unto JAMES COLQUHOUN & COMPY., their heirs paying therefor unto said SHORE & McCONNICO their heris yearly on the first day of January for ever; the sum of Ten pounds current money Ground Rent to commence from the first day of January next ensuing; which will be in the year one thousand seven hundred and Eighty seven; In Witness whereof the parties aforesaid have hereunto set their hands and affixed their seals the day and year first above written
Sealed and Delivered in the presence of
          ROBT. HEBLETHWAITE,   SHORE & McCONNICO
          FRED: NANCE JR.,   for JAMES COLQUHOUN & CO.
          BELFEILD STARK   ROBERT COLQUHOUN

At a Hustings Court held for the Town of Petersburg at the House of WM. DURELL in the
said Town Wednesday the Fifth day of July 1786   An Indenture of Bargain and Sale
between SHORE & McCONNICO, Merchants and Partners, of the Town of Petersburg of
one part and JAMES COLQUHOUN & COMPANY of NORFOLK of the other part was acknowledged by the said parties and ordered to be recorded
                        Teste J. GRAMMER, Clk. C. Hs.

p.   THIS INDENTURE made this first day of March in year of our Lord one thousand
222   seven hundred and Eighty six Between RICHARD WITTON of LUNENBURG County
          of one part and HENRY MORRISS of Town of Petersburg of other part. Witnesseth
that RICHARD WITTON for sum of Twenty five pounds current money in hand paid by
HENRY MORRISS, by these presents doth bargain sell and confirm unto HENRY MORRISS
his heirs one lot situated in that part of the Town of Petersburg called POCOHONTASS and
distinguished in the plan thereof by the number Sixty seven with all the piece of
Marsh and vacant ground adjoining KENNONs Line and the said lott & lotts 66 & 65 wth:
the appertenances; To have and to hold the said lot unto HENRY MORRISS his heirs; And
RICHARD WITTON for himself and his heirs the bargained and sold premises unto
HENRY MORRISS his heirs against all persons shall warrent and for ever defend by
these presents; In Witness whereof the said RICHARD WITTON hath hereunto set his
hand and affixed his seal the day & year first above written
Signed Sealed and Delivered in presence of
        ARMISTEAD DAVES,   RICHARD WITTON
        ALEX: McNABB,   J. ROAN,
        THOMAS HOLT,   ROB: COLQUHOUN
Received of HENRY MORRISS Twenty five pounds in full for the within bargained pre-
mises as witness my hand & seal this first day of March 1786
                             (no signatures recorded)
At a Court of Hustings held for the Town of Petersburg at the House of WM. DURELL
Wednesday the Fifth day of July 1786   An Indenture of Bargain and Sale between
RICHARD WITTON of LUNENBURG County of one part and HENRY MORRISS of other part
was proved by the Oath of ROBERT COLQUHOUN a witness thereto and the same having
been before proved by the Oaths of ARMISTEAD DAVES & ALEXANDER McNABB two of the
witnesses thereto, is ordered to be recorded
                        Teste J. GRAMMER, Clk. C. Hs.

pp.   THIS INDENTURE made this Second day of May in the year of our Lord one thou-
223-   sand seven hundred and Eighty six Between CHARLES DUNCAN of the County of
224   CHESTERFEILD of the one part and PETER RANDOLPH of County of AMELIA of the
          other part; Witnesseth that CHARLES DUNCAN in consideration of the quantity
of Six thousand pounds weight of Crop Tobacco paid by PETER RANDOLPH, said CHARLES
DUNCAN by these presents doth bargain sell and confirm unto PETER RANDOLPH his
heirs three lotts of ground number Fifty three, Sixty Nine & Eighty Eight, lying within
the Borough of Petersburg and in that part of the Town known by the name of NEW
BLANDFORD; To have and to hold the said lotts of ground and all the advantages and
appertenances thereto unto PETER RANDOLPH his heirs; And CHARLES DUNCAN for himself his heirs doth covenant with PETER RANDOLPH his heirs that he will for ever warrant and defend the said lotts against all persons; In Witness whereof the said CHARLES
DUNCAN hath hereunto set his hand and Seal the day & year as above written
Sealed & Delivered in presence of
        RICHARD GREGORY, JAMES GEDDY   CHARLES DUNCAN
        WILLIAM DAVIES,   U. MARCK,

The Commonwealth of Virginia to CHRISTOPHER McCONNICO, JOHN SHORE and ROBERT
BOLLING Gentlemen, Greeting, Whereas (the Commission for the privy examination of JANE,
the Wife of CHARLES DUNCAN); Witness JOHN GRAMMER Clerk of our said Court this third
day of May A. D. 1786   J. GRAMMER
   In Obedience to the above Commission to us directed, we have personally applied to the
said JANE DUNCAN & received her acknowledgment of the Indenture hereto annexed
and have examined her privily & apart from her Husband (the return of the execution of
the privy examination of JANE DUNCAN); Certified under our hands & seals this 3d. day of
May A. D. 1786   CHR: McCONNICO
                                   ROBERT BOLLING JR.
   At a Court of Hustings held for the Town of Petersburg at the House of WM. DURELL
Wednesday the 5th day of July 1786   An Indenture of Bargain and Sale between
CHARLES DUNCAN of the County of CHESTERFEILD of one part and PETER RANDOLPH of
AMELIA County of the other part was proved by the Oaths of RICHARD GREGORY, WIL-
LIAM DAVIES & UBRICK MARCK, three of the witnessels thereto and together with the
Commission annexed and the Certificate of the execution thereof are ordered to be
recorded   Teste J. GRAMMER, Clk. C. Hs.

p.   THIS INDENTURE made this third day of May one thousand seven hundred &
225   Eighty six Between CHARLES DUNCAN of CHESTERFEILD County of one part and
          ALEXANDER TAYLOR of Town of Petersburg of other part; Witnesseth that in
consideration of the quantity of Two thousand weight of tobacco to said CHARLES by said
ALEXANDER in hand paid, by these presents doth bargain & sell unto ALEXANDER TAY-
LOR his heirs all that certain lott of ground situate in that part of the Town of Petersburg called NEW BLANDFORD and distinguished by the number (49), Forty Nine; Together with all advantages and priviledges to the same belonging; To have and to hold the
above granted lot with the appertenances unto ALEXANDER TAYLOR his heirs; And
CHARLES DUNCAN for himself his heirs doth covenant with ALEXANDER TAYLOR his
heirs that he will warrant and by these presents forever defend; In Witness whereof
the said CHARLES DUNCAN hath hereunto set his hand and seal the day & year first
above written
Sealed & Delivered in the presence of
     ISAAC HALL, WILLIAM COLEMAN,   CHARLES DUNCAN
     U. MARCK, RO: WATKINS   JANE DUNCAN
   At a Court of Hustings held for the Town of Petersburg at the House of WILLIAM
DURELL Wednesday the fifth day of July 1786   An Indenture of Bargain and Sale
between CHARLES DUNCAN of CHESTERFEILD County of one part and ALEXANDER TAY-
LOR of the Town of Petersburg of the other part was proved by the Oaths of ISAAC HALL,
WILLIAM COLEMAN and UBRICE MARCK witnesses thereto and is ordered to be recorded
                      Teste J. GRAMMER, Clk. C. Hs.

p.   THIS INDENTURE made this third day of May in year of our Lord one thousand
226   seven hundred and Eighty six Between CHARLES DUNCAN of County of CHESTER-
          FEILD of one part and ANDREW HAMILTON of the Borough of Petersburg of the
other part; Witnesseth taht CHARLES DUNCAN for the sum of Twenty hundred pounds
weight of Crop Tobacco paid by ANDREW HAMILTON said CHARLES DUNCAN by these
presents doth bargain sell and confirm unto ANDREW HAMILTON his heirs a lott of
ground number Eighty Nine lying within the Borough of Petersburg and in that part of
the Town known by the name of NEW BLANDFORD; To have and to hold the lott of ground
and all the advantages appertaining thereto unto ANDREW HAMILTON his heirs, And

CHARLES DUNCAN will forever warrant and defend the Title of said lott of ground unto ANDREW HAMILTON his heirs against all persons; In Witness whereof the said CHARLES DUNCAN hath hereunto set his hand & fixed his seal the day and year as above written Sealed and Delivered in presence of

WILLIAM COLE,   JOS: WESTMORE,   CHARLES DUNCAN
JOHN FISHER,   WILL: COLEMAN

At a Court of Hustings held for the Town of Petersburg at the House of WILLIAM DURELL Wednesday the Fifth day of July 1786   An Indenture of bargain and sale between CHARLES DUNCAN of CHESTERFEILD County of one part and ANDREW HAMILTON of the other part was proved by the Oaths of WILLIAM COLE, JOSEPH WESTMORE and WILLIAM COLEMAN, witnesses thereto, and is ordered to be recorded
Teste J. GRAMMER, Clk. C. Hs.

pp.   THIS INDENTURE made the Twenty second day of June in year of our Lord one
227-   thousand seven hundred and Eighty six Between RICHARD YARBROUGH and
228   SARAH his Wife of Town of Petersburg of one part and Messrs. CUGNEAU &
             SUBERCASAUX and PETER JOHN CAUVY of said Town of other part; Witnesseth
that RICHARD YARBROUGH and SARAH his Wife for sum of Two hundred pounds current money of Virginia to them in hand paid by the said CUGNEAU & SUBERCASAUX and PETER JOHN CAUVY, said RICHARD YARBROUGH and SARAH his Wife by these presents do bargain & sell unto the said CUGNEAU & SUBERCASAUX and PETER JOHN CAUVY their heirs a certain plot of land lying in Town of Petersburg adjacent to CEDAR POINT WAREHOUSE on the South side of the Main Street and on the West of Cross Street, bounded by said Streets, BACK STREET and a plott of land which said YARBROUGH con-veyed to JOEL FENN, containing Forty five feet front & back & two hundred & seventeen feet in length, it being part of a lott of land which said YARBROUGH purchased of ROBERT BOLLING Esqr., Together with the buildings and every thing appertaining to the same, And also all right title and demand of said RICHARD & SARAH his Wife in the same premises; To have and to hold the tenement with the appurtenances unto said CUGNEAU & SUBERCASAUX and PETER JOHN CAUVY their heirs in severalty and not as joint tenants saving and reserving unto ROBERT BOLLING his heirs an annual Ground Rent of Six pounds current money of Virginia payable the first day of January every year; In Witness whereof the parties within named have hereunto set their hands & affixed their Seals the day & year above written
Signed Sealed & Delivered in the presence of

JNO: BAIRD JR.   RICHD. YARBROUGH
WM. BIGELOW,   SARAH YARBROUGH
BOSWELL GOODWIN   CUGNEAU & SUBERCASAUX
NORMAN BIGELOW   PR. JN. CAUVY

Received of Messrs. CUGNEAU & SUBERCASAUX & PETER JOHN CAUVY Fifty five pounds Cash & their Bonds for the balance of the within sum of Two hundred pounds June 22d. 1786

Test J. BAIRD JR.   RD. YARBROUGH
WM. BIGELOW, BOSWELL GOODWYN

At a Court of Hustings held for the Town of Petersburg at the House of WM. DURELL Wednesday the fifth day of July 1786   An Indenture of Bargain & Sale between RICHARD YARBROUGH & SARAH his Wife of the one part and CUGNEAU & SUBERCASAUX & PETER JOHN CAUVY of the other part; was proved by the Oaths of WILLIAM BIGELOW, BOSWELL GOODWIN and NORMAN BIGELOW three of the witnesses thereto and the memo-randum and Receipt thereon endorsed were proved by the Oaths of WILLIAM BIGELOW and BOSWELL GOODWIN witnesses thereto and together with the said Indenture, are ordered to be recorded Teste J. GRAMMER, Clk. C. Hs.

p. 229
THIS INDENTURE made third day of February one thousand seven hundred & Eighty six Between WILLIAM HARRISON of Petersburg of one part & HENRY VAUGHAN of County of DINWIDDIE of other part; Witnesseth that for the sum of One hundred pounds to said HARRISON paid by said VAUGHAN, by these presents doth bargain sell & conmfirm two certain lots of land containing each One hundred & twenty feet by one hundred & sixty feet lying & being in that part of Petersburg called RAVENSCROFT TOWN, being part of the lots number (9 & 10), Nine and Ten, which two lots were divided into six small lotts of one hundred & twenty feet by one hundred & sixty feet each by said HARRISON & numbered from one to twelve inclusive, which two pieces lye together & upon the Main Street going to PORTER HILL where said HARRISON lately lived. Together with all waters & all other priviledges thereunto belonging; To have & to hold the said lotts of land unto said VAUGHAN his heirs; And said HARRISON his heirs against the claim of every person shall warrant and forever defend; In Witness whereof the said HARRISON the day & year above written set his hand and affixed his seal

Signed Sealed and Delivered in the presence of
JNO: HARE, JAMES DURELL,   WM. HARRISON
JOEL HAMMON, EMD. COOPER

At a Court of Hustings held for the Town of Petersburg at the House of WM. DURELL Wednesday the fifth day of July 1786   An Indenture of Bargain and Sale between WILLIAM HARRISON of the Town of Petersburg of one part and HENRY VAUGHAN of DINWIDDIE County of other part was proved by the Oaths of JOHN HARE, JOEL HAMMON and EDMOND COOPER witnesses thereto and ordered to be recorded
Teste J. GRAMMER, Clk. C. Hs.

(Pages 230, 231 and 232 are blank.)

p. 233
THIS INDENTURE made this Eighteenth of March in year of our Lord one thousand seven hundred and Eighty four Between THOMAS GORDON of County of PRINCE GEORGE of the one part and ANN PORTLOCK of County of DINWIDDIE of other part; Witnesseth that THOMAS GORDON for sum of One hundred pounds specie by ANN PORTLOCK to him in hand paid, said THOMAS GORDON hath bargained and sold unto ANN PORTLOCK one lott and half acre of land lying in the County of DINWIDDIE in the Town of Petersburg known by the number Thirty Seven (it being a lott and half acre of land formerly the property of JAMES MURRAY deceas'd of the County of PRINCE GEORGE) and bounded by the lotts or lands of PETER WARREN deced., and RICHD. SPENCER. And also all houses gardens grees profits commodities and appurtenances unto said lott or half acre of land belonging; To have and to hold the lott or half acre of land unto ANN PORTLOCK her heirs; And THOMAS GORDON will by these presents warrant and forever defend all the above premises; In Witness whereof the said THOMAS GORDON hath hereunto set his hand and seal the day and year first above written

Signed Seal'd & delivd. in presence of
JNO: BAIRD JR.,   THOMAS GORDON
GEORGE DUDGEON, JAMES ANDREWS

At a Court of Hustings held for the Town of Petersburg at the House of WILLIAM DURELL Wednesday the Second day of August 1786   An Indenture of Bargain and Sale between THOMAS GORDON of PRINCE GEORGE County of one part and ANN PORTLOCK of DINWIDDIE County of the other part was acknowledged by the said THOMAS GORDON and is ordered to be recorded Teste J. GRAMMER, Clk. C. Hs.

p.   I HEREBY Certify that WILLIAM MAYNARD is at liberty to sell a certain House
234   built by him near CEDAR POINT WAREHOUSE provided the purchaser thereof will
        comply with the conditions agreed to on the part of said MAYNARD with ROBERT
BOLLING JR., which are as follows, vizt., said WILLIAM MAYNARD agrees and obliges
himself to build a House on a certain spot of ground near CEDAR POINT WAREHOUSE
twelve feet wide and fourteen feet long for the use of which said House and the ground
on which it stands he obliges himself to pay the sum of Fourteen pounds annually on
the 1st day of May for five years to commence from the 1st day of May 1786; And it is
further agreed that if said MAYNARD shou'd fail to pay the annual ground rent for the
space of ten days in any year (during the term of five years) in that case it shall be
lawfull for ROBERT BOLLING to enter into the said House & Ground and take the same to
his own sue and benefit in as full and compleat a manner as if no such bargain or Contract had every been entered into between the parties hereto; Sealed Signed and agreed
to this 20th day of April 1786   ROBERT BOLLING JR.
  N. B. If the said BOLLING shou'd (at any time during the within term of Five years)
think proper to erect a better house upon or near the within mentioned ground, then
and in that case the said House is to be removed at the joint expence of the parties to
some place on the said Street to be then pointed out by the said ROBERT BOLLING JR.
                           RO: BOLLING JR. ·
  I hereby certify that I have bargained sold and do hereby set over and sign over unto
JANE BURCH and her assigns all my right and title of this within agreement with the
House that I have all ready built on the said Ground for the full and just sum of Twenty
pounds good and lawfull money of Virginia to him in hand paid; As Witness my hand
and seal this 20th day of July 1786
Sign in the presence of us
      MARY her mark ✕ CORNS,   WILLIAM MAYNARD
      NATHAN GREEN
  Received of JANE BURCH the full and just sum of Twenty pounds good and lawful
money of Virginia it being the consideration money for a House and Lott on a parcell of
Ground sold her by me this 20th day of July 1786
Witness present NATHAN GREEN   WILLIAM MAYNARD
  At a Court of Hustings held for the Town of Petersburg at the House of WM. DURELL
Wednesday the Second day of August 1786   A Memorandum of Agrement between
ROBERT BOLLING JR. and WILLIAM MAYNARD for a spot of land and House near CEDAR
POINT WAREHOUSE signed by the said ROBERT BOLLING, together with the said MAY-
NARDs Relinquishment or conveyance of the same to JANE BURCH which was proved by
the Oaths of MARY CORNS and NATHAN GREEN witnesses thereto and his receipt for the
payment thereof was proved by the Oath of NATHAN GREEN, a witness thereto, are
ordered to be recorded   Teste J. GRAMMER, Clk. C. Hs,

p.   TO ALL TO WHOM these presents shall come, I THOMAS MASTERSON of the County
235   of DINWIDDIE send Greeting. Whereas I find it necessary for me to appoint some
        proper person to manage and settle all my affairs and disputes now depending
and undetermined between me and ANDREW HAMILTON, JAMES CAMPBELL and JOHN
BAIRD JUNIOR, as Executors of the Last Will and Testament of JAMES TURNBULL deceased; NOW KNOW YE that I THOMAS MASTERSON do by these presents ordain and appoint my Friend, INSTANCE HALL of County of PRINCE GEORGE, my true and lawfull Attorney for me and in my name to settle, adjust or to compromise (as to my said Attorney
shall seem best) all disputes, controversies, lawsuits, quarrells, demands, contracts,
agreements & disagreements of every kind and sort that have arisen and are now depen-

ding & undetermined between me & the Executors of JAMES TURNBULL deced., and more
particularly all disputes between the said Exors. & myself concerning the ORDINARY
laying in the Town of Petersburg and the disagrements & disputes conerning the same
in consequence of an agrement enterd into by me and the said TURNBULL in his life
time and the conduct or proceedings of the said Executors since the death of the said
TURNBULL, and upon such settlement to be made either by arbitratrion or any other
way that may seem best to my said Attorney my said Attorney for me tosue for or
receive the balances that may appear to be due or thought reasonable to be paid to me,
ratifying & holding firm all whatsoever my said Attorney shall lawfully do or cause to
be done in the premises by virtue of these presents; In Witness whereof I have hereunto set my hand & affixed my seal this Sixth day of July Anno Domini one thousand
seven hundred & Eighty six
Test   JAMES VAUGHAN   THOMAS MASTERSON
        JAMES HARRIS
     At a Court of Hustings held for the Town of Petersburg at the House of WM. DURELL in
the said Town Wednesday the Second day of August 1786   A Power of Attorney from
THOMAS MASTERSON to INSTANCE HALL was proved by the Oaths of JAMES VAUGHAN and
JAMES HARRIS witnesses thereto and is ordered to be recorded
                              Teste J. GRAMMER. Clk. C. Hs.
(Pages 236 and 237 are blank.)

pp.   THIS INDENTURE made this first day of May in the year of our Our Lord one
238-   thousand seven hundred and Eighty six Between CHARLES DUNCAN & JANE his
239   Wife of County of CHESTERFEILD of one part and WILLIAM STARK JR. of County
        of DINWIDDIE of other part; Witnesseth that for sum of One hundred pounds
current money specia to him said CHARLES DUNCAN in hand paid by WILLIAM STARK
JR., said CHARLES DUNCAN & JANE his Wife have bargained and sold unto WILLIAM
STARK JR. his heirs one certain lot of land situate in that part of the Town of Petersburg called NEW BLANDFORD and is distinguished in the plan of the same now of Record
in the Hustings Court of said Town by the number Forty (40), To have and to hld the
premises and appurtenances to WILLIAM STARK JR. and his heirs; And CHARLES DUN-
CAN and JANE his Wife for themselves & their heirs the parcel of land Iwill warrant and
forever defend against the title and demand of every person; In Witness whereof they
have hereunto set their hands and affixed their seals the day & year above written
Signed Sealed & Delivered in presence of
        CHR: McCONNICO, THOS: SHORE,   CHARLES DUNCAN
        PETER BAIRD, MATTHEW FERNANDO   JANE DUNCAN
     The Commonwealth of Virginia to ISAAC HALL, CHRISTOPHER McCONNICO & JOHN
SHORE Gent., Greeting. Whereas (the Commission for the privy Examination of JANE, the Wife
of CHARLES DUNCAN); Witness JOHN GRAMMER Clerk of our said Court this third day of
May 1786   J. GRAMMER
     In Obedience to the within Commission to us directed, we have personally applied to
the said JANE DUNCAN and received her acknowledgment of the Indenture hereunto
annexed and have also examined her privily and apart from her said Husband, (the
return of the execution of the privy examination of JANE DUNCAN); Certified under our hands
and seals this 3d. day of March 1786   CHR: McCONNICO
                                                ISAAC HALL
     At a Court of Hustings continued & held for the Town of Petersburg at the House of WM.
DURELL Thursday the Seventh day of September 1786   An Indenture of Bargain &
Sale between CHARLES DUNCAN & JANE his Wife of CHESTERFEILD County of one part

and WILLIAM STARK JR. of DINWIDDIE County of the other part was proved by the Oaths
of CHRISTOPHER McCONNICO and THOMAS SHORE, two of the witnesses thereto, and the
same having been before proved by the Oath of MATTHEW FERNANDO another witness
thereto, together with the Commission and the Certificate of execution thereof are
ordered to be recorded   Teste J. GRAMMER, Clk. C. Hs.

p.   TO ALL TO WHOM these presents shall come. Whereas ROBERT BOLLING Esquire
240   late of BOLLING BROOK in the County of DINWIDDIE deceased, did by his Last Will
             and Testament in writing bearing date the 30th day of January one thousand
seven hundred and seventy five recorded in the Court of DINWIDDIE devise unto his
Wife, MARY, his Executrix therein named (among other things, his Negro slaves with
power to dispose of the same amongst the Children of the said Testator at such time and
in such proportions as she shou'd think proper. NOW KNOW YE that by virtue of the
power aforesaid, I the said MARY BOLLING of BOLLINGBROOK in the County aforesaid do
give grant and set over unto my Son, THOS: TABB BOLLING, one of the Children of the
said ROBT. BOLLING deceased, Thirty nine Negro slaves whose names are as follows; to
wit, Stephen, Cate, Harry, Arthur, David, Cellar, Frank, Will, Will, Okey, Battis,
Toney, Charles, Tull, Sampson, Joe, Penoie, Hannah, Frank, Hannah, Amey, Isabel
Iris, Sarah, Chener, Syphax, Nicholas, Bob, David, Prince, Jenny, Sarah, Jellicah,
Aggy, Elizabeth, Beck, Milly, Patience, Annaca, Moll thirty nine, To have and to hold
the thirty nine Negro slaves and all the future increase of the female slaves to the said
THOMAS TABB BOLLING and his heirs as his full share and proportion of the slaves
which were the Estate of the said ROBERT BOLLING deceased; And I said THOMAS TABB
BOLLING do hereby acknowledge the said thirty nine Negro slaves are accepted by me
as my full and equal proportion of the Negro slaves to which I am intitled out of the
Estate of said ROBERT BOLLING deceased, my late Father. In Witness whereof the parties
aforesaid have hereunto set their hands and affixed their seals this Twenty eighth day
of August one thousand seven hundred and Eighty six
Sealed and Delivered in the presence of
           JOHN IMRAY,   MARY BOLLING
           ROBERT BOLLING JR.   THOMAS T. BOLLING
           F. ANDERSON JR.
   At a Court of Hustings continued & held for the Town of Petersburg at the house of WM.
DURELL in the said Town Thursday the Seventh day of September 1786   A Deed of Gift
between MARY BOLLING of BOLLINGBROOK in the Town of Petersburg of one part and
THOMAS TABB BOLLING of the other part was proved by the Oaths of JOHN IMRAY and
ROBERT BOLLING JR. two of the witnesses thereto, and the same having been proved by
the Oath of FRANCIS ANDERSON JR. another witness thereto is ordered to be recorded
                         Teste J. GRAMMER, Clk. C. Hs.

pp.   THIS INDENTURE made this Twenty seventh day of June in year of our Lord one
241   thousand seven hundred & Eighty six Between CHRISTOPHER McCONNICO Esqr.,,
             Merchant, of the Town of Petersburg of one part and JNO: BAIRD JR. of the same
plce of other part; Witnesseth that CHRISTOPHER McCONNICO for the full and just sum of
Three hundred and Seventy five pounds current money of Virginia to him in hand paid
(or secured to be paid) doth by these presents bargain sell & confirm unto JOHN BAIRD
JR. and to his heirs one certain half acre lott of land lying in the Old Town of Petersburg on the South side of the Stree thereof, in County of DINWIDDIE, and is more particularly and better known by the number Twenty four (or 24), and is called THE
YELLOW HOUSE, and is the lott and house lately occupied by GOLOTHON WALKER; To have

and to hold the said half acre lott of land number 24 with the appurtenances to JOHN
BAIRD JR., his heirs; and CHRISTOPHER McCONNICO for himself his heirs doth promise
JOHN BAIRD JR. his heirs that he will warrent and for ever defend by these presents;
In Witness whereof the said CHRISTOPHER McCONNICO hath hereunto set his hand &
affixed his seal the day & year at first within written in the presence of those whose
names are hereunto annexed as the witnesses thereof

HENRY MORRISS,   CHR: McCONNICO
WILLIAM STARKE, WILL: ELLIOTT

At a Court of Hustings continued and held for the Town of Petersburg at the House of
WILLIAM DURELL Thursday the Seventh day of September 1786   An Indenture of Bargain and Sale between CHRISTOPHER McCONNICO of the Town of Petersburg of one part
and JOHN BAIRD JR. of the same place of other part was acknowledged by the said
CHRISTOPHER McCONNICO and is ordered to be recorded

Teste J. GRAMMER, Clk. C. Hs.

p.   THIS INDENTURE made this Twentieth dy of March in year of our Lord one
242   thousand seven hundred and Eighty Six Between CHARLES DUNCAN of the one
            part and JOHN SHORE of PRINCE GEORGE County of other part; Witnesseth that
for the sum of Forty pounds by JOHN SHORE unto CHARLES DUNCAN in hand paid, said
CHARLES DUNCAN by these presents doth bargain sell and confirm unto JOHN SHORE his
heirs all those two lotts or parcells of land lying on BLANDFORD HILL known in the
plan by the numbers (1 & 22), One and Twenty Two, To have and to hold the said lotts of
land and all the advantages apertaining thereunto unto JOHN SHORE his heirs, And
CHARLES DUNCAN for himself and his heirs doth covenant with JOHN SHORE his heirs
that he will for ever warrant and defend the title to said lotts of land (No. 1 & 22), num--
ber One and Twenty Two unto JOHN SHORE and his heirs against the lawfull claim of
every person; In Witness whereof the said CHARLES DUNCAN hath hereunto set his
hand and seal the day & year above written
Sign'd Sealed & deliv'd. in presence of

WILLIAM COLE, JOHN ANGUS,   CHARLES DUNCAN
PATK. WALKER, DAVID MAITLAND

Memorandum. The lotts of land within mentioned mark'd in the recorded plan of that
part of the Town of Petersburg call'd NEW BLANDFORD with the numbers (1 & 22), One
and Twenty Two, and noted thereon as the property of WILLIAM MURRAY and ROBERT
TURNBULL whereas in fact we the said WILLIAM MURRAY and ROBERT TURNBULL
never had the said lotts conveyed to us by the within granter or any other person.

Now we the said WILLIAM MURRAY and ROBERT TURNBULL to prevent all disputes
respecting the same and in consideration of the sum of Five shillings to each of us in
hand paid do hereby for ourselves our heirs release and for ever quit claim unto the
within named JOHN SHORE his heirs all our right title and demand in and to the said
lotts and all their appurtenances. In Witness whereof we have hereunto set our hand &
seals this Twenty second day of March one thousand seven hundred & Eighty six
Signed and Delivered in presence of

WILLIAM COLE,   WM. MURRAY
JAMES KING, THOS: WITHERS,   ROBT. TURNBULL
WILLIAM STAINBACK, PATRICK WALKER

At a Court of Hustings continued and held for the Town of Petersburg at the House of
WM. DURELL Thursday the Seventh day of September 1786   An Indenture of Bargain &
sale between CHARLES DUNCAN of CHESTERFEILD County of one part and JOHN SHORE of
PRINCE GEORGE County of other part was proved by the Oaths of WILLIAM COLE, JOHN

ANGUS & PATRICK WALKER, witnesses thereto, And the Memorandum of Relinquishment of WM. MURRAY & ROBERT TURNBULL which is thereon indorsed was proved by
the Oaths of WILLIAM COLE, THOS: WITHERS and PATRICK WALKER witnesses thereto &
together with the sd. Indenture are ordered to be recorded
                              Teste J. GRAMMER, Clk. C. Hs.

pp.   THIS INDENTURE made this Twenty third day of January in year of our Lord one
243-   thousand seven hundred & Eighty six Between ROBERT TURNBULL late of the
244   County of DINWIDDIE but now of the County of PRINCE GEORGE and Merchant in
           the Town of Petersburg of one part and JOHN BAIRD JR. and ALEXANDER McNABB
of County of DINWIDDIE & Town of Petersburg of other part; Witnesseth that ROBERT
TURNBULL for sum of One hundred & Seventy four pounds specia or hard money to him
in hand paid by JOHN BAIRD JR. & ALEXANDER McNABB, by these presents doth bargain
sell and confirm unto JNO: BAIRD JR. and ALEXANDER McNABB their heirs one certain
lott or half acre of land lying in the Old Town of Petersburg and on the North side of the
Street thereof and distinguished by the number Eighteen (18) extending in front on
said Street ninety feet and in the rear or depth thereof two hundred and sixty seven
feet according to the most ancient know & reputed plan thereof. And all houses profits
commodities and appertenances thereon; To have and to hold the lott of land No. 18
with appertenances unto JNO: BAIRD JR. and ALEXANDER McNABB their heirs as tenants
in common and not as joint tenants that is to say said JOHN BAIRD JR. one moiety or half
part thereof and ALEXANDER McNABB the other moiety or half part thereof; And
ROBERT TURNBULL and his heirs unto JOHN BAIRD JR. and ALEXANDER McNABB their
heirs as tenants in common as aforesaid against every person shall warrant and for
ever defend by these presents; In Witness whereof said ROBERT TURNBULL & MARY his
Wife have hereunto set their hands & affixed their seals the day and year at first within
written
Sealed & Delivered in presence of
         THOS: WITHERS,   ROBERT TURNBULL
         PATRICK WALKER,   JNO: FISHER
   Be it Known by all whom it may now or hereafter concern, that we the subscribers for
ourselves and our heirs have agreed to divide the within mentioned Lott No. 18 in the
following manner; that is to say, the said JOHN BAIRD JR. to have forty five (45) feet in
front on the lower corner of said lott and that width to the extreme depth thereof, it
being the half part wch: his adjoining Lott No. 17, And the said ALEXANDER McNABB to
have forty five (45) feet in front on the upper corner of said lott and that width to the
extreme depth thereof, it being the half part which his adjoining lott No. 19, the said
BAIRDs half of which lott is charged to him at L. 97; and the said McNABBs half of said
lott is charged to him at L. 87 or Eighty seven pounds in their Day Book of this days date
Witness our hands 31st January 1786   JNO: BAIRD JR.
                                              ALEXR. McNABB
   At a Court of Hustings continued and held for the Town of Petersburg at the House of
WM. DURELL in the said Town Thursday the Seventh day of September 1786
   An Indenture of Bargain and Sale between ROBERT TURNBULL of PRINCE GEORGE County of one part and JOHN BAIRD JR. & ALEXANDER McNABB of the Town of Petersburg of
other part was proved by the Oath of PATRICK WALKER, one of the witnesses thereto
and the same having been before proved by the Oaths of THOMAS WITHERS and JOHN
FISHER two other witnesses thereto, & the Memorandum thereon indorsed having been
before acknowledged by the said JOHN BAIRD JR. & ALEXANDER McNABB, parties thereto, together with the Indenture are ordered to be recorded
                              Teste J. GRAMMER, Clk. C. Hs.

pp.   THIS INDENTURE made the ninth day of July one thousand seven hundred and
245-   Eighty five Between ROBERT TURNBULL of County of PRINCE GEORGE in the
246   Commonwealth of Virginia, Merchant, of one part and SAINT GEORGE TUCKER of
          County of CHESTERFEILD of other part; Witnesseth that for the sum of Two hun-
dred pounds current money of Virginia by SAINT GEORGE TUCKER to ROBERT TURNBULL
in hand paid, said ROBERT TURNBULL by these presents doth bargain sell and confirm
unto SAINT GEORGE TUCKER his heirs those four lots of land which ROBERT TURNBULL
purchased of CHARLES DUNCAN situate in that part of the Town of Petersburg common-
ly called NEW BLANDFORD contiguous to each other and in the plan thereof
distinguished by the numbers Nine, Thirteen, Fourteen and Fifteen; as by said plan
now of Record may appear; the said lotts being situate as follows; that is to say, at a corner formed by two Streets intersecting each other at right angles in a point South fifty
seven and a half degrees West, three hundred and thirty three feet distant from the
South East corner of DOCTOR ISAAC HALLs lott where the same corners upon CHURCH
STREET and a Cross Street which intersect the same at right angles, and leads down to
the Meadow between NEW BLANDFORD and BOLLINGBROKE and from that corner first
mentioned extending South fifty seven and a half degrees West four hundred feet along
the said Cross Street, thence North fifty seven and a half degrees West two hundred and
thirty one feet, thence North thirty two and a half degrees East two hundred feet,
thence North fifty seven and a half degrees West to the Cross Street leading from the
South East corner of ALEXANDER TAYLORs lott in OLD BLANDFORD to the Meadow, thence
along that Street one hundred feet, thence South thirty two and a half degrees East to
the North West Corner of Lott number Fifteen, thence North thirty two and a half degrees East one hundred feet to the Street, thence South thirty two and a half degrees
East along the said Street to the first mentioned Corner, the said Four lotts containing
Two acres and a half of land and the rents issues & profits thereof; To have and to hold
the four lotts and each of them with appertenances unto SAINT GEORGE TUCKER his
heirs, And ROBERT TURNBULL and his heirs the lots unto SAINT GEORGE TUCKER his
heirs against every person shall warrant and defend for ever by these presents; In
Witness whereof the said ROBERT TURNBULL hath set his hand and affixed his seal to
these presents the day & year first above written
Sealed and Delivered in the presence of
          S. G. TUCKER Jr., TH: BRODNAX,   ROBERT TURNBULL
          B. STARK,
          FRANCIS MUIR, U. MARCK   ) Acknowledged March
          P. MINOR   ) PRINCE GEORGE Court
    Memorandum, July ninth 1785. Received of SAINT GEORGE TUCKER Two hundred
pounds current money of Virginia being the consideration money within mentioned
Witness S. G. TUCKER JR.   ROBERT TURNBULL
          TH: BRODNAX, B. STARK
          FRAS: MUIR, P. MINOR   ) Reacknowledged PRINCE
          U. MARCK   ) GEORGE March Court
    At a Court of Hustings continued & held for the Town of Petersburg at the House of WM.
DURELL in the said town Thursday the Seventh day of September 1786
    An Indenture of Bargain and Sale between ROBERT TURNBULL of the County of PRINCE
GEORGE of one part and ST. GEORGE TUCKER of CHESTERFEILD County of other part was
proved by the Oaths of FRANCIS MUIR, PETER MINOR and URICK MARCK witnesses
thereto and together with the receipt thereon indorsed are ordered to be recorded
                        Teste J. GRAMMER, Clk. C. Hs.

p.
247
THIS INDENTURE made this 30th day of September in year of our Lord one thousand seven hundred & Eighty five or 85 Between WM. DURELL & ELIZA: his Wife of the Town & Borough of Petersburg in the County of DINWIDDIE of one part and JOHN CRUMPLER of the same place of other part; Witnesseth that WILLIAM DURELL & ELIZA: his Wife in consideration of JOHN CRUMPLER having built and erected on the land and lot of said DURELL which lott is No. 45, one certain House 16 by 30 feet by these presents do bargain sell & confirm unto JOHN CRUMPLER and to his heirs a moiety or half of the aforesaid land or Lott No. 45 now to him the said WILLIAM DURELL properly belonging which Lott No. 45 lies in the Town of Petersburg and on South side of the Street thereof and which half of said lott is laid off to said CRUMPLER and bounded Begining at the North West corner of the sd. Lott No. 45 on the Street where it adjoins lott No. 44 belonging to MRS. ELIZA: SPENCER, and from thence in front on the Street Easterly forty five feet, and from thence in a direct line Southwardly to the extreme depth of the said lott and from thence Westwardly forty five feet where the said Lott No. 45 adjoins the lott No. 44 belonging to MRS. ELIZA: SPENCER, and from thence Northwardly as the lines of said lotts run to the place at first begun at on the Street, with all houses yards gardens profits & appertenances thereunto belonging; To have and to hold the said moiety or half of said lott No. 45 unto JOHN CRUMPLER his heirs, And WILLIAM DURELL & ELIZA: his Wife their heirs the half of sd. Lott No. 45 unto JOHN CRUMPLER his heirs shall warrant and for ever defend by these presents; In Witness whereof said WM. DURELL & ELIZA: his Wife have hereunto set their hands and affixed their seals the day & year first within written

Sealed & Delivered in presence of
     JNO: BAIRD JR.   WM. DURELL
     JNO MacRAE, THOMAS POLLARD

At a Court of Hustings continued and held for the Town of Petersburg at WM. DURELLs in said Town Thursday the Seventh day of September 1786   An Indenture of Bargain and Sale between WILLIAM DURELL & ELIZA: his Wife of the Town of Petersburg of one part and JOHN CRUMPLER of the other part was acknowledged by the said WILLIAM DURELL & together with the memorandum of Livery & Seizen thereon indorsed are ordered to be recorded   Teste J. GRAMMER, Clk. C. Hs.

(Pages 248 and 249 are blank.)

pp.
250-
252
THIS INDENTURE made this Twenty fifth day of May Anno Domini one thousand seven hundred and Eighty six Between RICHARD HILL Esquire of the Town of Petersburg of one part and JOHN KILLEN and JOHN JEFFERS, Merchants and Partners under the Firm of KILLEN & JEFFERS, of the same Town of other part: Witnesseth that RICHARD HILL for sum of Five hundred & fifty pounds current money to him in hand paid by said KILLEN & JEFFERS, And also for the Rents covenants and agrements hereinafter specified to be paid and performed by said KILLEN & JEFFERS their heirs, said RICHARD HILL by these presents doth bargin sell make over and confirm unto said KILLEN & JEFFERS their heirs all his title and term of years yet to come in one certain parcel of land situate In Town of Petersburg and is part of a lott of land which said RICHARD purchased & holds of ROBERT BOLLING Esquire as by Indenture bearing date the first day of June 1784 recorded in the Court of the County of DINWIDDIE distinguished by the number Forty Eight (No. 48), which portion or parcell of land is bounded; Beginning for the same at the South East corner of said Lott (No. 48), where it adjoins lott No. Forty Nine on the North side of BOLLINGBROOK STREET, thence Northerly binding on Lott (No. 49) one hundred feet to an Alley, thence West along the said Alley twenty four feet; thence Southly from the said Alley one hundred feet to BOL-

LINGBROOK STREET, thence East along said Street twenty four feet to the begining; Together with the benefits and priviledges in Common of an Alley on West side of the same comprehending the space of Ground to a Store House now erect next adjoining thereto; And all buildings Improvements streets alleys benefits and advantages to said portion of land belonging; To have and to hold the portion of land to KILLEN & JEFFERS and assigns during the term yet to come and expiration of Ninety nine years computing from the first day of January one thousand seven hundred and Eighty four on payment of one years Ground Rent over and above the Ground Rent reserved by this Indenture as a fine for the same; said KILLEN and JEFFERS and their assigns paying therefor to ROBERT BOLLING Esqr. of BOLLINGBROOK and his assigns (for and on account of said RICHARD HILL his heirs) the sum of Fourteen pounds three shillings current money per annum Ground Rent; In Witness whereof the parties hereto have set their hands and their seals the day & year first above written

Sealed & Delivered in the presence of this seventeenth day
of August Anno Domini one thousand seven hundred &
Eighty six   PATRICK WHITE,   RICHD. HILL.
     JOHN ONEILL, DOMINICK JEFFERS   KILLEN & JEFFERS

Petersburg the 25th May 1786. Received of KILLEN & JEFFERS the sum of Five hundred & fifty pounds in full of the consideration money within mentioned
                              RD. HILL

At a Court of Hustings continued & held for the Town of Petersburg at the House of WM. DURELL in the said Town Thursday the Seventh day of September 1786

An Indenture of Bargain and Sale between RICHARD HILL of Town of Petersburg oe one part and KILLEN & JEFFERS of the same place of the other part was proved by the Oaths of PATRICK WHITE, JOHN ONEILL and DOMINICK JEFFERS witnesses thereto and ordered to be recorded   Teste J. GRAMMER, Clk. C. Hs.

p.   THIS INDENTURE made this Seventh day of September in year of our Lord one
253   thousand seven hundred and Eighty five Between CHARLES DUNCAN of CHESTER-
          FEILD County (Merchant) of one part and JOHN ANGUS of County of DINWIDDIE & Town of Petersburg of other part; Witnesseth that CHARLES DUNCAN for the full sum of Forty pounds to him in hand paid by JOHN ANGUS, by these presents do bargain sell & confirm unto JOHN ANGUS his heirs all that lott of ground lying in the New Town of BLANDFORD being the lott number Ninety Seven; To have & to hold the said parcell of ground with all improvements & appertenances thereunto belonging to JOHN ANGUS his heirs; And CHARLES DUNCAN his heirs the lott of ground unto JOHN ANGUS his heirs shall warrant and forever defend against any person claiming any right or title to the same; In Witness whereof he (the said CHARLES DUNCAN) have hereunto set his hand & seal the day & year above written

Sign'd Seal'd & Deliver'd in presence of
     HENRY MORRISS,   CHARLES DUNCAN
     ALEXR. GLASS STRACHAN, ERASMUS GILL

Whereas the Lott within mentioned and marked upon the Plan within mentioned Town of NEW BLANDFORD as the property of WILLIAM COLEMAN, Now I thesaid WILLIAM COLEMAN do by these presents relinquish all right and title to the said lott to the within named JOHN ANGUS, In Testimony thereof I the sd. WILLIAM COLEMAN hereunto set my hand & afixed my seal this third day of May one thousand seven hundred & eighty six
Test T. G. PEACHY   WILLIAM COLEMAN
     ALEXANDER WILL

At a Court of Hustings continued and held for the Town of Petersburg at the House of WM. DURELL in the said Town Thursday the Seventh day of September 1786

An Indenture of Bargain and Sale between CHARLES DUNCAN of the County of CHESTERFEILD of one part and JOHN ANGUS of the Town of Petersburg of the other part was proved by the Oath of ERASMUS GILL a witness thereto and the same having been before proved by the Oaths of HENRY MORRISS and ALEXANDER GLASS STRACHAN other witnesses thereto, together with the Relinquishment of WM. COLEMAN thereon indorsed which was proved by the Oaths of THOMAS GRIFFIN PEACHY and ALEXANDER WILL witnesses thereto are ordered to be recorded

Teste J. GRAMMER, Clk. C. Hs.

(Page 254 is blank.)

pp.   A MEMORIAL of all Bargains, Sales, Mortgages and other Conveyances acknow-
255-   ledged or proved and recorded in the Hustings Court of the Town of Petersburg
256   between 1st day of April and the first day of October 1786.

(The headings of various columns are as follows: Deed & Date; Names Surnames & addition of parties; consideration expressed, Quantity & situation of the Land, number & names of the slaves, discription of the personal Estate; When acknowledged or proved & recorded).

Bargain & Sale June 1st 1786. JOSEPH HARDWAY & MARY his Wife to DAVID VAUGHAN. L. 175. One lott land in RAVENSCROFT No. 33 containing three acres; 7th June 1786;

Lease for 99 years 5th June 1786. MARY BOLLING & ROBT. BOLLING to JOHN ANDREWS LAUSATT, L. 200 purchase & L. 28 p annum; one lott 100 feet square near BLANDFORD WAREHOUSE, 7th June 1786.

Bargain & Sale 12th April 1786. PHILIP W. JACKSON to JOHN ANGUS, L. 40., one lott in NEW BLANDFORD No.48; 7th June 1786

Bargain & Sale 7th Sept. 1785. JOHN ANGUS to SAMUEL DEMOVELL, L. 80; one lott in NEW BLANDFORD No. 37; 7th June 1786;

Bargain & Sale 8th Sept. 1786 JOHN McCLOUD to WM. PARSONS JR., L. 100; one Lott in NEW BLANDFORD No. 54; 7th June 1786.

Bargain & Sale 20th Jany. 1786. THOMAS RICHARDS & MARTHA his Wife to SILAS SANDFORD. L. 40., One Lott in POCOHONTASS No. 8 and one ditto on the River No. 8, 7th June 1786.

Bargain & Sale 1st May 1786. CHARLES DUNCAN to the Revd. JNO: CAMERON, 2000 lbs. Inspected Tobacco; One lott NEW BLANDFORD No. 83., 7th June 1786.

Bargain & Sale 22d. March 1786. CHARLES DUNCAN to JOSEPH SELDEN, 2000 lbs. Tobacco; One lott NEW BLANDFORD No. 96, 7th June 1786.

Mortgage 9th April 1786. WILLIAM HART to THOMAS HOPE, 5/ & for securing paymt. of L. 150; The remainder of a Lease for a House on PHILIP OTTs Lott, also 2 Negroes a boy Stephen & girl Violet 7th June 1786.

Bargain & Sale 11th May 1786. RICHARD WITTON to WM. ROWLETT JR. L. 15. One lott or half acre in POCOHONTAS No. 31, 7th June 1786

Bargain & Sale 11th May 1786. RICHARD WITTON to ROYALL BRITTON, L. 15. One lott or 1/2 acre in POCOHONTAS No. 14, 7th June 1786.

Bargain & Sale 28th June 1785. ANDREW HAMILTON, JAS. CAMPBELL & JOHN BAIRD JR., Exors. of JAS: TURNBULL deced. to WM. GREGG, L. 900; a House & part of Lott No. 19 on BOLLING BROOK STREET, 7th June 1786.

Bargain & Sale 26th April 1786. RICHARD YARBROUGH to SAMUEL LOGAN, L. 600 & 40/ p annum Ground Rent for ever; part of Lott No. 27 on B. BROOK STREET, 7th June 1786

Bargain & Sale 20th March 1786. CHARLES DUNCAN & JANE his Wife to DANIEL FISHER, L. 40. Two lotts land NEW BLANDFORD No. 68 7 91. 7th June 1786

Bargain & Sale 22d. April 1785; SHORE & McCONNICO to JAMES COLQUHOUN & CO., L. 150 purchase & L. 10 p annum for ever; part of Lott on BOOLING BOOK No. 38; 5th July 1786

Bargain & Sale March 1st 1786. RICHARD WITTON to HENRY MORRISS, L. 25., one lott in POCO-HONTASS No. 67 & Marsh adjoining, 5th July 1786

Bargain & Sale 2d. May 1786. CHARLES DUNCAN to PETER RANDOLPH; 6000 lbs. Tobacco; Three lotts in NEW BLANDFORD No. 53, 69 & 88; 5th July 1786

Bargain & Sale 3d. May 1786; CHARLES DUNCAN to ALEXANDER TAYLOR, 2000 lbs. Tobacco, one lott in New Blandord No. 49; 5th July 1786.

Bargain & Sale 3d. May 1786. CHARLES DUNCAN to ANDREW HAMILTON, 2000 lbs. Tobacco. one Lott in NEW BLANDFORD, No. 89. 5th July 1786

Bargain & Sale 2d. June 1786; RICHARD YARBROUGH & SARAH his Wife to CUGNEAU & SUBER-CASAUX & PETER JOHN CAUVY; L. 200 purchase, & L. 6 p annum for ever; part of a lott purchased of ROBERT BOLLING on BOLLING BROOK; 5th July 1786;

Bargain & Sale 3d. Feb: 1786. WILLIAM HARRISON to HENRY VAUGHAN, L. 100; Part of two Lotts in RAVENSCROFT No. 9 & 10; 5th July 1786;

Bargain & Sale 11th March 1784. THOMAS GORDON to ANN PORTLOCK, L. 100; one lott or 1/2 acre in OLD PETERSBURG No. 37, August 2d. 1786

Bargain & Sale 1st Maya 1786. CHARLES DUNCAN & JANE his Wife to WILLIAM STARK JR., L. 100 one Lott NEW BLANDFORD No. 40. 7th Sept. 1786

Deed of gift 28th Augt. 1786. MARY BOLLING to THOMAS TABB BOLLING; 39 Negroes (named as in the Deed); 7th Sept. 1786;

Bargain & Sale 27th June 1786; CHRISTOPHER McCONNICO to JOHN BAIRD JR., L. 375; one lott or half acre in OLD REVENSCROFT No. 24; 7th Sept. 1786

Bargain & Sale 20th March 1786. CHARLES DUNCAN to JOHN SHORE, L. 40., Two lotts NEW BLANDFORD No. 1 & 22; 7th Septembr. 1786.

Bargain & Sale 3d. Jany. 1786. ROBERT TURNBULL to JOHN BAIRD JR. & ALEXR. McNABB, L. 174; One lott or 1/2 acre in OLD PETERSBURG No. 18; 7th Septembr. 1786;

Bargain & Sale 12d. July 1785; ROBERT TURNBULL to ST. GEORGE TUCKER L. 200; Four lotts NEW BLANDFORD No. 9, 13, 14, & 15. 7th Septembr: 1786;

Bargain & Sale 30th Sept. 1785; WILLIAM DURELL & ELIZABETH his Wife to JOHN CRUMPLER, Building a House 30 by 16 feet, half of a lott or 1/2 acre in OLD PETERSBURG No. 48; 7th Sept. 1786;

Lease for 99 years renewable &c., 25th May 1786; RICHARD HILL to KILLEN & JEFFERS, L. 550 purchase, L. 14/3 p annum; part of Lott on B. BROOK No. 48. 7th Septembr. 1786

Bargain & Sale 7th Sept. 1785. CHARLES DUNCAN to JOHN ANGUS. L. 40. One Lott NEW BLAND-FORD No. 97; 7th September 1786.

pp. 257-258   THIS INDENTURE made this Twenty first day of January one thousand seven hundred and Eighty six Between the REVD. WILLIAM HARRISON and LUCY his Wife of Town of Petersburg of one part and JAMES BROMLY of said Town of other part; Witnesseth that for the sum of Three hundred pounds specia by said JAMES to said WILLIAM in hand paid, said WILLIAM HARRISON & LUCY his Wife by these presents do bargain and sell unto JAMES BROMLY his heirs one lott of land lying in Town of Petersburg and in that part of said Town known by the name of RAVENSCROFT and distinguished in the plan by the number (11), say Eleven, containing by estimation three acres be the same more or less, & further said WILLIAM & LUCY his Wife do hereby bargain and sell unto said JAMES his heirs one small lott of land lying in said Town & also in that part known by name of RAVENSCROFT adjoining said lott number Eleven, & begining on the line between numbers Eleven and Twelve five feet above where the Spring which is on number Twelve now stands, and extending thence in a right angle with the dividing line which divides numbers Eleven & Twelve into said lott number

Twelve untill it passes the South side of the Gum which which is now in the Spring on
lott number Twelve; thence on lott number Twelve paralel with the dividing line ten
feet, thence on said lott number Twelve in a line which shall intersect the said dividing
line of number Eleven & Twelve in a right angle & shall include the Spring which is
on Lott number Twelve, And the rents profits and issues thereof; To have and to hold
the lot of land unto JAMES BROMLY his heirs and WILLIAM HARRISON & LUCY his Wife
for themselves & their heirs the said lotts of land to JAMES BROMLY his heirs will warrant & forever defend; In Witness whereof said WM. HARRISON & LUCY his Wife have
hereunto set their hands and affixed their seals the day & year first above written
Signed Sealed & Delivered in presence of

WILLIAM COLE, BAKER PEGRAM,   WILLIAM HARRISON
NOEL WADDILL,   JOHN HICKS   LUCY HARRISON

The Commonwealth of Virginia to ROBERT BOLLING and ALEXANDER McNABB Gentlemen Greeting; Whereas (the Commission for the privy Examination of LUCY, the Wife of
WILLIAM HARRISON); Witness JOHN GRAMMER Clerk of our said Court this Tenth day of
February in the Tenth year of the Commonwealth   J. GRAMMER
By Virtue of the Commission hereto annexed, this Indenture was acknowledged by the
hereto subscribed LUCY HARRISON on the Eleventh day of February 1786, the said LUCY
being first privily and apart from the said WILLIAM HARRISON her Husband examined;
(the return of the execution of the privy Examination of LUCY HARRISON); before us

ROBERT BOLLING JR.
ALEXR: McNABB

At a Court of Hustings held for the Town of Petersburg at DURELLs in the said Town
Wednesday the Fourth day of October 1786   An Indenture of Bargain and Sale between the REVD. WILLIAM HARRISON & LUCY his Wife of one part and JAMES BROMLY
of the other part was proved by the Oaths of WILLIAM COLE, NOEL WADDILL and JOHN
HICKS witnesses thereto and with the Commission annexed & the Certificate of the execution thereof are ordered to be recorded

Teste J. GRAMMER, Clk, C. Hs.

pp.   THIS INDENTURe made this Twenty first day of January one thousand seven
259-   hundred and Eighty six Between WILLIAM HARRISON & LUCY his Wife of one
260   part & JAMES BROMLY of the Town of Petersburg of other part; Witnesseth that
        in consideration of the sum of One hundred pounds paid by said BROMLY to said
HARRISON, by these presents doth bargain sell & confirm two certain pieces of land
lying in Town of Petersburg & situated in that part of it called RAVENSCROFT, each piece
containing One hundred & twenty feet by One hundred and Sixty, the one piece being
the North East corner of lot number Ten in the plot of RAVENSCROFT TOWN, & the other
piece lying in the South East corner of lot number Nine of the same PLot; Together with
all houses & priviledges belonging; To have & to hold the two pieces of land & all the
appertenances unto JAMES BROMLY his heirs. And WILLIAM HARRISON and LUCY his
Wife for themselves & their heirs &c. the pieces of land unto said BROMLY shall warrant & forever defend by these presents against the claims of all persons; In Witness
whereof they have hereunto set their hands and affixed their seals the day & year
above written
Signed Sealed & delivered in the presence of

NOEL WADDILL, WILLIAM COLE,   WILLIAM HARRISON
BAKER PEGRAM,   JOHN HICKS   LUCY HARRISON

The Commonwealth of Virginia to ROBERT BOLLING and ALEXR. McNABB Gentlemen
Greeting, Whereas (the Commission for the privy Examination of LUCY, the Wife of WILLIAM

HARRISON): Witness JOHN GRAMMER Clerk of our said Court the Tenth day of February in the tenth year of the Commonwealth   J. GRAMMER

By Virtue of the Commission hereunto annexed, this Indenture was acknowledged by the thereto subscribed LUCY HARRISON on the 11th day of February 1786, she the said LUCY being first privily and apart from the said WILLIAM HARRISON her Husband examined; (the return of the execution of the privy Examination of LUCY HARRISON), before us

ROBERT BOLLING JR.
ALEXR. McNABB

At a Court of Hustings held for the Town of Petersburg at DURELLs in the said Town Wednesday the Fourth day of October 1786   An Indenture of Bargain and Sale between the REVD. WILLIAM HARRISON and LUCY his Wife of one part and JAMES BROMLY of the other part was proved by the Oaths of NOEL WADDILL, WILLIAM COLE and JOHN HICKS witnesses thereto and together with the Commission annexed and the Certificate of execution thereof are ordered to be recorded

Teste J. GRAMMER, Clk. C. Hs.

pp.   THIS INDENTURE made this Twenty eighth day of September one thousand
261-   seven hundred and Eighty five Between RICHARD HILL Esquire of the Town of
262   Petersburg of one part and WILLIAM WADDILL of CITY of RICHMOND of other
           part: Witnesseth that in consideration of One hundred and Eighty pounds, Ten
shillings current money to said RICHARD HILL in hand paid by WILLIAM WADDILL, said RICHARD HILL by these presents doth bargain sell and to Farm Lett unto WILLIAM WADDILL his heirs a certain part of a lott of land in Town of Petersburg laid out into Lotts by ROBERT BOLLING Esquire by the number (43), Forty Three, and is bounded, Begining at the South West corner of said lott on BOLLINGBROOK STREET, from thence along the Street Easterly Forty six feet, thence Northerly one hundred and twenty feet to the back line of said lott, thence along the same Westerly forty six feet to the Northwest corner thereof, and from thence Southerly to BOLLINGBROOK STREET the begining; Together with all priviledges & appertenances belonging; To have and to hold the portion of land dto WILLIAM WADDILL his heirs during the full term of Ninety nine years to commence from the first day of January next, paying therefor unto ROBERT BOLLING Esquire of BOLLING BROOK his heirs (for and on account of RICHARD HILL his heirs & for no other purpose) the Rent of Five pounds current money annually, the first years rent to grow due and payable on the first day of January one thousand seven hundred & Eighty seven; In Witness whereof the parties aforesaid have hereunto set their hands and affixed their seals the day and year first above written
Sealed and Delivered in the presence of

JAMES GEDDY, RO: WATKINS.   RD. HILL
JOHN GRAMMER   )   WM. WADDILL
WILLIAM BARR   ) on part of WADDILL
ROBERT GRAMMER   )

At a Hustings Court held for the Town of Petersburg at DURRELLs in the said Town Wednesday the fourth day of October 1786   An Indenture of Lease between RICHARD HILL of one part and WILLIAM WADDILL of other part ws proved on the part of WILLIAM WADDILL by the Oaths of JAMES GEDDY, JOHN GRAMMER and ROBERT GRAMMER, witnesses thereto and the same having been acknowledged by said RICHARD HILL, together with the memorandum of livery & seizen thereon indorsed are ordered to be recorded   Teste J. GRAMMER, Clk. C. Hs.

(Pages 263 and 264 are blank.)

p.   THIS INDENTURE made this Eleventh day of November in year of our Lord one
265   thousand seven hundred and Eighty six Between RICHARD WITTON of County of
          MECKLENBURG and THOMAS SHORE of County of CHESTERFEILD, Witnesseth that
for the sum of Five pounds in hand paid by THOMAS SHORE said RICHARD WITTON hath
bargained and sold unto THOMAS SHORE his heirs one certain lott of land lying in that
part of the Corporation of Petersburg called POAKAHUNTAS and known by (No. 5), Five,
with a small lott of the same number & belonging to said lott on the side of APPOMATTOX
RIVER; To have and to hold the parcells of land with the appurtainances unto THOMAS
SHORE his heirs; and RICHARD WITTON for himself his heirs will warrant and forever
defend the title of said parcells of land unto THOMAS SHROE his heirs against the claims
of every person; In Witness whereof the said RICHARD WITTON have hereunto set his
hand and affixed his seal the day & year above written
     Witness HENRY MORRISS, WILLIAM STARK JR.,   RICHARD WITTON
          FREDRICK ADLER, CHARLES JOHNSTON
Petersburg November 11th 1786. Recd. of THOMAS SHORE Five pounds in full of the
within consideration and have given full and peaceable possession of the within
mentioned lotts unto the said THOMAS SHORE   RICHD. WITTON
At a Hustings Court held for the Town of Petersburg at DURELLs in the said Town
Wednesday the Sixth day of December 1786   An Indenture of Bargain and Sale be-
tween RICHARD WITTON of the County of MECKLENBURG and THOMAS SHORE of the
County of CHESTERFEILD was proved by the Oaths of HENRY MORRISS, WILLIAM STARK
JR. and FREDRICK ADLER witnesses thereto and together with the Receipt thereon in-
dorsed are ordered to be recorded   Teste J. GRAMMER, Clk. C. Hs.

p.   THIS INDENTURE made this third day of May in year of our Lord one thousand
266   seven hundred and Eighty six Between CHARLES DUNCAN of CHESTERFEILD
          County of one part and WILLIAM COLVIN of County of CHESTERFEILD of other
part; Witnesseth that CHARLES DUNCAN for sum of Two thousand pounds weight of Merchantable Crop Tobacco in hand paid to CHARLES DUNCAN, by these presents doth bargain sell and confirm unto WILLIAM COLVIN his heirs all those lotts of ground lying on
BLANDFORD HILL known in the plan of a Town lately laid out on said Hill by the number
Thirty Eight, To have and to hold the said lott of ground with all advantages appertaining thereto to WILLIAM COLVIN his heirs; And CHARLES DUNCAN doth for himself
his heirs covenant with WILLIAM COLVIN his heirs that he will for ever warrant and
defend the lott of ground unto WILLIAM COLVIN his heirs against the lawfull claim of
every person; In Witness whereof the said CHARLES DUNCAN hath hereunto set his
hand and seal the day and year above written
Sealed & Delivered in presence of
          WILLIAM COLEMAN, JOSEPH WESTMORE,   CHARLES DUNCAN
          WILLIAM COLE, JOHN FISHER
Whereas the Lott within mentioned is marked upon the plan of the within mentioend
Town of NEW BLANDFORD as the property of WILLIAM GILLIAM, Now I said WM.
GILLIAM do by these presents relinquish all right & title to the said lott to the within
named WILLIAM COLVIN his heirs & assigns, In Testimony whereof I the said WILLIAM
GILLIAM have hereunto set my hand & affixed my seal this Third day of May in year
one thousand seven hudnred & Eighty six
Test WILLIAM COLE,   WILLIAM GILLIAM
     JOHN FISHER, A. WALKER
At a Hustings Court held for the Town of Petersburg at DURELLs in the said Town
Wednesday the Sixth day of December 1786   An Indenture of Bargain and Sale between

CHARLES DUNCAN of CHESTERFEILD County of one part and WILLIAM COLVIN of the same County of other part was proved by the Oath of JOHN FISHER a witness thereto & haveing been before proved by the Oaths of WILLIAM COLE, JOSEPH WESTMORE and WILLIAM COLEMAN, other witnesses thereto, And the Relinquishment of WM. GILLIAM thereon indorsed was also proved by the Oath of JOHN FISHER & ALEXANDER WALKER witnesses thereto & the same having been before proved by the Oath of WILLIAM COLE another witness thereto, together with the said Indenture are ordered to be recorded
Teste J. GRAMMER, Clk. C. Hs.

p.   THIS INDENTURE made the 3d. day of May in year of our Lord one thousand
267   seven hundred and Eight six Between CHARLES DUNCAN of County of CHESTER-
       FEILD of one part and NATHANIEL COCKE of State of GEORGIA of other part; Witnesseth that for sum of Five Shillings by said NATHANIEL to said CHARLES in hand paid said CHARLES DUNCAN by these presents doth bargain and sell unto NATHANIEL COCKE his heirs three lots of land lying in that part of Petersburg called NEW BLANDFORD and in the plan by the number Thirty Two, Thirty Five and Thirty Five: To have and to hold the three lotts of land unto NATHANIEL COCKE his heirs and CHARLES DUNCAN for himself & his heirs the three lotts of land unto NATHANIEL COCKE his heirs will warrant & forever defend. In Witness whereof the said CHARLES DUNCAN hath hereunto set his hand and affixed his Seal the day and year first above written
Signed Sealed & Delivd. in presence of
    THOS: WITHERS, PATRICK WALKER,   CHARLES DUNCAN
    NOEL WADDILL, JOHN FISHER
At a Hustings Court held for the Town of Petersburg at DURELLs in the said Town Wednesday the Sixth day of December 1786   An Indenture of Bargain and Sale between CHARLES DUNCAN of CHESTERFEILD County of one part and NATHANIEL COCKE of the State of GEORGIA of other part was proved by the Oaths of THOMAS WITHERS, PATRICK WALKER and JOHN FISHER, witnesses thereto and is ordered to be recorded
Teste J. GRAMMER, Clk. C. Hs.

p.   KNOW ALL MEN by these presents that I GEORGE C. LEACY of PRINCE GEORGE
268   County in consideration of the sum of Six hundred & three pounds, Six shillings
       &7d., Virga. currency to me in hand paid by WILLIAM DAVIES of the same County, by these presents do bargain sell or confirm unto WILLIAM DAVIES his heirs one Negro woman slave named Phillis & her increase, one Negro boy called George & one other Negro boy named Edmunds, on other boy named Archer, and one other boy called Miles; To have and to hold the said Negro Phillis and the said Negro boy slaves to WILLIAM DAVIES his heirs; Provided always & it is hereby agreed between the said parties, that if GEORGE C. LEACY or assigns shall truly pay or cause to be paid unto WILLIAM DAVIES or assigns the sum of Six hundred & three pounds, Six shillings & 7d., afsd. agreable payable at the option of said GEORGE C. LEACY his heirs in Military Audited Certificates of the State of Virginia with all the Interest then due therefor on or before the Eighteenth day of September next for the Redemption of the said slaves, for which sum I have executed my Bond bearing even date with these presents, then these presents shall cease & be void otherwise to remain in full force & effect. In Witness whereof I the said GEORGE C. LEACY have hereunto set my hand and seal this Eighteenth day of April 1786
Sealed & Delivered in presence of
    W. COLMAN, PEGGY DAVIES,   GEORGE C. LEACY
    ALEXR. TAYLOR, MICAJAH H. HOLLINSHEAD

At a Court of Hustings held for the Town of Petersburg at DURELLs in the said Town,
Wednesday the Sixth day of December 1786   A Mortgage of GEORGE C. LEACY of the
County of PRINCE GEORGE to WILLIAM DAVIES of the same County was acknowled: by the
said GEORGE C. LEACY and is ordered to be recorded
                              Teste J. GRAMMER, Clk. C. Hs.

p.   KNOW ALL MEN by these presents that I GEORGE C. LEACY of PRINCE GEORGE
269   County am held & firmly bound unto WILLIAM DAVIES of the same County in the
          just & full sum of Six hundred and Three pounds, six shillings & 7d., payable at
my option in Military Audited Certificates of Virginia to be paid to said WILLIAM
DAVIES & assigns, which payment well & truly to be made I bind myself my heirs by
these presents; Sealed with my seal this Eighteenth day of April 1786
   The Condition of the above obligation is such that if the above bounded GEORGE C. LACY
shall on or before the Eighteenth day of September next pay or cause to be paid to the
said WILLIAM DAVIES or assigns the sum of Six hundred & three pounds, six shillings &
7d., payable at the option of said LACY his heirs in Military Audited Certificates of Virginia with the interest due thereon from the first day of January last, then the above
obligation to be void or else to remain in full force & virtue
Sealed & Delivered in presence of
          ALEXR. TAYLOR,   PEGGY DAVIES,   GEORGE C. LEACY
          WM. COLEMAN, MICAJAH H. HOLLINSHEAD
   At a Hustings Court held for the Town of Petersburg at DURELLs in the said Town,
Wednesday the Sixth day of December 1786   An Obligation or Bond from GEORGE C.
LEACY of the County of PRINCE GEORGE to WILLIAM DAVIES of the same County was ack-
nowledged by the said GEORGE C.LEACY and ordered to be recorded
                              Teste J. GRAMMER, Clk. C. Hs.

p.   KNOW ALL MEN by these presents that I ROBT. BOLLING of County of DINWIDDIE
270   for divers good causes me thereunto moving hath (by Virtue of a certain Act of
          General Assembly passed at RICHMOND in the month of May & Anno Domini one
thousand seven hundred & Eighty two, intitled "An Act to Authorise the Manumission of
slaves," do by these presents emancipate & set free a certain woman slave named Betty
and I do hereby for myself my heirs release all claim property interest or demand
which I now have ever had or may hereafter have in & to the service of the said Betty
& her future increase, hereby declaring her emancipated & free to all intents & purposes whatsoever & entitled to enjoy every advantage of Freedom which is in my power
to give or grant her by virtue of the aforesaid Act of Assembly; And I do hereby oblige
myself my heirs never to disturb molest or interupt the said Betty or her future
increase in the full enjoyment of every the aforesaid priviledges and immunities; In
Witness whereof I have hereunto set my hand & affixed my Seal this Fourth day of July
Anno Domini one thousand seven hundred & Eighty six
Test RICHD. GREGORY   ROBERT BOLLING
   At a Hustings Court held for the Town of Petesburg at DURELLs in the said Town,
Wednesday the Sixth day of December 1786   A Deed of Emanumission or Emancipation
from ROBERT BOLLING to his Negroe slave Betty was presented in Court and acknow-
ledged by the said ROBERT BOLLING and ordered to be recorded
                              Teste J. GRAMMER, Clk. C. Hs.

p.   THIS INDENTURE made the Twenty Ninth day of November in year of our Lord
271   one thousand seven hundred and Eighty six Between ERASMUS GILL and SARAH
          his Wife of Town of Petersburg of one part and ANN THOMSON of said Town of

other part; Witnesseth that ERASMUS GILL and SARAH his Wife for sum of Three hundred pounds current money to them in hand paid by ANN THOMPSON, by these presents
do bargain sell and confirm unto ANN THOMSON and to her heirs one lott of land containing One Acre adjoining the lotts of the late JOHN THOMPSON deced. in the Town of
Petersburg and numbered Fifteen, also One Acre of land adjoining said Lott extending
forty six yards and an half from the corner of said lott along the Road towards the
GRAVE YARD, and then a course parellel with the lotts of the Town one hundred yards
three inches to the BRICKHOUSE RUN, then the same course as the back line of the Town
to a corner Stone of said lott, and along the line of the lott to the beginning on the
Street, To have and to hold the Two Acres of land with all the premises belonging unto
ANN THOMPSON her heirs; And ERASMUS GILL and SARAH his Wife for themselves and
their heirs the two acres of land with the appertenances to ANN THOMPSON and her
heirs will warrant and forever by these presents defend against the claim of all
persons whatsoever; In Witness whereof the said ERASMUS GILL and SARAH his Wife
have hereunto set their hands and seals the day and year first above written.
Signed Sealed and Delivered in presence of

        CHARLES LOGAN,   ERASMUS GILL

        E. JNO: COLLETT,   SARAH GILL

        THOS: SHORE

Petersburg 29th November 1786. The recieved of ANN THOMPSON the sum of Three
hundred pounds specia in full consideration of the within as witness our hands & seals
the day & date before written

Witness THOS: SHORE   ERASMUS GILL

                                     SARAH GILL

  At a Hustings Court held for the Town of Petersburg at DURELLs in the said Town,
Wednesday the Sixth day of December 1786   An Indenture of Bargain and Sale be-
tween ERASMUS GILL and SARAH his Wife of Town of Petersburg of one part and ANN
THOMPSON of the same Town of other part was acknowledged by the said ERASMUS GILL
& SARAH his Wife (she the said SARAH being first privily examined as the Law directs)
and together with the receipt thereon indorsed are ordered to be recorded

                       Atteste J. GRAMMER, Clk. C. Hs.

pp.   THIS INDENTURE made this 31st day of October in year of our Lord one thousand
272-   seven hundred and Eighty six between JNO: BAIRD JR. of Town of Petersburg and
273   County of DINWIDDIE of one part and JNO: DOUGLASS, Stone Mason by Trade of
        the same place but late from IRELAND of the other part; Witnesseth that JNO:
BAIRD JR. for sum of Forty pounds specia, Dollars at Six shillings each, to him in hand
paid or secured to be paid by JNO: DOUGLASS, by these presents doth bargain sell and
confirm unto JOHN DOUGLASS and to his heirs Twenty two & 1/2 feet in front and one
hundred feet in the rear or depth of Lott number Eighteen or (18), lying in the Old
Town of Petersburg and which said Lott No. 18 the said BAIRD purchased of ROBERT
TURNBULL Gentleman, which 22 1/2 feet in front of said lott No. 18 is laid off next adjoining Lott No. 17; on the Street and thence in a direct line back 100 feet rear ward as
above mentioned & thence Easterly to the line of lott No. 17, in which lines lies and is
comprehended the ground or land sold and meant to be sold the said DOUGLASS by the
said BAIRD by this Indenture, the spot of ground containing, as is usually termed & expressed, 22 1/2 feet by 100 feet; With all houses profits commodities and appurtenances
thereon; To have and to hold the land with appurtenances unto JOHN DOUGLASS his
heirs and JOHN BAIRD doth covenant that the premises now are and shall remain & be
free and clear of and from all incumbrances whatsoever; (the Fee Rent of Eight pounds

Specia or hard money dollars at six shillings each) per annum due and payable to said JNO: BARID JR. his heirs on the first day of May each year; And if the said Fee Rent be unpaid it may be lawfull for JNO: BAIRD JR. his heirs into the said lott to re enter and have as if this Indenture had never been made; In Witness whereof the said JOHN BAIRD JR. and JOHN DOUGLASS, the parties thereto, have mutually set their hands and affixed their seals the day & year at first within written
Sealed & Delivered in presence of

WILLM. CAUDILL, ABSALUM VAUGHAN	JNO: BAIRD JR.
JOHN JONES, JAS. CAMPBELL	JOHN DOUGLASS

At a Hustings Court held for the Town of Petersburg at DURELLs in the said Town, Wednesday the Sixth day of December 1786 An Indenture of Bargain and Sale between JOHN BAIRD JR. of Town of Petersburg of one part and JOHN DOUGLASS of the same place of other part was acknowledged by the said parties whose names are thereunto subscribed and is ordered to be recorded   Atteste J. GRAMMER, Clk. C. Hs.

pp.   THIS INDENTURE made this 26th day of April in the year of our Lord one thou-
274-   sand seven hundred and Eighty six Between CHARLES DUNCAN of CHESTERFEILD
275   County of one part and THOMAS GRIFFIN PEACHY of AMELIA County of other part
       Witnesseth that for the sum of Two hundred and Forty pounds current money by
THOMAS GRIFFIN PEACHY to CHARLES DUNCAN in hand paid, by these presents doth bargain sell and confirm unto THOMAS GRIFFIN PEACHY his heirs all those lotts or parcels of land lying on BLANDFORD HILL known in the plan of the Town lately laid out on the said Hill, (now part of the Town of Petersburg) by the numbers Three, Four, Twenty, Twenty Six, Thirty Six, Forty Two, Fifty One, Fifty Seven, Sixty Three, Seventy One, Seventy Two and Ninety Eight (Nos. 3, 4, 20, 26, 36, 42, 51, 57, 63, 71, 72 & 98); To have and to hold the lotts and all advantages appertaining thereto unto THOMAS GRIFFIN PEACHY his heirs; And CHARLES DUNCAN doth for himself and his heirs covenant with THOS: GRIFFIN PEACHY his heirs that the severall lotts unto THOMAS GRIFFIN PEACHY his heirs against the title claim and demand of all persons will warrant and forever defend by these presents; In Witness whereof the said CHARLES DUNCAN hath hereunto set his hand and affixed his seal the day and year above written
Sealed and Delivered in presence of

JOHN ANGUS, JOHN CONWAY,	CHARLES DUNCAN
RICHD. WILLIAMS, THOS: WITHERS	

Memorandum; The lotts of land within mentioned are mark'd in the recorded Plan of that part of the Town of Petersburg called NEW BLANDFORD with the numbers Four, Thirty Six and Forty Two (No. 4, 36, & 42), and noted thereon as the property of JAMES FRENCH & THOMAS GORDON when in fact the lotts were never conveyed to us the said JAMES FRENCH & THOMAS GORDON by the within granter or any other person; Now we the said JAMES FRENCH & THOMAS GORDON to prevent all disputes respecting the same and in consideration of the sum of Five shillings current money to us paid doe hereby for ourselves our heirs release and for ever quit claim unto the within named THOS. GRIFFIN PEACHY his heirs all our right title interest and demand whatsoever of in and to the said lotts and all their appertenances; In Witness whereof we have hereunto set our hands & seals this Twenty sixth day of April 1786

(no signatures)

I WILLIAM COLEMAN do by these presents relinquish all my right & title to the lott number Seventy two (72) having exchang'd the same for Lott No. 84 with THOMAS GRIFFIN PEACHY Esqr., Witness my hand & seal this first day of May one thousand seven hundred and Eighty six

Sealed & Delivered by WM. COLEMAN in presence
    JOHN ANGUS, ALEXANDER WILL   WILLIAM COLE
    WILLIAM COLE for COLEMAN & FRENCH
    ROBERT TURNBULL, HENRY TATUM for JAS. FRENCH
At a Hustings Court held for the Town of Petersburg at DURELLs in the said Town,
Wednesday the Sixth day of December 1786   An Indenture of Bargain and Sale between
CHARLES DUNCAN of CHESTERFEILD County of one part and THOMAS GRIFFIN PEACHY of
AMELIA County of other part was proved by the Oath of JOHN CONWAY, a witness thereto
and the same having been before proved by the Oath of JOHN ANGUS and THOMAS
WITHERS other witnesses thereto, Together with the Relinquishment of WILLIAM COLE-
MAN and JAMES FRENCH thereon indorsed (which hath been before proved by the
Oaths of JOHN ANGUS, ALEXANDER WILL and WILLIAM COLE witnesses thereto) and also
the Relinquishment of THOMAS GORDON as also thereon indorsed and hath been before
acknowledged by the said THOMAS GORDON are ordered to be recorded
                Atteste J. GRAMMER, Clk. C. Hs.

p.   THIS INDENTURE made the Second day of May in year of our Lord one thousand
276   seven hundred and Eighty six Between CHARLES DUNCAN of County of CHESTER-
          FEILD of one part and THOMAS GORDON of Town of Petersburg of other part; Wit-
nesseth that for the sum of Sixty pounds current money by THOMAS GORDON to CHARLES
DUNCAN in hand paid, by these presentsdoth bargain & sell unto THOMAS GORDON his
heirs all those lotts of land lying in BLANDFORD HILL known in the plan of a Town
lately laid out on the said Hill (which is now a part of the Town of Petersburg) by the
numbers Fifty Nine, Seventy Five & Seventy Six (No. 59, 75 & 76); To have and to hold
the lotts and all the advantages appertaining thereto unto THOMAS GORDON his heirs
and CHARLES DUNCAN for himself his heirs doth covenant with THOMAS GORDON his
heirs that he the severall lotts unto THOMAS GORDON his heirs against the title &
demand of all persons shall warrant & forever defend by these presents; In Witness
whereof the said CHARLES DUNCAN hath hereunto set his hand and seal the day & year
above written
Sealed & Delivered in presence of
    JOHN ANGUS, JOHN CONWAY,   CHARLES DUNCAN
    RICHD: WILLIAMS, THOS: WITHERS
Memorandum that the lotts within mentioned are noted in the recorded Plan of
BLANDFORD HILL or NEW BLANDFORD as the Property of THOMAS GRIFFIN PEACHY when
in fact they never were conveyed to him by the within named CHARLES DUNCAN in
whom the Fee Simple Estate thereof was vested but to prevent all disputes respecting
the same & in consideration of Five shillings, I the said PEACHY do hereby for myself
my heirs release and forever quit unto the within named THOMAS GORDON his heirs all
my right title & interst property & demand of & in the lotts aforesaid and every of their
apperlenances. Witness my hand & seal this 2d. day of May 1786
Sealed & Delivered in presence of
    (no witnesses recorded)   T. G. PEACHY
At a Hustings court held for the Town of Petersburg at DURELLs in the said Town,
Wednesday the Sixth day of December 1786   An Indenture of Bargain and Sale between
CHARLES DUNCAN of CHESTERFEILD County of one part and THOMAS GORDON of the Town
of Petersburg of the other part was proved by the Oath of JOHN CONWAY, a witness
thereto and the same having been before proved by the Oaths of JOHN ANGUS and
THOMAS WITHERS other witnesses thereto, together with the Relinquishment of
THOMAS GRIFFIN PEACHY thereon indorsed, which hath been acknowledged by the said

THOMAS GRIFFIN PEACY are ordered to be recorded
                    Atteste J. GRAMMER, Clk. C. Hs.

p.   THIS INDENTURE made this fifth day of December in year of our Lord one thou-
277   sand seven hundred & Eighty six Between ROBERT KIRKHAM and REBECCA his
          Wife of Town of Petersburg of one part and WILLIAM BARKSDALE of the same
Town of other part; Witnesseth that ROBERT KIRKHAM and REBECCA his Wife for the
sum of One hundred and Thirty eight pounds, seven shillings current money to them in
hand paid by WILLIAM BARKSDALE, by these presents do bargain sell and confirm unto
WILLIAM BARKSDALE his heirs, one certain lott of land situate in Town of Petersburg
containing Three acres more or less distinguished in the plan of the land laid out in
Lotts by ROBERT RAVENSCROFT by the number Sixteen (excepting only a small portion
of said lott which said ROBERT hath conveyed to JOHN LOVE containing Eight yards in
width on the North side of the said Lott & in length from the Street to the Ditch the
whole length of the lott as by Deed bearing date the Eighteenth day of January last
(1786), will more fully shew) To have and to hold the lott number (16) together with all
yards gardens pastures and appertenances thereunto belonging (the small portion as
before discribed only always excepted), And ROBERT KIRKHAM and REBECCA his Wife
and their heirs the lott of land (except as herein before excepted) against the lawfull
claims of all persons will warrant and defend unto WILLIAM BARKSDALE his heirs for
ever; In Witness whereof they the said ROBERT KIRKHAM and REBECCA his Wife have
hereunto set their hands and affixed their seals the day & year above written
Sealed & Delivered in the presence of
          HENRY MORRISS,   ROBERT KIRKHAM
          FREDRICK ADLER, THOS: SHORE   REBECKA KIRKHAM
At a Hustings Court held for the Town of Petersburg at DURELLs in the said Town,
Wednesday the Sixth day of December 1786   An Indenture of Bargain and Sale between
ROBERT KIRKHAM and REBECKA his Wife of the Town of Petersburg of one part and
WILLIAM BARKSDALE of the same Town of the other part was proved by the Oaths of
HENRY MORRISS, FREDRICK ADLER and THOMAS SHORE, witnesses thereto (she the said
REBECKA being first privily and apart from the said ROBERT her Husband examined as
the Law directs) and is ordered to be recorded
                    Teste J. GRAMMER, Clk. C. Hs.

pp.   THIS INDENTURE made on the Eighth day of April Anno Domini 1785 Between
278-   SHORE & McCONNICO, Merchants in Petersburg of one part & ANDREW JOHNSTON,
279   Merchant in Petersburg, of other part; Witnesseth that for the sum of Four
          hundred pounds current money in hand paid to the said SHORE & McCONNICO by
ANDREW JOHNSTON & for and in consideration of the sum of Twenty pounds paid them
the said SHORE & McCONNICO by ALEXANDER HORSBURGH also of Petersburg, Merchant,
have granted to bargain Lease & confirm in free tack for the space of seven years to
the said ANDREW JOHNSTON and his heirs to be reckoned from the date of possession
given to the following subject & houses contracted for on the Ninth day of June seventeen hundred & Eighty four in manner following to be built for theuse of said JOHNSTON
hisheirs for & in consideration of the sums above stated; that is to say, a Stone House to
be situated in front on the Street whre their present Store stands, vizt., BOLLING BROOK
STREET & to the Eastward of their lot in that Street forty feet long & twenty four feet
wide, two story high with a Brick Cellar underneath the size of the House, The Store
House to be finished in the same manner as the Store they at present possess with a Bed
room & Counting Room adjoining, plaistered & finished as their own, the upper story to
be calculated for the reception of goods with a Door in the front for hoisting them up

to be finished by the fifteenth of November Seventeen hundred & Eighty four or
sooner if possible & possession given; A Lumber House back of and adjoining to the said
Store House of the same size, height, breadth & length so as in appearance to make but
one house of Eighty feet long & twenty four feet wide with a Chimney in the middle & a
door from the Counting Room in the Store House into said Lumber House; which last
house to be built joined to the former & possession given by the first day of June next
ensuing the date of finishing the Store House or sooner if possible; binding themselves
that if from delay of the Carpenter possession is not given on the respective dates above
mentioned for finishing both houses to the payment of whatever Rent the said JOHN-
STON or his assigns shall have occasion or be under the necessity of giving for a suitable Store House &c., untill the said Store House is made Tenantable and no longer;
   Which Houses agreable to the above Contract well & truely finished to be held by said
ANDREW JOHNSTON his heirs in fee Tack for the space of seven years from the day possession is given clear of Rent other than the aforesaid Four hundred & Twenty pounds
to them SHORE & McCONNICO already paid, subject nevertheless tosuch dues that may be
imposed by the Corporation or Publick; they bind themselves their heirs to warrant and
defend unto ANDREW JOHNSTON his heirs for the term of seven years against the claim
of all persons keeping him the said JOHNSTON his assigns &c. in full & free possession
thereof during that period accident excepted; In Witness whereof they the said SHORE
& McCONNICO do hereunto sell the name of their Firm & afix their seal the date above
written. having previously ascertained with ALEXANDER HORSBURGH assignee of said
ANDREW JOHNSTON that the commencement of the term of seven years as above recited
shall be accounted & dated from the Fifteenth of February last past, the Lumber House
to be finished & possession given as above on the first day of June ensuing
Witness RT. HEBLETHWAITE   CHRISTOPHER McCONNICO
       BELFEILD STARK   for self & THOS: SHORE
   I do hereby sell unto ALEXANDER HORSBURG of Petersburg, Mercht., for the consideration of the sum of Three hundred pounds currt. money of Virginia to me in hand paid
and for the further sum of Three hundred pounds currt. money to be paid to me by said
ALEXR. HORSBURGH his heirs before the fifteenth day of February next ensuing all my
right title & property in & to the fee Tack & Lease of the premises above bargained to
me by the above named Messrs. SHORE & McCONNICO; And I do hereby for myself my
heirs &c. warrant and defend the same unto the said HORSBURGH his heirs; In Witness
whereof I have afixed my name and seal the date above written
Signed Sealed & Delivered in presence of
       WILLIAM McKINNON,   ANDW. JOHNSTON
       DUNCAN MacRAE
   At a Court of Hustings held for the Town of Petersburg Wednesday & by adjournment
continued Thursday the 8th day of September 1785   This Indenture of Lease between
SHORE & McCONNICO of one part and ANDREW JOHNSTON of the other part was acknowledged by CHRISTOPHER McCONNICO for and in behalf of the said SHORE & McCONNICO
and the conveyance and Relinquishment of the same by said ANDREW JOHNSTON to
ALEXANDER HORSBURG which is thereto annexed was by the Oaths of WILLIAM McKIN-
NON and DUNCAN MacRAE witnesses thereto and together with the said Indenture are
ordered to be recorded   Teste J. GRAMMER, Clk. C. Hs.

p.   Petersburg June 20th 1786. I ALEXR. HORSBURGH of Petersburg, Mercht., for
279   the sum of Twenty shillings current money & other valuable considerations by
           these presents do bargain & sellunto DANIEL WARDROP of Petersburg all my
right title & property in and to the above free Tack & Lease of the premises within

bargained, And I do for myself my heirs &c. warrant & defend the dame unto the said WARDROP his heirs. In Witness whereof I have afixed my name & seal the date above
                                    ALEXR. HORSBURGH
At a Hustings Court held for the Town of Petersburg at DURELLs in the said Town the Sixth day of December 1786   A Conveyance or Relinquishment from ALEXANDER HORSBURG, Merchant of the Town of Petersburg, to DANIEL WARDROP of the same Town (of a certain Indenture of Lease between Messrs. SHORE & McCONNICO of one part & ANDREW JOHNSTON of the other part, which was conveyed by the said JOHNSTON to ALEXANDER HORSBURG & recorded in the Hustings Court of said Town) was acknowledged by said ALEXANDER HORSBURG and together with the Indenture, JOHNSTONs Conveyance & the Certificate of the Records, are ordered to be recorded
                    Atteste J. GRAMMER, Clk. C. Hs.

p.   THIS INDENTURE made the 12th day of October in year of our Lord one thousand
280   seven hundred and Eighty six Between ROGER ATKINSON of County of DINWIDDIE
        of one part and JOSEPH JONES of same County of other part; Witnesseth that
ROGER ATKINSON for the sum of Two hundred & fifty pounds current money of Virginia to him in hand paid, by these presents hath bargained & sold unto JOSEPH JONES his heirs one lot containing half an acre of land in the Old Town of Petersburg and County of DINWIDDIE which lot is marked by the number (Four); Also one other lot in the Town of Petersburg adjoining the said JOSEPH JONES Tenements which was escheated for the Commonwealth and lately the property of GEORGE YOUNGER, a British Subject, lying on the North side of the Street, Begining at the said JONES Tenement and runing down the Street till it comes opposite to the lower end of the Chimney of the Store House which said JONES had built on said lot, thence runing in a direct line till it strikes the South East corner of the Lumber House vch: the said JONES hath built, thence North 27 degrees East six poles 17 links to a Gum on the BRICK HOUSE RUN, thence down the Run to STITH BOLLINGs Lot, thence along BOLLINGs line till it strikes the land of the Estate of PETER JONES, thence along his line to the Tenement of said JOSEPH JONES, thence along the sd. JONES line to the begining; containing by estimation one quarter of an acre be the same more or less, And all right title and demand of ROGER ATKINSON in the said lands; To have and to hold the lots or parcels of land with appurtenances unto JOSEPH JONES his heirs; And ROGER ATKINSON for himself and his heirs the said lots unto JOSEPH JONES his heirs against all persons shall warrant and forever defend by these presents; In Witness whereof the said ROGER ATKINSON hath hereunto set his hand and seal the day and year above written
Signed Sealed and delivered in presence of
        CHARLES LOGAN,   ROGER ATKINSON
        THOMAS J. HUNTER, ROGER ATKINSON JUNR.
    At a Hustings Court held for the Town of Petersburg at DURELLS in the said Town Wednesday the Sixth day of December 1786   An Indenture of Bargain and Sale between ROGER ATKINSON of DINWIDDIE County of one part and JOSEPH JONES of the same County of other part was proved by the Oaths of CHARLES LOGAN, THOMAS J. HUNTER & ROGER ATKINSON JUNR. witnesses thereto and is ordered to be recorded
                    Atteste J. GRAMMER, Clk. C. Hs.

pp.   THIS INDENTURE made this first day of May in year of our Lord one thousand
281-   seven hundred and Eighty six Between CHARLES DUNCAN of County of CHESTER-
282   FEILD and JANE his Wife of one part and WILLIAM CALL of County of PRINCE
        GEORGE of other part; Witnesseth that for sum of Eight pounds currt. money of

Virginia to him said CHARLES DUNCAN in hand paid by WILLIAM CALL, said CHARLES
DUNCAN by these presents doth bargain sell and confirm unto WILLIAM CALL his heirs
a certain parcell of land lying in County of CHESTERFEILD containing by estimation Two
acres be the same more or less, according to the boundaries lying on the North side of
APPOMATTAX RIVER, Beginning at the mouth of a Creek or Gutt making out of said
River below the Town called POCOHUNTAS or WITTON TOWN, thence up the Creek or Gutt
as it meanders (adjoining the Swamp or Marsh Land of said CALL) untill it meets the
line of said DUNCAN, runing from the lower end of said Town to said Creek, thence
along down the Ridge or Neck of Highland below said Town along the Edge of said Neck
of Highland or Marsh so far as any Swamp or Marsh Land extends, thence up the said
River as it meanders to the mouth of said Creek or Gutt, the said Neck of Highland and
the said RIVER APPOMATTOX contained within the boundaries aforesaid with all the
rights priviledges and appurtenances thereunto belonging; and the rents issues and
profits thereof; To have and to hold the said Two acres of land more or less hereby conveyed and appurtenances unto WILLIAM CALL his heirs; And CHARLES DUNCAN for
himself his heirs doth covenant with WILLIAM CALL his heirs the two acres of land
unto WILLIAM CALL and to his heirs shall warrant and forever defend against every
person and shall warrant and defend by these presents; In Witness whereof the said
CHARLES DUNCAN and JANE his Wife hath hereunto set their hands and affixed their
seals the day and year first above written
Sealed and Delivered in presence of
    CHR: McCONNICO,   CHARLES DUNCAN
    JNO: SHORE JUNR.,   JANE DUNCAN
    ROBERT BOLLING JR.
 Received May 1st 1786 the sum of Eight pounds current money in full consideration of
the within mentioned land and premises   CHARLES DUNCAN
 At a Hustings Court held for the Town of Petersburg at DURELLs in the said Town
Wednesday the Sixth day of December 1786   An Indenture of Bargain and Sale between
CHARLES DUNCAN of CHESTERFEILD County and JANE his Wife of one part and WILLIAM
CALL of PRINCE GEORGE County of other part was proved by the Oaths of CHRISTOPHER
McCONNICO, JOHN SHORE and ROBERT BOLLING JR., witnesses thereto and together with
the memorandum of Livery and Seizen and receipt thereon indorsed are ordered to be
recorded   Atteste J. GRAMMER, Clk. C. Hs.

pp.   THIS INDENTURE made this fifth day of December in year of our Lord one thou-
283-   sand seven hundred and Eighty six Between THOMAS MATHIS of PRINCE GEORGE
285   County and SARAH his Wife of one part and ALLING MAY of County of DINWID-
       DIE of other part; Witnesseth that THOMAS MATHIS and SARAH his Wife for the
sum of Thirty pounds current money of Virginia to them in hand paid by ALLEN MAY
And also in consideration of the rents covenants and agrements hereinafter mentioned
to be paid and performed by said ALLEN MAY his heirs said THOMAS MATHIS and SARAH
his Wife by these presents doth bargain sell and confirm unto ALLEN MAY his heirs
one quarter acre lott of land on the Ridge of the Hill adjoining the New Town of BLAND-
FORD, being part of the first lott laid off into lotts by Mr. NICHOLAS PARHAM adjoining
the New Town of BLANDFORD in County of PRINCE GEORGE and sold by NICHOLAS PAR-
HAM to said THOMAS MATHIS and all ways and appurtainances to the one quarter or one
fourth part of above named acre lott of land belonging; To have and to hold the land
hereby granted with the appurtenances unto ALLEN MAY and his heirs paying therefor unto THOMAS MATHIS his heirs yearly from the first day of January for ever the
Fee Rent of Twenty five shillings current money, the first years rent to grow due and

payable on the first day of January which shall be in the year one thousand seven hundred and Eighty seven; free and clear of and from all former and other sails and incumbrances, the Fee Rent of twenty five shillings pr. annum always foreprized and excepted, and THOMAS MATHIS and SARAH his Wife and their heirs the premises unto ALLEN MAY his heirs against every person shall warrant and for ever defend by these presents: In Witness whereof the parties aforesaid have hereunto set their hands and affixed their seals the day and year first above written
Signed Sealed and Delivered in the presence of

SILAS SANDFORD,   THOS: MATHIS
HENRY LINCH,   WM. COLVIN

Received this Fifth day of December one thousand seven hundred and Eighty six of ALLEN MAY the sum of Thirty pounds the conditions or consideration money for the quarter acre lott of land within mentioned

SILAS SANDFORD,   THOS: MATHIS
HENRY LINCH,   WM. COLVIN

At a Hustings Court held for the Town of Petersburg at DURELLs in the said Town Wednesday the Sixth day of December 1786   An Indenture of Bargain and Sale between THOMAS MATHIS of PRINCE GEORGE County and SARAH his Wife of one part and ALLEN MAY of DINWIDDIE County of other part was acknowledged by the said THOMAS MATHIS and together with a memorandum and receipt thereon indorsed are ordered to be recorded   Atteste J. GRAMMER, Clk. C. Hs.
(Page 286 is blank.)

p.   THIS INDENTURE made this Eleventh day of May in year of our Lord one thou-
287   sand seven hundred and Eighty six Between RICHARD WITTON of County of
         MECKLENBURG of one part and ROWLETT GILL of County of CHESTERFEILD of
other part; Witnesseth that for sum of Twelve pounds current money of Virginia to RICHARD WITTON in hand paid by ROWLETT GILL, said RICHARD WITTON doth bargain sell and confirm unto ROWLETT GILL his heirs one certain lott of land containing half an acre more or less situate in CHESTERFEILD County in that part of Petersburg at present called POAKAHUNTAS and is distinguished in the plan of the lands laid out by RICHARD WITTON and heretofore known as WITTON TOWN by the number Seventeen, No. 17. To have and to hold the lott of land number Seventeen with all appurtenances thereunto belonging; together with all priviledges and advantages unto ROWLET GILL his heirs free and clear from all incumbrances and RICHARD WITTON at all times will warrant anddefend the title of said lott unto ROWLET GILL his heirs forever; In Witness whereof RICHARD WITTON hath hereunto set his hand and affixed his seal the day and year first above written
Sealed and Delivered in presents of us

GAWIN BROWN,   RICHARD WITTON
JOHN JACKSON, SAM: HINTON

Received of ROWLET GILL Twelve pounds current money in full of the within consideration
Teste JOHN JACKSON,   RICHARD WITTON

At a Hustings Court held for the Town of Petersburg at DURELLs in the said Town Wednesday the Seventh day of February 1787   An Indenture of Bargain and Sale between RICHARD WITTON of County of MECKLENBURG of one part and ROWLET GILL of CHESTERFEILD County of other part was proved by the Oath of JOHN JACKSON a witness thereto and the same having been before proved by the Oaths of GAWIN BROWN and SAMUEL HINTON other witnesses thereto together with the Receipt thereon indorsed are ordered to be recorded   Atteste J. GRAMMER, Clk. C. Hs.

(Page 288 is blank.)

p.   THIS INDENTURE made this 7th day of March one thousand seven hundred and
289   Eighty seven Between WILLIAM COLE of County of PRINCE GEORGE of one part
        and ANTONIO SEPARK of Town of Petersburg of other part; Witnesseth that for
sum of Five shillings by said ANTONIO to said WILLIAM in hand paid, said WILLIAM by
these presents doth bargain & sell unto ANTONIO SEPARK one lott of land lying in Town
of Petersburg & in that part of the Town known by the name of NEW BLANDFORD, & in
the plan by the number (35), say Thirty five, which lott of Land was drawn in the
Lottery for laying off NEW BLANDFORD by NATHL. COCKE as appears bythe plan now of
Record in the Court of Hustings of Petersbg. and was conveyed to him by Deed from
CHARLES DUNCAN & by said COCKEs Attorneys to WILLIAM COLE, reference being had to
the several Deeds all of Record in the Hustings Court of Petersburg may appear; the
said lott of land with issues and profits thereof unto ANTONIO SEPARK his heirs and
WILLIAM COLE for himself his heirs the lot of land unto ANTONIO SEPARK his heirs
against the lawfull claim of all persons will warrnt & forever defend. In Witness
whereof said WILLIAM COLE hath hereunto set his hand and affixed his seal the day &
year first above written
Signed Sealed & Delivd. in presence of
    THOMAS WITHERS,   WILLIAM COLE
    JOHN FISHER, ROBERT TORRENCE
  At a Hustings Court held for the Town of Petersburg the Seventh day of March 1787
An Indenture of Bargain and Sale between WILLIAM COLE of PRINCE GEORGE County of
one part and ANTONIO SEPARK of the Town of Petersburg of other part was acknowledged by the said WILLIAM COLE and ordered to be recorded
                Atteste J. GRAMMER, Clk. C. Hs.

p.   THIS INDENTURE made this Ninth day of Feby. one thousand seven hundred &
290   Eighty six Between RICHARD YARBROUGH of County of SURRY of one part and
        JOEL FENN & JOHN FENN of County of PRINCE GEORGE of other part; Witnesseth
that RICHARD YARBROUGH for the sum of Fifty pounds current money of Virginia to
him in hand paid by JOEL & JOHN FENN, said RICHARD YARBROUGH by these presents
doth bargain & sell unto JOEL & JOHN FENN their heirs one certain parcell of land lying
in Town of Petersburg on South side of BOLLINGBROOK STREET and bounded by the
Street in front and back by SUPEREASORY & COMPANY on the East and LOGAN &
McELDERRY on the West, containing Thirty feet front and back & two hundred & seven-
teen feet in depth from Street to Street & all the appurtenances belonging; To have & to
hold the parcell of land with appurtenances unto JOEL & JOHN FENN their heirs and
RICHARD YARBROUGH for himself his heirs the parcell of land against all persons to
JOEL & JOHN FENN their heirs shall warrant & forever defend by these presents; In
Witness whereof said RICHARD YARBROUGH hath hereunto set his hand and affixed his
Seal the day & year above written
Sealed & Delivered in presence of
    RICHD. DENNIS,   RICHD. YARBROUGH
    WM. TIMBERLAKE, ARMT. DAVES
  At a Hustings Court held for the Town of Petersburg the Seventh day of March 1787
An Indenture of Bargain and Sale between RICHARD YARBROUGH of SURRY County of
one part and JOEL FENN & JOHN FENN of PRINCE GEORGE County of other part together
with the memorandum thereon indorsed were acknowledged by the said RICHARD
YARBROUGH and by the said Court ordered to be recorded
                Atteste J. GRAMMER, Clk. C. Hs.

p.   THIS INDENTURE made this first day of December in year of our Lord one thou-
291   sand seven hundred and Eighty six Between PETER MINOR & JOHN BROWN of the
      State of Virginia of one part and ERASMUS GILL of Town of Petersburg in the
same State of other part; Witnesseth that whereas ROBERT BOLLING of said Town by Deed
of Indenture bearing date the first day of January in year one thousand seven hundred
& Eighty five for the consideration therein mentioned and for the rents covenants &
agreements therein stipulated to be kept paid and performed did demise & to farm lett
unto the parties to these presents for the term of Twenty years to be computed from the
date of said Indenture, a part of a lot therein mentioned and hereinafter particularly
described, And whereas PETER MINOR & JOHN BROWN are desirous to part with their
interest in the demised premises, Now Therefore This Indenture Witnesseth that PETER
MINOR & JOHN BROWN for sum of Six hundred pounds current money to them in hand
paid by said GILL, by these presents do release & for ever quit claim unto ERASMUS
GILL his heirs for so much of said term of years as now remain unexpired all that part
of one certain lot of land situate in Town of Petersburg and on North side of BOLLING-
BROOK street which lot whereof the premises are a part is known in the Platt of lands
made by ROBERT BOLLING by the number (46), Forty Six; which said part of number
(46) extends in front on BOLLING BROOK STREET begining at the West end of a twenty
foot Alley laid off between the said MINOR, GILL & BROWN and BLODGET & EUSTIS upon
BOLLINGBROOK STREET, thence Northwardly along the said Street sixty four feet, thence
Eastward parallel with BOLLINGBROOK STREET twenty two feet, thence Northward one
hundred & thirty feet parallel with CEDAR POINT down to a twelve feet Alley to be laid
off parellel with BOLLINGBROOK STREET so as to communicate with the aforesaid twenty
feet Alley and CEDAR POINT STREET, thence Eastward along the said twelve foot Alley
twenty two feet, thence South along the twenty feet Alley one hundred and ninety four
feet to BOLLINGBROOK STREET and the begining with free use and benefit of said twenty
foot Alley in common with BLODGET & EUSTIS their heirs so far as the above described
land extends: And also free use & benefit of the twelve foot Alley in common with
ROBERT BOLLING his heirs so far as to have communication through the Alley to CEDAR
POINT or THIRD STREET, Together with the rents issues and profits thereof; the Ground
rents now chargeable thereon alone being excepted, To have and to hold the released
premises with the appurtenances unto ERASMUS GILL his heirs untill the full end of
the residue of the aforesaid Term of Twenty years agreable to the expressions conditions & stipulations in the Original Lease granted by ROBERT BOLLING and recorded in
the Hustings Court of said Town; In Witness whereof the parties to these presents have
hereunto set their hands and seals the day & year first before written
Signed Sealed & Delivered in presence of
    J. GRAMMER,   PETER MINOR for self and
    THOS: ARMISTEAD, HENRY GEE   JOHN BROWN
  At a Hustings Court held for the Town of Petersburg the Seventh day of March 1787
An Indenture of Release between PETER MINOR & JOHN BROWN of one part & ERASMUS
GILL of other part was proved by the oaths of JOHN GRAMMER, THOMAS ARMISTEAD &
HENRY GEE witnesses thereto and ordered to be recorded
               Atteste J. GRAMMER, Clk C. Hs.

p.   KNOW ALL MEN by these presents that I WILLIAM HARRISON, Clerk, of Town of
292   Petersburg have named & constituted EDWARD PEGRAM Esqr. of County of DIN-
      WIDDIE my true & faithfull Attorney for me & in my name to demand sue for
recover & receive of all persons all sums of money due & owing to me granting my
Attorney full power & authority to exercise all such acts things & devices in the Law as

shall be necessary for recovering all debts & give discharges in my name, and
generally to do & execute in the premises as fully as I myself might or could do being
personally present; ratifying and allowing all my said Attorney shall lawfull do or
cause to be done threin by virtue of these presents; In Witness whereof I have
hereunto set my hand and seal this Sixth day of February 1786
Test ERASMUS GILL,   WILLM. HARRISON
    HESTER ARBUCKLE
At a Hustings Court held for the Town of Petersburg the Seventh day of March 1787
A Letter of Attorney from WILLIAM HARRISON of the Town of Petersburg to EDWARD
PEGRAM Esqr. of DINWIDDIE County was proved by the Oaths of ERASMUS GILL and
HESTER ARBUCKLE witnesses thereto and ordered to be recorded
    Atteste J. GRAMMER, Clk. C. Hs.

pp.   THIS INDENTURE made the Twenty Seventh day of February in year of our Lord
293- one thousand seven hundred and Eighty seven Between GEORGE DUDGEON and
294   MARTHA his Wife of Town of Petersburg of one part and WILLIAM BUCHANAN,
Merchant, of the same Town of other part; Witnesseth that for sum of Two hundred & Fifty pounds Sterling money of Great Britain to GEORGE DUDGEON in hand paid by
WILLIAM BUCHANAN, said GEORGE DUDGEON and MARTHA his Wife by these presents do
bargain sell and confirm unto WILLIAM BUCHANAN and his heirs for ever one moiety
of one lott or half acre of land which was formerly the property of HUGH MILLER sold
by him to RICHARD KENNON, by said KENNONs Executors conveyed to JERMAN BAKER
and by him conveyed to GEORGE DUDGEON as by the several Deeds recorded in the Court
of DINWIDDIE County will appear, and is situate in Town of Petersburg in the County of
DINWIDDIE & numbered in the plan of said Town (9), Nine, as in the Plan is set forth;
which moiety or half part thereof is situate and bounded, Begining for the same on the
street at the Center or middle of the said lot No. 9, number Nine, thence runing
Northerly through the middle of the same to the back line thereof, thence along said
back line to the North East corner, thence along the East line Southerly to the South
East corner of the same on the Street and thence along the Street Westerly to the begining, comprehending & including one half part of said lott or half acre of land, Together with allhouses orchards profits commodities and appurtenances belonging; and
the rents issues and profits thereof; To have and to hold the land hereby conveyed with
appurtenances unto WILLIAM BUCHANAN his heirs free and clear from all incumbrances whatsoever; And GEORGE DUDGEON & MARTHA his Wife and their heirs unto
WILLIAM BUCHANAN his heirs against all persons shall warrent and for ever defend by
these presents; In Witness whereof the said GEORGE DUDGEON and MARTHA his Wife
have hereunto set their hands and seals the day and year first above written
Sealed and Delivered in the presence of
  (no witnesses recorded)   GEORGE DUDGEON
                    MARTHA her mark X DUDGEON
At a Hustings Court held for the Town of Petersburg at DURELLS in the said Town the
Seventh day of March 1787   An Indenture of Bargain and Sale between GEORGE
DUDGEON and MARTHA his Wife of the Town of Petersburg of one part and WILLIAM
BUCHANAN of the same Town of other part was acknowledged by the said GEORGE
DUDGEON and MARTHA his Wife (she the said MARTHA being first privily examined as
the Law directs) and by the said Court ordered to be recorded.
    Atteste J. GRAMMER, Clk. C. Hs.

p.   THIS INDENTURE made this 13th day of December Anno Domini one thousand
295   seven hundred and Eighty six Between EDWARD WATLINGTON & SARAH his Wife
        of one part & CUZNEAU & SUBERCAZEUX, Merchants & Partners of Town of
Petersburg of other part; Witnesseth that EDWARD WATLINGTON & SARAH his Wife for
sum of Six hundred pounds current money of Virginia to them in hand paid do by these
presents bargain & sell unto said CUZNEAU & SUBERCASEAUX their heirs one certain
parcel or half lot of land lying on the Old Main Street & being half of lot known by the
lot nubmer Eight (No. 8), & which said half lot of land is now occupied by and in the
possession of said CUZNEAU & SUBERCASEAUX & which said lot descended from a certain
JOHN WATLINGTON now deded. to the said EDWARD as Heir at Law; To have and to hold
the parcel or half of said lot number Eight (No. 8), agreable to the metes & bounderis
now in their possession together with all appertunances & profits & commodities thereunto belonging; And EDWARD WATLINGTON and SARAH his Wife will warrant and for
ever defend the aforesaid tenements from the claim of any person; In Witness whereof
the said EDWARD WATLINGTON & SARAH his Wife have hereunto set their hands and
affixed their seals the day & year first within written
Signed Sealed Delivered & acknowledged before us
        RICHD. GREGORY as to Edwd.   EDWD. WATLINGTON
        WM. WATLINGTON ditto
        RODCK. BIGELOW, ARMT. DAVES,
        THOMAS LANIER
    At a Hustings Court held for the Town of Petersburg the Seventh day of March 1787
An Indenture of Bargain and Sale lbetween EDWARD WATLINGTON & SARAH his Wife of
one part and CUZNEAU & SUBERCASEAUX, Merchants & Partners of the Town of Peters-
burg of the other part; was proved by the Oaths of RICHARD GREGORY, WM. WATLING-
TON and ARMISTED DAVES witnesses thereto and is ordered to be recorded
                    Atteste J. GRAMMER, Clk. C. Hs.

pp.   THIS INDENTURE made this Nineteenth day of February in year of our Lord one
296-   thousand seven hundred & Eighty seven Between JNO: DOUGLASS, Stone Mason,
297   of Town of Petersburg of one part and HECTOR McNEILL, Merchant, of the same
        place of other part; Witnesseth that JNO: DOUGLASS for the full & just sum of
Four hundred & fifty pounds specia to him in hand paid by HECTOR McNEILL, by these
presents do bargain sell and confirm unto HECTOR McNEILL and to his heirs Twenty two
and an half feet in front and one hundred foot in the rear of Lott No. Eighteen (or 18),
lying in the Old Town of Petersburg and on the North side of the Street thereof, together with all houses and improvements thereon which piece of land said JOHN DOUG-
LASS purchased of JNO: BAIRD JR. & is part of Lott No. 18 in the said Old Town of Petersburg as before described; To have and to hold the said lott of land hereby sold with
appertainances unto HECTOR McNEILL his heirs free & clear of all incumbrances made
done or committed by said JOHN DOUGLASS & SARAH DOUGLASS his Wife or his or their
heirs (the Fee Rent of Eight (or L. 8) pounds specia or hard money dollars at six shillings each per annum due & paiable to JNO: BARID JR. his heirs on the first day of May
in every year only excepted); In Witness whereof the parties have set their hands &
seals the day at first within written in presence of
        ROBERT STEWART, JOHN D. HALDANE,   JOHN DOUGLASS
        JOHN MacRAE, JOS: WEISIGER   SALLY DOUGLASS
                                                     HECTOR McNEILL
    At a Hustings Court held for the Town of Petersburg at DURELLS in the said Town the
Seventh day of March 1787   An Indenture of Bargain and Sale from JOHN DOUGLASS,

Stone Mason, of Town of Petersburg of one part and HECTOR McNEILL, Merchant, of the same place of other part was proved by the Oaths of ROBERT STEWART, JOHN D. HALDANE & JOHN Mac RAE witnesses thereto and is ordered to be recorded
                                 Atteste J. GRAMMER, Clk. H. C.

(Page 298 is blank.)

p.   A Memorial of all Bargains Sales Mortgages & other Conveyances acknow-
299   ledged or proved and recorded in the Hustings Court of the Town of Petersburg
          between the 1st day of October 1786 and the 1st day of April 1787

(The headings of the colums are, Deed and Date, Names surnames and addition of parties; Condition expressed, Quantity and Situation of the Land, number and names of the slaves and description of the personal Estate; when acknowledged or proved & recorded.)

Bargain & Sale 1st Jany. 1786. WILLIAM HARRISON & LUCY his Wife to JAMES BROMLY L. 300; One lott of 3 acres in RAVENSCROFT, one small lott adjoining; 4th October 1786

Bargain & Sale 21st Jany. 1786; WILLIAM HARRISON & LUCY his Wife to JAMES BROMLY, L. 100; Two pieces of land in RAVENSCROFT containing each 120 by 160 feet part of Lotts No. 9 & 10; 4th of October 1786.

Lease for 99 years &c. 28th Septemr. 1785; RICHARD HIL to WILLIAM WADDILL, L. 180...10 & L. 5 p annum; part of Lott on B. BROOK No. 43; 4th October 1786.

Bargain and Sale 11th Novr. 1786. RICHARD WITTON to THOMAS SHORE. L. 5. Two lotts in POCO-HONTASS No. 5; 6th Decr. 1786.

Bargain & Sale May 3d. 1786. CHARLES DUNCAN to WILLIAM COLVIN, 2000 lbs. Tobacco; One lott in NEW BLANDFORD No. 38; 6th Decr. 1786

Bargain & Sale May 3d. 1786. CHARLES DUNCAN to NATHANIEL COCKE, 5/; Three lotts in NEW BLANDFORD No. 32, 33, & 55; 6th Decr. 1786

Mortgage 18th April 1786. GEORGE C. LEACY to WILLIAM DAVIES. L. 603...6...7; 5 Negroes vizt. Philis, George, Edmund, Archer & Miles; 6th Decr. 1786

Bargain & Sale 29th Novr. 1786. ERASMUS GILL & SARAH his Wife to ANN THOMSON, L. 300; one lott in NEW PETERSBURG No. 15 and one acre of land adjoining thereto; 6th Decr. 1786

Bargain & Sale 31st Oct. 1786; JOHN BAIRD JR. to JOHN DOUGLASS, L. 40. & L. 8 p. annum; Part of lott in OLD PETERSBURG No. 18, 22 1/2 by 100 feet; 6th Decr. 1786

Bargain & Sale, 31st Octobr. 1786; CHARLES DUNCAN to THOMAS G. PEACHY, L. 240. Twelve lotts in NEW BLANDFORD No. 3, 4, 20, 26, 36, 42, 51, 57, 63, 71, 72 & 98; 6th Decr. 1786.

Bargain & Sale 2d. May 1786; CHARLES DUNCAN to THOMAS GORDON. L. 60; Three lotts in NEW BLANDFORD No. 59, 75, & 76; 6th Decr. 1786.

Bargain & Sale 5th Decr. 1786; ROBERT KIRKHAM & REBECKAH his Wife to WM. BARKSDALE, L. 138...7...0; part of Lott No. 16 in RAVENSCROFT; Decr. 6th 1786

Lease for 7 years 8th April 1785. SHORE & McCONNICO to DANIEL WALDROP. L. 420. A Store & Lumber House adjoining to SHORE & McCONNICO's Store; 6th Decr. 1786

Bargain & Sale 12th Octr. 1786; ROGER ATKINSON to JOSEPH JONES, L. 250; One lott 1/2 acre No. 4 in OLD PETERSBURG, also another Lott or parcel of land near ye BRICK HOUSE RUN; 6th Decr. 1786

Bargain & Sale 1st May 1786. CHARLES DUNCAN & JANE his Wife to WILLIAM CALL, L. 8; Two acres land by estimation of North side of the River; 6th Decr. 1786

Bargain & Sale 5th Decr. 1786; THOMAS MATHIS to ALLING MAY; L. 30 purchase, & 25/ per annum; Quarter of an acre part of the first lot of land laid out by NICHOLAS PARHAM adjoining NEW BLANDFORD; 6th Decr. 1786

Bargain & Sale, 11th May 1786. RICHARD WITTON to ROWLETT GILL; L. 12; One lott in POCO-HANTASS No. 17; 7th Feb. 1787

Bargain & Sale 7th March 1787. WILLIAM COLE to ANTONIO SEPARK; 5/; One lott in NEW BLANDFORD No.33, 7th March 1787.

Bargain & Sale 9th Feb: 1787. RICHARD YARBROUGH to JOEL FENN & JOHN FENN; L. 50; Part of a lott on BOLLING BROOK adjoining LOGAN & McELDERRY & SUBERCASEAUX; 7th March 1787

Release; 1st Decr. 1786. PETER MINOR & JOHN BROWN to ERASMUS GILL. L. 600; Part of lott No. 46 on BOLLING BROOK: 7th March 1787

Bargain & sale 27th Feb: 1787; GEORGE DUDGEON & MARTHA his Wife to WILLIAM BUCHANAN; L. 250 Sterling; Half a lott No. 9 in OLD PETERSBURG; 7th March1787

Bargain & Sale 3d. Decr. 1786; EDWARD WATLINGTON to CUZNEAU & SUBERCASEAUX, L. 600; Half of Lott No. 8 in OLD PETERSBURG, 7th March 1787;

Bargain & Sale Feby 1787. JOHN DOUGLASS to HECTOR McNEILL, L. 450 & L. 8 p. annum; Part of Lott No. 18 in OLD PETERSBURG bot. of JOHN BAIRD JR. 7th March 1787.

(Page 300 is blank.)

p. 301　　(On this page is another plat; at the top the heading; TOWN OF PETERSBURG APRIL COURT 1787. The lots run West to East along the APPOMATTOX RIVER and back Southward. Notes. The Plan above represents about 40 acres of Land laid off for ROBERT BOLLING Gentleman into Streets, Squares and 59 lotts all of which have 100 feet front on the River and Streets except such as are otherwise marked in the plan. All those South of BOLLING BROOK STREET, except numbers 35 & 36 hve 217 feet 9 inches depth. The Lotts No. 40, 41, 42, 46, 47, 48 49, 50, 51 & 52 are 400 feet in length from Street to Street and those from 47 to 52 inclusive extend to the River. The Nos. 43, 44, 45 have 120 fet depth.　　AUGUST 1783 Surveyed by WM. WATKINS

At a Hustings Court held for the Town of Petersburg the fourth day of April 1787 A Plan of Forty acres of land laid off by ROBERT BOLLING Gentleman into Streets squares and Fifty nine lotts signed by WILLIAM WATKINS, Surveyor thereof, was presented in Court by ROBERT BOLLING and is at his request and desire ordered to be recorded
　　　　　　　　　　Atteste J. GRAMMER, Clk. H. C.

(Page 302 is blank.)

p. 303　　KNOW ALL MEN by these presents that I ROBERT BOLLING for divers good causes me thereunto moving hath (by virtue of a certain Act of Assembly passed at RICHMOND in the month of May Anno Domini one thousand seven hundred & Eighty two intitled, "An Act to authorise the manumission of Slaves," emancipated and set free & do by these presents emancipate & set free a certain woman slave named Terressa, And I do hereby for my self my heirs release all claim property interest or demand which I now have or may hereafter have in & to the service of said Terressa & her future increase hereby declaring her emancipated and free to all intents & purposes & intitled to enjoy every advantage of Freedom which is in my power to give or grant her the said Terressa by virtue of the aforesaid Act of Assembly; And I do hereby obligate myself my heirs never to disturb molest or interrupt the said Terressa or her future increase in the full enjoyment of every the aforesaid priviledges & immunities; In Witness whereof I have hereunto set my hand & affixed my seal this Fourth day of July Anno Domini one thousand seven hundred and Eighty six
　　　　　　　　　　ROBERT BOLLING JR.

At a Hustings Court held for the Town of Petersburg the Fourth day of April 1787 A Deed of Emanumission or Emancipation from under the hand and seal of ROBERT BOLLING JR. setting free a Negro slave, Terressa, was presented in open Court and acknowledged by the said ROBERT BOLLING JR. and at his request is ordered to be recorded
　　　　　　　　　　Atteste J. GRAMMER, Clk. H. C.

p.   I do hereby acknowledge to have received from MRS. MARY BOLLING of DIN-
303   WIDDIE the sum of Seventy pounds in full for my Negro woman, TERRISSA, and
        do by these presents oblige myself my heirs &c. to warrant and defend the title
to the said Terrissa against all and every person whatsoever, as witness my hand & seal
this Seventh day of December 1786
Teste   R. ARMISTEAD; THOS: ARMISTEAD   WILLM. ARMISTEAD
   At a Hustings Court held for the Town of Petersburg Wednesday the fourth day of April
1787   A Receipt or Bill of Sale from WILLIAM ARMISTEAD to MRS. MARY BOLLING for a
Negro woman Terrissa was proved by the Oath of ROBERT ARMISTEAD, one of the witnesses thereto and is ordered to be recorded
                        Atteste J. GRAMMER, Clk. H. C.

p.   KNOW ALL MEN by these presents that I MARY BOLLING of Petersburg in con-
304   consideration of the love and affection I bear to my Son in Law, JOHN SHORE of
        the same Town and for the further consideration of Ten shillings to me in hand
paid, by these presents do bargain & sell unto JOHN SHORE the following Negroe slaves
with all their future increase, to wit, Doctor, Ned, Jack, Harry, Tom, Phoebe, Crease,
Irish & Lucy; To have and to hold the said slaves with all their future increase unto
JOHN SHORE his heirs; And I the said MARY BOLLING for myself my heirs the said slaves
to JOHN SHORE his heirs shall warrant & by these presents defend; In Witness whereof I
have hereunto set my hand & Seal this Thirtieth day of August in year one thousand
seven hundred and Eighty six
Sealed & Delivered in presence of
        THOMAS TABB BOLLING,   MARY BOLLING
        FREDERICK VICTOR, FRANS: ANDERSON
   At a Hustings Court held for the Town of Petersburg Wednesday the Fourth day of April
1787   A Deed of Gift from MARY BOLLING of the Town of Petersburg to JOHN SHORE of
the same Town was proved by the Oaths of THOMAS TABB BOLLING and FRANCIS ANDER-
SON, two of the witnesses thereto, and by the said Court is ordered to be recorded
                        Atteste J. GRAMMER, Clk. H. C.

p.   THIS INDENTURE made this Thirtieth day of August in year one thousand seven
305   hundred and Eighty six Between MARY BOLLING and ROBERT BOLLING of Peters-
        burg of one part and JOHN SHORE of the same Town of other part; Witnesseth
that for the sum of Five shillings current money to MARY & ROBERT BOLLING by said
JOHN in hand paid, by these presents do bargain sell & confirm unto JOHN SHORE his
heirs one lot or half acre of land situate in Town of Petersburg on BOLLINGBROOK
STREET distinguished by the number (21), Twenty One, together with all houses advantages priviledges and emoluments to the same belonging and all rents issues and profits
thereof; To have and to hld the lot & half acre of land unto JOHN SHORE his heirs,
paying therefor upon the decease of said MARY BOLLING after the expiration of one
year the yearly fee rent of Eight pounds current money to said ROBERT BOLLING his
heirs the same being demanded on the premises by said ROBERT BOLLING; And MARY
BOLLING & ROBERT BOLLING for themselves and their heirs the said lot with appurtenances unto JOHN SHORE his heirs by these presents shall warrant & forever defend;
In Witness whereof the parties hereto have set their hands and seals the day and year
first above written
Sealed and Delivered in presence of
        THOMAS TABB BOLLING,   MARY BOLLING,
        FREDERICK VICTOR,   ROBERT BOLLING JR.
        FRANCIS ANDERSON JR.   JOHN SHORE

At a Hustings Court held for the Town of Petersburg Wednesday the Fourth day of April
1787   An Indenture of Bargain and Sale between MARY BOLLING and ROBERT BOLLING
of the Town of Petersburg of one part and JOHN SHORE of the same Town of other part
was severally acknowledged by the said ROBERT BOLLING and JOHN SHORE on their parts
and on the part of MARY BOLLING was proved by the Oaths of THOMAS TABB BOLLING
and FRANCIS ANDERSON JR. two witnesses thereto and is ordered to be recorded
Atteste J. GRAMMER, Clk. H. C.

p.   THIS INDENTURE made this first day of January in year of our Lord Christ one
306   thousand seven hundred and Eighty seven Between JAMES BROMLY of County of
DINWIDDIE and Town of Petersburg of one part and JOHN SOMERSALL of County
of CHESTERFEILD and Town of Petersburg of other part; Witnesseth that JAMES BROMLY
doth Lease unto JOHN SOMERSALL his heirs part of Lot number Fifty Nine (59) which
said BROMLY purchased of ROBERT BOLLING Esqr., containing and runing South from
Mr. HENRY LINCHs line Stone twenty eight feet (28) in front and Forty feet back; To
have and to hold the said parcel of land & premises with all appurtenances and improvements unto JOHN SOMERSALL his heirs from the first day of January next unto the
full end & term of Eight years then next ensuing, and JOHN SOMERSALL for his part
doth promise tomove on aforesaid lot one House eighteen feet wide and twenty six feet
long (which house is now built) and to have the same underpined with Brick or Stone
three feet clear of the surface of the Earth and to have the said House returned unto
said BROMLY his heirs &c. (in a good & sufficient repair with a good Brick Chimney to
said House) at the expiration of the term of Eight years; In Witness whereof the said
JAMES BROMLY and JOHN SOMERSALL have interchangeably set their hands & seals this
day & date above written
In presence of us R. BIGELOW,   JAMES BRONLEY
     WILLIAM DURELL, WILLIAM BROADNAX   JOHN SOMERSALL
At a Hustings Court held for the Town of Petersburg Wednesday the Fourth day of April
1787   An Indenture of Lease between JAMES BROMLY of one part & JOHN SOMERSALL
of the other part was acknowled: by said parties and together with the memorandum of
seizen thereunto annexed (which was also acknowledged by said JAMES BROMLY) are
ordered to be recorded   Atteste J. GRAMMER, Clk. H. C.

p.   THIS INDENTURE made this 20th dy of March one thousand seven hundred and
307   Eighty seven Between JOHN SOMERSALL of the Town of Petersburg of one part
and PLEASENTS MAGANN of County of AMHERST of other part; Whereas by a
certain Writing made and dated the first day of January in year aforesaid between
JAMES BROMLY of one part and said SOMERSALL of the other part, said BROMLY Leased
to said SOMERSALL part of a lott of land in the Town of Petersburg No. 59 which the said
BROMLY purchased of ROBERT BOLLING Esqr., runing South from HENRY LYNCH's line
twenty eight feet in front and forty feet in back, the said Lease to continue from the
first day of January next ensuing unto the full end and term of Eight years then next
ensuing, NOW THIS INDENTURE Witnesseth that JOHN SOMERSALL for sum of Two hundred and Fifty pounds currt. money of Virginia to him discounted by said PLEASENTS
MAGANN out of a Debt due to him for the purchase of a tract of land in AMHERST County, by these presents doth bargain sell and set over unto said MAGANN and to his Executors or assigns all that parcell of land above mentioned with all houses and appurtainances thereto belonging; also all the title and demand of said SOMERSALL to the same; To
have and to hold the lott of ground to said MAGANN or assigns for and during the residue of the term yet to come and not already expired; In Witness whereof the said
SOMERSALL hath hereunto set his hand and affixed his seal the day and year first above

written
Sealed and Delivered in presence of

     JOS: ROGERS,   JOHN SOMERSALL
     HENRY LINCH, EDMUND HOLLIDAY

  At a Hustings Court held for the Town of Petersburg Wednesday the Fourth day of April
1787   An Indenture of Lease between JOHN SOMERSALL of Town of Petersburg of one
part and PLEASANTSMAGANN of AMHERST County of other part was acknowledged by
the said JOHN SOMERSALL and is ordered to be recorded
               Atteste J. GRAMMER, Clk. H. C.

pp.   THIS INDENTURE made this first day of December in year of our Lord one thou-
308-   sand seven hundred and Eighty six Between ERASMUS GILL of Town of Peters-
309   burg of one part and JAMES CAMPBELL & LUKE WHEELER, Merchants & Partners,
       of the same Town of other part; Witnesseth that for sum of Six hundred pounds
current money paid to said GILL by said CAMPBELL & WHEELER, by these presents doth
bargain sell & convey unto said CAMPBELL & WHEELER as Tenants in Common for the
residue of a term of Twenty years commencing on the first day of January which was
in the year one thousand seven hundred & Eighty five, all that part of a lott of land
lying on North side of BOLLING BROOK STREET in Town of Petersburg & County of DIN-
WIDDIE, which said lot whereof the premises are a part is distinguished in a platt of land
made by ROBERT BOLLING by number (46), Forty Six, which part of number (46) extends
in front on BOLLING BROOK STREET beginning at the West end of a twenty foot Alley laid
off between the premises and the land of BLODGET & EUSTIS, upon BOLLING BROOK
STREET, thence Westward along BOLLING BROOK STREET forty four feet to CEDAR POINT
or THIRD STREET, thence Northward along said Street sixty four feet, thence Eastward
parrallel with BOLLING BROOK STREET twenty two feet, thence Northward one hundred
and thirty feet parrallell with CEDAR POINT down to a twelve foot Alley to be laid off
parrallel with BOLLING BROOK STREET so as to communicate with the aforesaid Twenty
foot Alley and CEDAR POINT STREET, thence Eastward along the said Twelve foot Alley
twenty two feet, thence Southward along the twenty feet Alley One hundred & ninety
four feet to BOLLING BROOK STREET and the begining; with the free use and benefit of
said Twenty foot Alley in common with said BLODGET & EUSTIS their heirs so far as the
above discribed land extends, and also the free use & benefit of a twelve foot Alley in
common with ROBERT BOLLING his heirs so far as to have communication through the
Alley to CEDAR POINT or THIRD STREET; Together with all advantages profits rents &
issues thereof, the Original Ground Rent alone being excepted; To have and to hold the
premises with appurtenances unto JAMES CAMPBELL and LUKE WHEELER their heirs as
Tenants in Common until the end of the term of twenty years; In Testimony whereof
the said ERASMUS GILL hath hereunto set his hand & seal the day & year afore written
Signed Sealed & Delivered in presence of
     KEN: JONES,   ERASMUS GILL
     EDMUND FEILD, E. JNO: COLLETT
  Petersburg 1st December 1786. Received from Messrs. CAMPBELL & WHEELER the sum
of Six hundred pounds Virga. Curry., being the consideration money of the above Deed
on account of ERASMUS GILL & in part execution of a Bond of L. 1598...19...3; granted to
me by MINOR GILL & BROWN
Test W. PEACHY   E. JNO: COLLETT
  At a Hustings Court held for the Town of Petersburg Wednesday the Fourth day of April
1787   An Indenture of Lease and Release between ERASMUS GILL of Town of Petersburg of one part and JAMES CAMPBELL & LUKE WHEELER, Merchants & Partners, of the

same Town of other part was acknowledged by the said ERASMUS GILL and together
with the receipt thereon indorsed are ordered to be recorded
                          Atteste J. GRAMMER, Clk. H. C.

pp.   THIS INDENTURE made this Second day of September one thousand seven hun-
310-   dred and Eighty six Between ERASMUS GILL of Town of Petersburg of one part
311   and JOHN OSBOURNE of the same Town of other part; Witnesseth that whereas
          said ERASMUS GILL stands justly indebted to LUKE WHEELER of said Town by one
Bond bearing even date with these presents in the just and full quantity of Fifty thousand pounds of Nett Crop Tobacco inspected at Petersburg or the Inspections above it on
JAMES RIVER and to be praised in hogsheads not less than one thousand weight in each
to be paid and delivered to LUKE WHEELER on or before the first day of January next,
And Whereas said ERASMUS GILL is willing and desirous to make immediate provision
for securing the payment of the quantity of Tobacco to LUKE WHEELER whose consent
hereto is signified by his seal affixed and his name in his proper hand writing subscribed hereunto, said ERASMUS GILL for the considerations aforesaid and for the further consideration of Five shillings to ERASMUS GILL by said JOHN OSBOURNE in hand
paid, by these presents doth bargain & sell unto JOHN OSBOURNE his heirs one moiety of
a certain lot or half acre of land which is distinguished in the plan of the Town of
Petersburg laid out by (blank) JONES deceased by number (18), Eighteen, which said
moiety or half acre of land is situate and bounded begining at the middle or centre from
East to West of said lot number (18) Eighteen on the Street and from thence runing
Northerly parrallel with the Original Lines and equally dividing the same to the back
line thereof, thence along the back line Westwardly to the corner of said lot bounding
on Lot Number (17), Seventeen, thence along lot number (17), Seventeen, Southwardly
to the Street and thence along the Street Eastwardly to the place of begining; being the
same lot or half acre of land conveyed by WILLIAM WRIGHT to ERASMUS GILL by Deed
of Indenture bearing date the Twenty eighth day of September last, & duly recorded,
Together with all houses gardens priviledges advantages and emoluments belonging; To
have and to hold the lot with appurtenances unto JOHN OSBOURNE his heirs IN TRUST
nevertheless that JOHN OSBOURNE his heirs shall after the first day of January next as
soon as said LUKE WHEELER shall think fit or said ERASMUS GILL shall request sell for
the best price that can be had after giving Ten days publick previous notice thereof
and out of the money arising from such sale pay LUKE WHEELER hisheirs the aforementioned tobacco with interest thereon and also all expences of drawing and recor-
ding this Indenture and the contingent charges of the Sale or Sales and all other necessary expences that shall attend the securing and receiving of the aforesaid tobacco; In
Witness whereof the parties to these presents have hereunto set their hands & seals the
day & year first before written
Signed Sealed and Deliverd in presence of
          L. WILLIAMS,   ERASMUS GILL
          GEO: McFARLANE   LUKE WHEELER
                                                  JNO: OSBORNE
At a Hustings Court held for the Town of Petersburg the fourth day of April 1787
An Indenture in trust between ERASMUS GILL of Town of Petersburg of one part and
JOHN OSBOURNE of the same Town of the other part was acknowledged by the said
ERASMUS GILL and is ordered to be recorded
                          Atteste J. GRAMMER, Clk. H. C.
(Pages 312, 313 and 314 are blank.)

p.   The Commonwealth of Virginia to JOHN BAIRD, CHRISTOPHER McCONNICO &
315   ISAAC HALL Gentlemen Greeting; Whereas WILLIAM COLE of County of PRINCE
          GEORGE by his certain Indenture of Bargain and Sale bearing date the seventh
day of March last (1787) hath sold and conveyed unto ANTONIO SEPARK of Town of
Petersburg one lott of land lying in said Town number (35) Thirty five, And whereas
ANN COLE, the Wife of said WILLIAM COLE, cannot conveniently travell to our Hustings
Court of the Town of Petersburg to relinquish her right and make acknowledgment of
said conveyance; Therefore (the Commission for the privy Examination of ANN, the Wife of
WILLIAM COLE.) Witness JOHN GRAMMER Clerk of our said Court the Seventh day of April
in the eleventh year of the Commonwealth   J. GRAMMER, Clk. H. C.
     By Virtue of the Commission hereunto annexed, this Indenture was acknowledged by
ANN COLE, Wife of the within named WILLIAM COLE, on the Second day of June 1787, she
the said ANN being first privily and apart from the said WILLIAM, her Husband, examined; (the return of the execution of the privy examination of ANN COLE); before ue
                         CHRISTO: McCONNICO
                         ISAAC HALL
     At a Hustings Court held for the Town of Petersburg at the House of JOHN HARE in the
said Town Wednesday the Sixth day of June 1787   A Commission annexed to an Indenture of Bargain and Sale between WILLIAM COLE of PRINCE GEORGE County of one part
and ANTONIO SEPARK of the Town of Petersburg of other part was returned executed by
CHRISTOPHER McCONNICO and ISAAC HALL, Gentlemen, and together with the Certificate
of the Execution thereof are ordered to be recorded
                         Atteste J. GRAMMER, Clk. H. C.

p.   THIS INDENTURE made on the Twentieth day of November Anno Domini one
316   thousand seven hundred and Eighty six between BENJAMIN EDWARDS BROWNE
          and MASON BROWNE his Wife of SURRY County, State of Virginia, of one part and
NORMAN BIGELOW of Petersburg of other part; Witnesseth that BENJAMIN E. BROWNE
and MASON his Wife in consideration of One hundred and thirty three pounds, Six shillings and eight pence current money of Virginia to them in hand paid by said BIGELOW
by these presents do bargain sell and confirm unto said BIGELOW his heirs part of a
certain lott of land lying in Town of Petersburg which lott is marked in the plan of said
Town with the number Thirty five (35), To have and to hold the said lot, that is to say,
forty (40) feet in width thro the full length of said lott (being on the West side of
STEGAR's Tenement) to said BIGELOW his heirs; And the said BENJAMIN E. BROWNE and
MASON his Wife for themselves their heirs will warrant and forever defend; In Witness whereof they have hereunto set their hands and seals the day and year above
written
Signed sealed and delivered in the presence of
     BOSWELL GOODWYN,   BENJA: EDWDS. BROWNE
     THOS: HOPE, ROBERT STUART,   MARY MASON BROWNE
     WM. BROWNE, ROBERT TAYLOR
     At a Hustings Court held for the Town of Petersburg at the House of JOHN HARE in the
said Town Wednesday the Sixth day of June 1787   An Indenture of Bargain and Sale
between BENJAMIN EDWARDS BROWNE and MARY MASON his Wife of SURRY County of
one part and NORMAN BIGELOW of the Town of Petersburg of other part was proved by
the Oaths of BOSWELL GOODWYN, THOMAS HOPE and ROBERT STUART, witnesses thereto,
and is ordered to be recorded   Atteste J. GRAMMER, Clk. H. C.

pp. THIS INDENTURE made this Seventh day of May in year of our Lord one thou-
317- sand seven hundred and Eighty seven (say 1787), Between JOHN BAIRD JR. of
318 the Town of Petersburg of one part and JOHN WARDROP & JOHN DRUMMOND of
the same place of other part; Witnesseth that JOHN BAIRD JR. for the full & just
sum of Four hundred pounds specie or hard money to him in hand paid or secured to be
paid by JOHN WARDROP & JNO: DRUMMOND by these presents doth bargain and sell unto
JNO: WARDROP & JNO: DRUMMOND and to their heirs as Tenants in Common & not as
Joint Tenants one certain lott of ground lying in Town of Petersburg on South side of
the Street thereof, it being a part of Lott No. 29 & 30, which said land or ground said
BAIRD bought of Mr. THOMAS GORDON & Mr. JNO: JONES the Elder, as will more fully
appear by the Records of the County Court of DINWIDDIE where a good and lawfull Deed
for the same is duly recorded, said spot of ground begins at and upon the North East
corner of the Stone Wall of the House now occupied by said DRUMMOND (which said
House stands and is situated on said lott number 30 or Thirty, and said ground runs &
extends in front & on the sd. Street from said Corner of sd. Wall of the aforesaid House,
sixty four feet in front & in the rear or depth of the sd. two lotts, No. 29 & 30, 242 feet or
the full & extreme depth thereof, the said spot of ground together with all appurtenances thereto belonging more plainly and simply described by calling it a part of Lott
No. 29 & 30 and is in front of the South side of the Street of sd. Old Town of Petersburg
and is sixty four feet by two hundred & forty two; Together with all houses profits
commodities & appurtenances appertaining; To have and to hold the bargained part
unto JOHN WARDROP & JNO: DRUMMOND as Tenants in Common and not as Joint Tenants
their heirs; free and clear from all incumbrances (the usual and lawful taxes of the
Country to grow due & payable to the Publick in respect to the premises only excepted
and foreprized), In Witness whereof the said JOHN BAIRD JR. hath hereunto set his
hand and affixed his seal the day and year first within written
Sealed and Delivered in presence of
JAS. CAMPBELL, PETER THWEATT   JNO: BAIRD JR.
JAMES STURDEVANT, JOHN THOMPSON
At a Hustings Court held for the Town of Petersburg at the House of JOHN HARE in the
said Town, Wednesday the Sixth day of June 1787   An Indenture of Bargain and Sale
between JOHN BAIRD JR. of the Town of Petersburg of one part and JOHN WARDROP &
JOHN DRUMMOND of the same place of the other part was acknowledged by the said JOHN
BAIRD JR. and is ordered to be recorded
Atteste J. GRAMMER, Clk. H. C.

p. THIS INDENTURE made this Tenth day of August in year of our Lord one thou-
319 sand seven hundred and Eighty six Between ROBERT FITZGERRALD and ANN his
Wife of County of AMELIA of one part and JOHN BLAND of County of PRINCE
GEORGE of other part; Witnesseth that for the just & full sum of Fifty pounds current
money by said JOHN BLAND to ROBERT FITZGERRALD and ANN his Wife in hand paid; by
these presents doth bargain sell and confirm unto JOHN BLAND his heirs one parcel of
land lying in the New Town of BLANDFORD known by the number (50) Fifty which plan
is recorded in the Borough Court of Petersburg; To have and to hold the parcel of land
and all the advantages thereunto unto JOHN BLAND his heirs and ROBERT FITZGERRALD
and ANN his Wife will forever warrant and defend the title of said parcel of land unto
JOHN BLAND his heirs against the claims of every person; In Witness whereof said
ROBERT FITZGERRALD and ANN his Wife hath hereunto set their hands and seals the day
and year above written

Sealed and Delivered in the presence of
SIMON FRASER,   ROBERT FITZGERALD
ROBERT TURNBULL,   ANNE FITZGERALD
WILLIAM DOUGLASS

At a Hustings Court held for the Town of Petersburg at the House of JOHN HARE in the said Town Wednesday the Sixth day of June 1787   An Indenture of Bargain and Sale between ROBERT FITZGERALD and ANNE his Wife of AMELIA County of one part and JOHN BLAND of PRINCE GEORGE County of other part was proved by the Oath of ROBERT TURNBULL a Witness thereto and the same having been before proved by the Oaths of SIMON FRASER and WILLIAM DOUGLASS witnesses thereto is ordered to be recorded
Atteste J. GRAMMER, Clk. H. C.

pp.   THIS INDENTURE made the Nineteenth dy of May in the year of our Lord one
320-   thousand seven hundred and Eighty seven Between ROBERT BOLLING Esquire of
323   BOLLING BROOKE in the County of DINWIDDIE and MARY BOLLING, Widow and Relict of ROBERT BOLLING Esquire deceased of the same County of one part and JAMES GIBBON of Town of Petersburg on the other part; Whereas ROBERT BOLLING Esquire deceased did by his last Will and Testament among other things devise to said MARY BOLLING the use of all his lands in and adjoining the Town of Petersburg during her natural life with remainder in fee to said ROBERT BOLLING(party hereto) as by the said Will duly proved and recorded in the Court of the County of DINWIDDIE may appear; And ROBERT BOLLING having agreed with the privity and assent of said MARY BOLLING (signified by her being party hereto and sealing and delivering this Indenture) to sell and convey in fee simple to JAMES GIBBON part of one certain lott of land number (blank) lying in that part of the Town of Petersburg heretofore called BLANDFORD, Begining at the South East corner of the House or Store now in occupation of Messrs. GORDON, WESTMORE & MAITLAND, thence up the Street along the whole front of said Store to the line of Land held by NICHOLAS PARHAM, thence down said line to the River, thence down along the river shore twenty seven feet, thence in a straight line up to the North East corner of said Store, thence along the East end of said Store to the begining, which lott was conveyed by ROGER ATKINSON to ROBERT BOLLING deceased by Deed duly proved and recorded in the Court of the County of PRINCE GEORGE as will appear; NOW THIS INDENTURE WITNESSETH that ROBERT BOLLING and MARY BOLLING for the sum of Fifty five pounds current money of Virginia to them or one of them in hand paid by JAMES GIBBON and also in consideration of the Rents covenants and agrements hereinafter mentioned to be kept and performed by JAMES GIBBON his heirs, ROBERT BOLLING and MARY BOLLING by these presents do bargain sell and confirm unto JAMES GIBBON his heirs all that parcel of land part of lott number (blank), and all ways and appurtenances to the same belonging; (the ground rents hereafter mentioned to be reserved by and payable to ROBERT BOLLING his heirs excepted), To have and to hold lthe parcel of land hereby conveyed unto JAMES GIBBON his heirs, said JAMES GIBBON paying therefor unto ROBERT BOLLING his heirs on the first day of January every year the fee or ground rent of Five pounds current money of Virginia; the first years rent to become due and payable the first day of January one thousand seven hundred and Eighty eight; In Witness whereof the parties to this Indenture have hereunto set their hands and affixed their seals the day and year first above written
Sealed and Delivered in the presence of
WM. HAXALL,   MARY BOLLING
WM. KNOX,   ROBERT BOLLING JR.
JOS; WESTMORE   J. GIBBON

Received the Nineteenth day of May 1787, of JAMES GIBBON the sum of Fifty pounds current money of Virginia the consideration money for the parcel of land and premises convey'd to said GIBBON by the Indenture hereto annexed

In presence of WM. HAXALL,   ROBERT BOLLING JR.
    WM. KNOX, JOS: WESTMORE

    At a Hustings Court held for the Town of Petersburg at the House of JOHN HARE Wednesday the Sixth day of June 1787   An Indenture of Bargain and Sale between ROBERT BOLLING Esquire of BOLLING BROOK in County of DINWIDDIE and MARY BOLLING Widow & Relict of ROBERT BOLLING Esqr., deceas'd, of the same County of one part and JAMES GIBBON of Town of Petersburg of other part was proved by the Oaths of WILLIAM HAXALL and JOSEPH WESTMORE witnesses thereto and together with the memorandum of livery and seizen & receipt thereon indorsed are ordered to be recorded
                Atteste J. GRAMMER, Clk. H. C.

p.
324

    THIS INDENTURE made the Sixth of June in year of our Lord one thousand seven hundred and Eighty seven Between GEORGE ROBERTSON of County of CHESTERFEILD of one part and HENRY LINCH of County of DINWIDDIE of other part & Town of Petersburg of other part: Witnesseth that GEORGE ROBERTSON for the sum of Seventeen pounds current money of Virginia to him in hand paid by HENRY LINCH, doth grant and confirm unto HENRY LINCH hisheirs one lott of land containing by estimation half an acre lying in a certain Town call'd WITTON TOWN, but now is known by the name of POCOHONTAS layed off by RICHARD WITTON, which lott is marked in the plan of said Town by No. 35 as appears upon the Records of CHESTERFEILD; To have and to hold the lott of land with all priviledges and advantages thereunto belonging unto HENRY LINCH his heirs, And GEORGE ROBERTSON doth for himself his heirs &c. warrant the said lott of land to HENRY LINCH against all persons claiming under him: In Witness whereof the said GEORGE ROBERTSON hath hereunto set his hand and fixed his seal the day and year above mentioned

Sign'd Seal'd & Delivered in presence of
    JOHN HILL,   GEORGE ROBERTSON
    PARKER HARE, ELERMOR HEALY

    At a Hustings Court held for the Town of Petersburg at the House of JOHN HARE Wednesday the Sixth day of June 1787   An Indenture of Bargain and Sale between GEORGE ROBERTSON of CHESTERFEILD County of the one part and HENRY LINCH of the County of DINWIDDIE and Town of Petersburg of the other part was proved by the Oaths of JOHN HILL, PARKER HARE & ELERMOR HEALY witnesses therto and by order of said Court is truly recorded   Atteste J. GRAMMER, Clk. H. C.

(Pages 325 and 326 are blank.)

pp.
327-
328

    THIS INDENTURE made the Twenty fifth day of May Anno Domini one thousand seven hundred and Eighty seven Between NATHANIEL COCKE of the State of GEORGIA of one part and WILLIAM COLE of PRINCE GEORGE COUNTY of the other part: Whereas WILLIAM THOMPSON and WILLIAM TARRY, Attorneys for the said NATHANIEL COCKE have by their certain Indenture made & executed & bearing date the 25th day of November last past conveyed the same to WILLIAMCOLE three lotts of land situate in that part of the Town of Petersburg called NEW BLANDFORD and distinguished in the plan of the same by the numbers (32), (35) & (55), Thirty Two, Thirty Five & Fifty Five, belonging to and the property of said NATHANIEL COCK as will appear by a Deed from CHARLES DUNCAN to him bearing date the 3d. day of May 1786, duly recorded in the Hustings Court of said Town; And Whereas the Indenture made by the said Attorneys

hath been partly proved only and lodged with the Clerk of the Hustings Court of the
said Town, and as some difficulties may attend procuring the witnesses so as to have the
same fully proved and the said NATHANIEL COCKE being now present to act in his own
proper person and being willing and desirous of confirming to said WILLIAM COLE a
sufficient title to the three lotts of land and to avoid any disputes or doubts that may
hereafter arise respecting the same; THIS INDENTURE WITNESSETH that NATHANIEL
COCKE for the sum of Six thousand pounds weight of tobacco to him in hand paid by said
WILLIAM by these presents doth bargain sell and confirm unto WILLIAM COLE his
heirs three lotts of land situate in Town of Petersburg as aforesaid; To have and to hold
the three lotts of land with their appurtenances unto WILLIAM COLE his heirs and
NATHANIEL COCKE and his heirs the three lotts of land to WILLIAM COLE his heirs will
warrant and forever defend against every person claiming under him; And it is hereby agreed that the conveyance made by WILLIAM THOMPSON & WILLIAM TARRY, Attorneys of said NATHANIEL COCKE as hereinbefore mentioned of the three lotts of land and
premises is hereby set aside made void and of none effect; In Witness whereof the
parties aforesaid have hereunto set their hands and affixed their seals the day and year
first within written
N. B. It is agreed on by and betwixt the paties that in case it should hereafter appear
that CHAS. DUNCAN's Title to the aforesaid Lotts shou'd be contested & found insuf-
ficient that then said NATHL. COCKE & his heirs shall not be answerable to the said Cole
or his assigns, it being only intended that the said COCKE shall warrant from his heirs
or any person claiming under him or them
Signed Sealed & Delivered in presence of
    JNO: HARE, THOS: ROWLETT,   NATHL. COCKE
    JAMES DURELL, CAD: JONES
At a Hustings Court held for the Town of Petersburg at the House of JOHN HARE in the
said Town Wednesday the Fourth day of July 1787   An Indenture of Bargain and Sale
between NATHANIEL COOKE of the State of GEORGIA of one part and WILLIAM COLE of
County of PRINCE GEORGE of other part was proved by the Oaths of JOHN HARE, THOMAS
ROWLETT and CADWALLADER JONES witnesses thereto and is ordered to be recorded
    Atteste J. GRAMMER, Clk. H. C.

p.
329
    THIS INDENTURE made this 25th day of April Anno Dom: 1787 Witnesseth that I
ALEXANDER HORSBURGH of DINWIDDIE County & Borough of Petersburg for certain good and valid considerations me thereunto specially moving did in the
year of our Lord one thousand seven hundred & Seventy four lend unto MRS. ANN
BAKER, Wife of MARTIN BAKER, then of BRUNSWICK now of HALIFAX County a Negro
girl slave named Charlote to have and to hold the Negroe girl Charlotte her issue in
posterity free of rent or charge during the period of her natural life and after her
decease to her Husband, MARTIN BAKER, during the period of his natural life in case of
his surviving his Wife, which loan in its full extent and meaning (the Original Deed
made by me for that purpose in the year above specified being lossed or mislaid) I do
now for myself my heirs fully ratify and confirm, saving to me my heirs that nothing
herein contained shall tend or be construed to vest in said MARTIN BAKER & his said
Wife any other claim to the service of the said slave and her issue or to vest in them
any right title & claim in and to the property of the said Negro, reserving to my heirs
&c. the full and entire right of property in the said slave and her issue subject only to
the incumbrance of the loan hereby made and which under the penalty of forfiture of
said Loan I hereby prohibit the said MARTIN and his Wife from conveyed to any other
person whatsoever the above specified right of service in consequence of this Deed,

declaring the above conditions to be the terms on which I originally lent the said slave & her issue & which by these presents are recited and confirmed; Given under my hand & seal the day and year above written
Signed Sealed & Delivered in presence of
     SHADRACK YOAMAN,   ALEXR: HORSBURGH
     JAMES CHALMERS, ROBERT KENNON
  At a Hustings Court held for the Town of Petersburg at the House of JOHN HARE in the said Town Wednesday the fourth day of July 1787   An Indenture of Loan from ALEXAN-DER HORSBURGH of the Town of Petersburg of one part and ANN BAKER, Wife of MAR-TIN BAKER, formerly of BRUNSWICK but now of HALIFAX County and the said MARTIN BAKER of the other part was acknowledged by the said ALEXANDER HORSBURGH and is ordered to be recorded .   Atteste J. GRAMMER, Clk. H. C.

pp.   THIS INDENTURE made this first day of December one thousand seven hundred
330- and Eighty six Between CLARISA LAMB of one part and JOHN BAIRD JR. of the
331   other part; Witnesseth that whereas the said CLARISA LAMB stands indebted to
         sd. BAIRD the full & just sum of Eight hundred pounds specia which she is obli-gated to pay at Eighty yearly or annual payments, the first of which payments is due & payable on the 25th day of December 1787, as per a written agrement signed & witnes-sed bearing date October 28th 1786, which said sum of L. 800 specia is and will become due & payable at the respective times and periods in the manner and form in the above recited agremt., set forth and expressed;
  NOW THIS INDENTURE Witnesseth that CLARISA LAMB for the better securing and more sure payment of the said L. 800 specia, as it shall hereafter become due, And also in consideration of the sum of Five shillings specia to her in hand paid by said BAIRD, by these presents doth bargain sell and deliver unto JOHN BAIRD JR. and to his heirs during her natural life the following Negro slaves, that is to say; Jemima, Lydda, Grace, Isaac, Osbourne, Ned & Will, which Negro slaves are and were given to me by my Father by a Deed of Gift bearingd ate the 10th day of January 1775 in Trust to GEORGE ELLIOTT, reference to sd. Deed of Gift which is duly recorded in the County Court of CHESTERFEILD will better appear; To have and to hold the sd. Negro slaves & increase In Trust to pay and satisfy the aforesaid L. 800 specia, as it shall become due; Now This Indenture further Witnesseth that it is agreed by and between the parties to these pre-sents that if the L. 800 specia be not paid annually as it shall become due that then it shall be lawful for sd. BAIRD JR. his heirs to take possession of said Negroe slaves or any part of them and advertise and sell at publick sale the whole or so much or such part thereof as may be sufficient to pay the L. 800 or whatever part thereof as shall be behind in arrear; Now this Indenture further Witnesseth that if CLARISA LAMB her heirs shall pay or cause to be paid the sd. L. 800 as the same become due that then this Indenture shall cease and be utterly void, otherwise to be & remain in full force and virtue; In Witness whereof I have hereunto set my hand and affixed my seal the day and year first within written
Sealed & Delivered in presence of
     SALLY HALDANE,   CLARISSA LAMB
     JOHN DRUMMON, BENJA. SPENCER
  Note; MRS. CLARISSA LAMB is to give me Eight seperate Bond for the payment of the L. 800 specia and on her paying the same or part thereof before they become due, I agree to allow her to discount of seven and a half per cent for such advanced payment, And it is agreed by me that should the Assembly of Virginia at any time during the term of eight years for which she has to pay me the L. 800 specia issue and emission of paper

money, I do agree to take it at its comparative value as it passes betwixt man and man in lieu of the L. 800 specia.

SALLY HALDANE   JNO: BAIRD JR.

At a Hustings Court held for the Town of Petersburg at the House of JOHN HARE in the said Town Wednesday the Fourth day of July 1787   An Indenture or Mortgage between CLARISA LAMB of the one part and JOHN BAIRD JR. of other part was proved by the Oath of SALLY HALDANE, a witness thereto, and having been before partly proved by the Oath of JOHN DRUMMOND, another witness thereto, is ordered to be recorded

Atteste J. GRAMMER, Clk. H. C.

(Page 332 is blank.)

pp
333-
334

THIS INDENTURE made on the Twenty first day of June in year of our Lord one thousand seven hundred and Eighty seven Between ERASMUS GILL and SARAH his Wife of Town of Petersburg in the County of DINWIDDIE of one part and WILLIAM RANDOLPH of the County of CHARLES CITY of other part; Witnesseth that ERASMUS GILL and SARAH his Wife for sum of Two thousand Eight hundred pounds paid to said ERASMUS by said WILLIAM at the time of execution of these presents; and for other good causes and considerations them thereunto moving by these presents do and each of them doth bargain and sell unto WILLIAM RANDOLPH and his heirs a half acre Lot adjoining EDWARD STABLERs property in said Town and lying on East side thereof and number sixteen; Also Eight acre lotts lying near the property of ROBERT ARMISTEAD in said Town and partly bounded on the East by the Road which divides the land of JOHN TABB from that of said GILL on the South by WASHINGTON STREET on the West by MARKET STREET and on the North and partly on the East by the lotts of DOUGLASS and FREELAND and LENOX which lotts are numbers 3, 4, 5, 10, 11, 12, 13 and 14, also all the Meadow Land belonging to said GILL and SARAH his Wife lying between HIGH STREET and the Old Town containing Nine acres by estimation begining a little West of the corner of SPENCERs WAREHOUSEs and runing West to EDWARD STABLERs Land and bounded by STABLERs land on the West, by DANIEL DODSONs on the East and on the North and South by the lotts laid off in the Old and New Streets, To have and to hold the lands herein with appurtenances unto WILLIAM RANDOLPH and his heirs; And ERASMUS GILL hereby covenants for himself his heirs that if the title to the premises should at any time hereafter proved defective said ERASMUS his heirs will make WILLIAM RANDOLPH and his heirs compensation for the loss or damage thereby sustained; In Testimony whereof the parties have hereunto set their hands and seals the day and year above mentioned

Signed Sealed & Delivered in the presence of

JAMES VERRELL,   ERASMUS GILL
ADAM JOHNSTON,   SARAH GILL
GEO: HAY

The Commonwealth of Virginia to JOHN SHORE, SAMUEL DAVIES, THOMAS GRIFFIN PEACHY and ALEXANDER McNABB Gentlemen, Greeting. Whereas (the Commission for the privy examination of SARAH, the Wife of ERASMUS GILL); Witness JOHN GRAMMER Clerk of our said Hustings Court the Fourth day of July in the Twelfth year of the Commonwealth

By Virtue of the Commission hereunto annexed the within Indenture was acknowledged by the thereto subscribed SARAH GILL on the 5th day of July 1787, she the said SARAH being first privily and apart from the said ERASMUS GILL her Husband, examined; (the return of the execution of the privy Examination of SARAH GILL); before us

JNO: SHORE
SAML. DAVIES

At a Hustings Court continued and held for the Town of Petersburg at the House of
JOHN HARE in the said Town. Thursday the Fifth day of July 1787   An Indenture of Bargain and Sale between ERASMUS GILL and SARAH his Wife of Town of Petersburg of one
part and WILLIAM RANDOLPH of CHARLES CITY County of other part was acknowledged
by the said ERASMUS GILL and together with the Commission annexed and the Certificate of the execution thereof are ordered to be recorded
Atteste J. GRAMMER, Clk. H. C.

p.   THIS INDENTURE made on the Twenty second day of June in year of our Lord
335   one thousand seven hundred and Eighty seven Between JOHN OSBOURNE and
     LUKE WHEELER of Town of Petersburg of one part and WILLIAM RANDOLPH of
County of CHARLES CITY of other part. Whereas WILLIAM RANDOLPH is now in possession of a half acre lot with a two story house in HIGH STREET in Petersburg in which
ERASMUS GILL lately lived, which said half acre lott is part of number Eighteen in the
plan of the said Town, and together with the two story house thereon was lately conveyed to him by said ERASMUS GILL: NOW THIS INDENTURE WITNESSETH that LUKE
WHEELER and JOHN OSBURN in consideration of having received from ERASMUS GILL
other sufficient security for the payment and discharge of a Debt due from the said
GILL to LUKE WHEELER and which was formerly secured by a Deed of Trust for the
premises prior to the date of said RANDOLPHs conveyance, and also in consideration of
the sum of Five shillings in hand paid by said RANDOLPH to said LUKE WHEELER and
JOHN OSBOURNE by these presents do bargain sell and confirm release and for ever quit
claim unto WILLIAM RANDOLPH and his heirs all their right title claim and demand in
and to the premises to WILLIAM RANDOLPH and his heirs; In Testimony whereof the
parties have hereunto subscribed their names and affixed their seals the day and year
above men-tioned
Signed Sealed and Delivered in the presence of
    GEO: McFARLANE, witness to JOHN OSBORNE   JOHN OSBORNE
    STITH HARDAWAY. CAD: JONES,   LUKE WHEELER
    THOS: ARMISTEAD
At a Hustings Court continued and held for the Town of Petersburg at the House of
JOHN HARE in the said Town Thursday the Fifth day of July 1787. An Indenture of Release between JOHN OSBOURNE and LUKE WHEELER of the Town of Petersburg of one
part and WILLIAM RANDOLPH of the County of CHARLES CITY of the other part was
acknowledged by the said JOHN OSBORNE and LUKE WHEELER and ordered to be recorded
Atteste J. GRAMMER, Clk. H. C.

p.   THIS INDENTURE made this Eighteenth day of Jany. one thousand seven hun-
336   dred & Eighty six Between WILLIAM WRIGHT & ROBERT KIRKHAM of the Town of
     Petersburg of one part & JOHN LOVE of said place of other part; Witnesseth that
for sum of Eleven pounds thirteen shillings to them in hand paid by said LOVE, by these
presents do sell release & confirm unto JOHN LOVE a certain piece of land lying in that
part of Petersburg called RAVENSCROFT, being a part of the lott number (16), say Sixteen, containing Eight yards in width of the North side of said lott & in length from the
Street to the Ditch being all the length of the lott (in its present situation) which piece
of land joins lot number seventeen, now the property of JOHN LOVE, together with all
woods waters & water courses houses & preveledges also the right title & Estate in said
piece of land with the appurtenances thereunto belonging; To have & to hold the piece
of land unto JOHN LOVE his heirs, And WILLIAM WRIGHT & ROBERT KIRKHAM do for
themselves & their heirs agree with JOHN LOVE the piece of land against the claim of

every person will warrant & forever defend; In Witness whereof they have hereunto
set their hands and affixed their seals the day & year above written
Signed Sealed & Delivered in the presence of

WILLIAM DOUGLASS,	)	WM. WRIGHT
PARHAM MABRY	) as to WRIGHT	ROBERT KERKHAM
JNO: GRAMMER	)	

Memorandum made this First day of February 1786.

   That the piece of Land conveyed by this Deed was purchased by WILLIAM HARRISON,
Clerk, of Petersburg and given to the said JOHN LOVE mentioned in the said Deed for a
full compensation for the deficiency occasioned by a New Survey of RAVENSCROFT by
consent of Proprietors; in the lot number 17 sold by said HARRISON to FREDK.
WILLIAMS and by WILLIAMS to JAMES YOUNG, by YOUNG to ANDREW JOHNSTON, by the
Exrs. of ANDREW JOHNSTON to JOHN LOVE who hereby acknowledges the said piece of
land as full compensation for the deficiency of the said lot and acquits the parties of all
further claim in consequence thereof, Witness my hand the day and year above written
                              JOHN LOVE

   At a Hustings Court continued and held for the Town of Petersburg at the House of
JOHN HARE in the said Town, Thursday the Fifth day of July 1787   An Indenture of Bargain and Sale between WILLIAM WRIGHT & ROBERT KERKHAM of Town of Petersburg of
one part & JOHN LOVE of the same Town of other part was acknowledged by the said
WILLIAM WRIGHT and having been before acknowledged by the said ROBERT KIRKHAM
together with the memorandum thereon indorsed are by order of said Court truly
recorded   Atteste J. GRAMMER, Clk. H. C.

(Pages 337 and 338 are blank)

(Petersburg City Hustings Court Deed Book No. 1, 1784-1790, contains 550 pages. This Book will be
continued in our next book.)

COUNTIES. Amelia 39, 50, 66, 78, 98, 99, 116, 117; Amherst 112, 113; Brunswick 45, 49, 119, 120; Charles City 121, 122; Chesterfield 7, 10, 30, 37, 44-46, 50, 54, 55, 68, 69, 72, 75, 78, 79, 83, 85, 87, 90, 94, 95, 98, 99, 102-104, 118, 120; Greensville 34; Halifax 119, 120; Henrico 9; Lunenburg 78; Mecklenburg 72, 94, 104; Norfolk 27; Prince George 3, 7, 21, 24, 25, 28-30, 37, 41, 46, 52, 55, 59, 61, 62, 65, 67, 69, 81, 82, 85-87, 95, 96, 102-105, 116-119; Surry 105, 113.
CRUMPLER. John 12, 13, 88, 91.
CUGNEAU & SUBERCASCAUX. Messr. (Merchts. -80), 91, 108, 110.
CUMING. James 42.

DALYETT. David 48, 49.
DAVES. ARmstreat 26, 78, 105.
DAVIES. Peggy 95, 96; Samuel (of Prince George Co. -24), 28, 29, 39, 121; William (of Prince George Co. -24), 28, 29, 43, 51, 75, 78, 95, 96, 109.
DAVIS. Gressett 9, 23, 26, 47-49, 60, 61, 63, 76, 77; John 47, 48; L. 18; Martha 48, 60, 61, 63; P. 20.
DEMOVEL. Samuel (of Prince George Co. -67), 90.
DENNIS. Richard 105.
DODSON. Daniel 34, 64, 121.
DONOLD. Robert 56, 67.
DONOLDSON. Samuel 67.
DORTON. John 54.
DOUGLAS. James 50; John (Sone Mason late from Ireland -97), 98, 108-110; Sally 108; William 117, 123.
DOWNMAN. (blank) 76.
DRUMMOND. John 116, 120, 121.
DUDGEON. George 6, 62, 81, 107, 110; Martha 107, 110.
DUNCAN. Charles (Mercht. of Chesterfield Co. -7), 37-39, 44-46, 50, 51, 54, 55, 61, 62, 69-71, 73, 76, 78-80, 83, 85, 89-91, 94, 95, 98, 99, 102, 103, 105, 109, 118; Jane 70, 71, 75, 76, 79, 83, 90, 91, 102, 103, 109.
DURRELL. Elizabeth 88, 91; James 16, (Taylor -32), 33, 36, 42, 43, 81, 119; William 6, 7, 12-14, 16, 21, 24, 41, 62, 88, 91, 112.
DYSART. John 28, (Mercht. -40), 57, 58.

EDWARDS. Lewis 22, 29; William 76.
ELLIOTT. George 120; William 35, 85.
EVANS. Abram: 24, 41, 59, 60.

FARRELL. Joseph (of Bristol, Mercht., deced. -57)
FAUX. Joseph 31, 52.
FAWCETT. James 8, 9, 11, 36, 66; Molly 66.
FENN. Joel 80, (of Prince George Co. -105), 110; John (of Prince George Co. -105), 110; Thomas F. 28.
FERNANDD. Matthew 38, (of Prince George Co. -41), 62, 83; William (of Prince George Co. -41), 62.
FIELD. Edmund 113; James (of Prince George Co. -37), 38; John S. 4, 27; Nanny (Widow of Theophilus -3); Theophilus (the Younger, deced. -3); Theophilus Senr., (deced. -3).
FISHER. Daniel 38, 75, 76, 90; John 62, 86, 94, 95, 105.
FITZGERALD. Ann 116, 117; Robert 38, 50, 67, 76, (of Amelia Co. -116), 117.
FOWLER. Joseph 4.
FRASER. Simon 28, 38; (of Prince George Co. -52), 54, 56, 59, 67, 76, 117.
FREELAND. James 58.
FRENCH. James 38, 76, 98, 99.
FRIEND. Thomas 30.

GALBRAITH. Charles 58.
GALLIGO. Jb. 7.
GARRETTSON. Richard 22, 23.
GEDDY. James 9, 11, 66, 78, 93.
GEE. Henry 106.
GEORGIA. State of 95, 118.
GIBBON. James 42, 117.
GILL. Elizabeth (of Chesterfield Co. -10); Erasmus 53, 54, 89, 90, 96, 97, 106, 107, 109, 110, 113, 114, 121, 122; Rowlett (of Chesterfield Co. -104), 109; Sarah 96, 97, 109, 121, 122.
GILLIAM. Robert 38, 69; William 7, 38, 76, 94, 95.
GOODWYN/GOODWIN. Boswell 3, 10, 22, 80, 81, 115; Peterson 4.
GORDON. Alexander 17, 34; Thomas 17, 38, 61, 62, 76, (of Prince George Co. -81), 91, 98, 99, 109, 116, 117.
GRAMMER. John (Clerk of Hustings Court -1), 3, 4, 34, 45, 52, 54, 74, 75, 93, 106, 123; Robert 93.

Heritage Books by Ruth and Sam Sparacio:

Abstracts of Account Books of Edward Dixon, Merchant of Port Royal, Virginia, Volume I: 1743–1747

Abstracts of Account Books of Edward Dixon, Merchant of Port Royal, Virginia, Volume II

Albemarle County, Virginia Deed and Will Book Abstracts, 1748–1752

Albemarle County, Virginia Deed Book Abstracts, 1758–1761

Albemarle County, Virginia Deed Book Abstracts, 1761–1764

Albemarle County, Virginia Deed Book Abstracts, 1764–1768

Albemarle County, Virginia Deed Book Abstracts, 1768–1770

Albemarle County, Virginia Deed Book Abstracts, 1776–1778

Albemarle County, Virginia Deed Book Abstracts, 1778–1780

Albemarle County, Virginia Deed Book Abstracts, 1780–1783

Albemarle County, Virginia Deed Book Abstracts, 1787–1790

Albemarle County, Virginia Deed Book Abstracts, 1790–1791

Albemarle County, Virginia Deed Book Abstracts, 1791–1793

Augusta County, Virginia Land Tax Books, 1782–1788

Augusta County, Virginia Land Tax Books, 1788–1790

Amherst County, Virginia Land Tax Books, 1789–1791

Caroline County, Virginia Order Book Abstracts, 1765

Caroline County, Virginia Order Book Abstracts, 1767–1768

Caroline County, Virginia Order Book Abstracts, 1768–1770

Caroline County, Virginia Order Book Abstracts, 1770–1771

Caroline County, Virginia Order Book, 1765–1767

Caroline County, Virginia Order Book, 1771–1772

Caroline County, Virginia Order Book, 1772–1773

Caroline County, Virginia Order Book, 1773

Caroline County, Virginia Order Book, 1773–1774

Caroline County, Virginia Order Book, 1774–1778

Caroline County, Virginia Order Book, 1778–1781

Caroline County, Virginia Order Book, 1781–1783

Caroline County, Virginia Order Book, 1786–1787

Caroline County, Virginia Order Book, 1787, Part 1

Caroline County, Virginia Order Book, 1788

Culpeper County, Virginia Deed Book Abstracts, 1795–1796

Culpeper County, Virginia Land Tax Book, 1782–1786

Culpeper County, Virginia Land Tax Book, 1787–1789

Culpeper County, Virginia Minute Book, 1763–1764

Digest of Family Relationships, 1650–1692, from Virginia County Court Records

Digest of Family Relationships, 1720–1750, from Virginia County Court Records

Digest of Family Relationships, 1750–1763, from Virginia County Court Records

Digest of Family Relationships, 1764–1775, from Virginia County Court Records

Essex County, Virginia Deed and Will Abstracts, 1695–1697

Essex County, Virginia Deed and Will Abstracts, 1697–1699

Essex County, Virginia Deed and Will Abstracts, 1699–1701

Essex County, Virginia Deed and Will Abstracts, 1701–1703

Essex County, Virginia Deed and Will Abstracts, 1745–1749

Essex County, Virginia Deed and Will Book, 1692–1693

Essex County, Virginia Deed and Will Book, 1693–1694

Essex County, Virginia Deed and Will Book, 1694–1695

Essex County, Virginia Deed and Will Book, 1753–1754 and 1750

Essex County, Virginia Deed Book, 1724–1728

Essex County, Virginia Deed Book, 1728–1733

Essex County, Virginia Deed Book, 1733–1738

Essex County, Virginia Deed Book, 1738–1742

Essex County, Virginia Deed Book, 1742–1745

Lancaster County, Virginia Order Book, 1701–1703

Lancaster County, Virginia Order Book, 1703–1706

Lancaster County, Virginia Order Book, 1732–1736

Lancaster County, Virginia Will Book, 1675–1689

Loudoun County, Virginia Order Book, 1763–1764

Loudoun County, Virginia Order Book, 1764

Louisa County, Virginia Deed Book, 1744–1746

Louisa County, Virginia Order Book, 1742–1744

Madison County, Virginia Deed Book Abstracts, 1793–1804

Madison County, Virginia Deed Book, 1793–1813, and Marriage Bonds, 1793–1800

Middlesex County, Virginia Deed Book, 1679–1688

Middlesex County, Virginia Deed Book, 1688–1694

Middlesex County, Virginia Deed Book, 1694–1703

Middlesex County, Virginia Deed Book, 1703–1709

Middlesex County, Virginia Deed Book, 1709–1720

Middlesex County, Virginia Order Book Abstracts, 1686–1690

Middlesex County, Virginia Order Book Abstracts, 1697–1700

Middlesex County, Virginia Record Book, 1721–1813

Northumberland County, Virginia Deed and Will Book, 1650–1655

Northumberland County, Virginia Deed and Will Book, 1655–1658

Northumberland County, Virginia Deed and Will Book, 1662–1666

Northumberland County, Virginia Deed and Will Book, 1666–1670

Northumberland County, Virginia Deed and Will Book, 1670–1672 and 1706–1711

Northumberland County, Virginia Deed and Will Book, 1711–1712

Northumberland County, Virginia Order Book, 1652–1657

Northumberland County, Virginia Order Book, 1657–1661

Northumberland County, Virginia Order Book, 1665–1669

Northumberland County, Virginia Order Book, 1669–1673

Northumberland County, Virginia Order Book, 1680–1683

Northumberland County, Virginia Order Book, 1683–1686

Northumberland County, Virginia Order Book, 1699–1700

Northumberland County, Virginia Order Book, 1700–1702

Northumberland County, Virginia Order Book, 1702–1704

Orange County, Virginia Deeds, 1743–1759

Orange County, Virginia Order Book Abstracts, 1747–1748

Orange County, Virginia Order Book Abstracts, 1752–1753

Petersburg City, Virginia Hustings Court Deed Book Abstracts, 1784–1787

Petersburg City, Virginia Hustings Court Deed Book Abstracts, 1787–1790

Petersburg City, Virginia Hustings Court Deed Book Abstracts, 1790–1793

Prince William County, Virginia Deed Book Abstracts, 1749–1752

Prince William County, Virginia Order Book Abstracts, 1752–1753

Prince William County, Virginia Order Book Abstracts, 1753–1757

(Old) Rappahannock County, Virginia Deed and Will Book Abstracts, 1656–1662

(Old) Rappahannock County, Virginia Deed and Will Book Abstracts, 1662–1665

(Old) Rappahannock County, Virginia Deed and Will Book Abstracts, 1663–1668

(Old) Rappahannock County, Virginia Deed and Will Book Abstracts, 1665–1677

(Old) Rappahannock County, Virginia Deed and Will Book Abstracts, 1668–1670

(Old) Rappahannock County, Virginia Deed and Will Book Abstracts, 1670–1672

(Old) Rappahannock County, Virginia Deed and Will Book Abstracts, 1672–1673/4

(Old) Rappahannock County, Virginia Deed and Will Book Abstracts, 1673/4–1676

(Old) Rappahannock County, Virginia Deed and Will Book Abstracts, 1677–1678/9

(Old) Rappahannock County, Virginia Deed and Will Book Abstracts, 1678/9–1682

(Old) Rappahannock County, Virginia Deed and Will Book Abstracts, 1682–1686

(Old) Rappahannock County, Virginia Deed and Will Book Abstracts, 1686–1688

(Old) Rappahannock County, Virginia Deed and Will Book Abstracts, 1688–1692

(Old) Rappahannock County, Virginia Order Book Abstracts, 1683–1685

(Old) Rappahannock County, Virginia Order Book Abstracts, 1689–1692

(Old) Rappahannock County, Virginia Will Book Abstracts, 1682–1687

Richmond County, Virginia Deed Book Abstracts, 1692–1695

Richmond County, Virginia Deed Book Abstracts, 1695–1701

Richmond County, Virginia Deed Book Abstracts, 1701–1704

Richmond County, Virginia Deed Book Abstracts, 1705–1708

Richmond County, Virginia Deed Book Abstracts, 1708–1711

Richmond County, Virginia Deed Book Abstracts, 1711–1714

Richmond County, Virginia Deed Book Abstracts, 1715–1718

Richmond County, Virginia Deed Book Abstracts, 1718–1719

Richmond County, Virginia Deed Book Abstracts, 1719–1721

Richmond County, Virginia Deed Book Abstracts, 1721–1725

Richmond County, Virginia Order Book Abstracts, 1694–1697

Richmond County, Virginia Order Book Abstracts, 1697–1699

Richmond County, Virginia Order Book abstracts, 1699–1701

Richmond County, Virginia Order Book Abstracts, 1714–1715

Richmond County, Virginia Order Book Abstracts, 1719–1721

Richmond County, Virginia Order Book, 1692–1694

Richmond County, Virginia Order Book, 1702–1704

Richmond County, Virginia Order Book, 1717–1718

Richmond County, Virginia Order Book, 1718–1719

Spotsylvania County, Virginia Deed Book, 1722–1725

Spotsylvania County, Virginia Deed Book, 1725–1728

Spotsylvania County, Virginia Deed Book: 1730–1731

Spotsylvania County, Virginia Order Book Abstracts, 1742–1744

Spotsylvania County, Virginia Order Book Abstracts, 1744–1746

Stafford County, Virginia Deed and Will Book, 1686–1689

Stafford County, Virginia Deed and Will Book, 1689–1693

Stafford County, Virginia Deed and Will Book, 1699–1709

Stafford County, Virginia Deed and Will Book, 1780–1786, and Scheme Book Orders, 1790–1793

Stafford County, Virginia Deed Book, 1722–1728 and 1755–1765

Stafford County, Virginia Order Book, 1664–1668 and 1689–1690

Stafford County, Virginia Order Book, 1691–1692

Stafford County, Virginia Order Book, 1692–1693

Stafford County, Virginia Will Book, 1729–1748

Stafford County, Virginia Will Book, 1748–1767

Westmoreland County, Virginia Deed and Will Abstracts, 1723–1726

Westmoreland County, Virginia Deed and Will Abstracts, 1726–1729

Westmoreland County, Virginia Deed and Will Abstracts, 1729–1732

Westmoreland County, Virginia Deed and Will Abstracts, 1732–1734

Westmoreland County, Virginia Deed and Will Abstracts, 1734–1736

Westmoreland County, Virginia Deed and Will Abstracts, 1736–1740

Westmoreland County, Virginia Deed and Will Abstracts, 1740–1742

Westmoreland County, Virginia Deed and Will Abstracts, 1742–1745

Westmoreland County, Virginia Deed and Will Abstracts, 1745–1747

Westmoreland County, Virginia Deed and Will Abstracts, 1747–1748

Westmoreland County, Virginia Deed and Will Abstracts, 1749–1751

Westmoreland County, Virginia Deed and Will Abstracts, 1751–1754

Westmoreland County, Virginia Deed and Will Abstracts, 1754–1756

Westmoreland County, Virginia Order Book, 1705–1707

Westmoreland County, Virginia Order Book, 1707–1709

Westmoreland County, Virginia Order Book, 1709–1712

www.ingramcontent.com/pod-product-compliance
Lightning Source LLC
Chambersburg PA
CBHW080335270326
41927CB00014B/3227